THEORIES OF CULTURE

GUIDES TO THEOLOGICAL INQUIRY

Edited by Kathryn Tanner of the University of Chicago and Paul Lakeland of Fairfield University, Guides to Theological Inquiry are intended to introduce students, scholars, clergy, and theologians to those academic methods, disciplines, and movements that are most germane to contemporary theology. Neither simple surveys nor exhaustive monographs, these short books provide solid, reliable, programmatic statements of the main lines or workings of their topics and assessments of their theological impact.

Already available are *Nonfoundationalism* by John E. Thiel, *Literary Theory* by David Dawson, *Postmodernity* by Paul Lakeland, and *Theories of Culture* by Kathryn Tanner. Forthcoming titles in the series include *Hermeneutics* by Francis Schüssler Fiorenza, *Feminist Theory* by Serene Jones, *Critical Social Theory* by Gary Simpson, and *African American Critical Thought* by Shawn Copeland.

THEORIES OF CULTURE

A NEW AGENDA
FOR THEOLOGY

KATHRYN TANNER

GUIDES TO
THEOLOGICAL
INQUIRY

FORTRESS PRESS / MINNEAPOLIS

THEORIES OF CULTURE
A New Agenda for Theology
Guides to Theological Inquiry series

Cover design: Craig Claeys
Text design: David Lott
Author photo: Kathryn Hanson
Cover photo: © 1997 Tony Stone Images

Library of Congress Cataloging-in-Publication Data

Tanner, Kathryn, 1957–
    Theories of culture : a new agenda for theology / Kathryn Tanner.
       p.   cm. — (Guides to theological inquiry)
    Includes bibliographical references.
    ISBN 0-8006-3097-1 (alk. paper)
    1. Christianity and culture. 2. Theology—Methodology.
  I. Title.   II. Series
  BR115.C8T36   1997
  261'.01—dc21   97-22497
                                         CIP

Manufactured in the U.S.A.   AF 1-3097

01   00   99   98   97   1   2   3   4   5   6   7   8   9   10

Contents

Foreword

Whether it is mere failure of nerve or a genuine and seismic shift in the intellectual landscape, today we have trouble finding our way around in the world of ideas. In the past, it was always *terra firma*. True, there might have been potholes, swamps, and even dragons, but there were maps to designate the precise locations in which these and other dangers to the traveler might be found. In our age, there can be no maps, because there is no agreement on what the terrain looks like, or even if there is any terrain at all. From the Copernican revolution that substituted the sun for the earth as the center of the universe, through the discoveries of modern physics and astronomy, we know now—cosmologically, philosophically, and culturally—that there is no center.

It is this pervasive absence of center, security, or certainty, and its profound implications for the study of religion, that the Guides to Theological Inquiry exist to investigate. Each volume in the series takes up one important theme in contemporary thought or culture, explains its origins and own internal logic, and examines critically its importance to and impact upon contemporary theological investigation and religious studies. No mere surveys, these texts aim to make constructive proposals for the theological usefulness of their particular focus.

Kathryn Tanner's text presented here takes up this challenge for the topic of culture itself. Differently from other volumes in the series, whose task is to explicate an unfamiliar notion or methodology, here Tanner leads the reader carefully into a deeper understanding of a word, *culture*, which trips off the tongue easily and is all too often assumed to need no explication at all. Focusing first of all on the history of the idea of culture, predominantly in the nineteenth century, she moves on to a fuller consideration of how twentieth-century cultural anthropology comes to understand the object of its inquiry. Having laid out this background with clarity and precision, Tanner goes on to a fascinating and suggestive proposal for the implications of this fuller notion of culture for the theological enterprise itself. Readers who know little or nothing of cultural anthropology, and those who do but who want to think more deeply about the theological import of contemporary theories of culture, have much to learn from this important volume.

—*Paul Lakeland*

Preface

Although less than one hundred years old, the modern anthropological meaning of "culture" now enjoys a remarkable influence within the humanistic disciplines of the academy and within commonsense discussions of daily life. "In explanatory importance and in generality of application it is comparable to such categories as gravity in physics, disease in medicine, evolution in biology."[1] Incorporating within its range of associations the notions of context, community, convention, and norm, "culture" has broken through the disciplinary boundaries of anthropology as one narrowly defined academic field. For example, the idea of culture has become a mainstay of social historians such as Natalie Davis, Carlo Ginsburg, Robert Darnton, Peter Burke, and R. W. Scribner.[2] These historians eschew both an event-centered political or institutional history and an intellectual history of elites in favor of a description of popular forms of life. Historical study becomes a kind of "retrospective cultural anthropology" that focuses on the cultural mediation of historical events and conflicts, and renders the strange particulars of past occurrences intelligible through the fullest possible description of their cultural context.[3] In literary studies the new historicists (for instance, Stephen Greenblatt and Louis Montrose) hope to understand texts "as part of the system of signs that constitute a given culture," as focal points for lines of force in the wider cultures in which they figure.[4] The bloom is on the rose of that interdisciplinary melange known as British and U.S. cultural studies, in which Superman comics and rap tunes compete for attention with works of "great" literature and the formal speeches of politicians. Economists and political scientists such as Charles Sabel and Michael Taussig deem structural and systematic accounts of global processes to be incomplete without attention to the way those processes are culturally construed in particular locations.[5] Cultural critics like David Reisman, Daniel Bell, Richard Sennett, and Christopher Lasch, and the followers of the Frankfurt School with their complaints about mass culture, continue in a tradition of critical self-consciousness about modern Western forms of behavior which anthropologists like Margaret Mead and Ruth Benedict fostered with their descriptions of other peoples' ways of living.[6] Philosophy merges with anthropology where, as they do for Richard Rorty, descriptions of what "we" do and believe displace preoccupations with supposedly perennial questions of human life. In Marxist-oriented accounts of the way power relations are constructed and sustained, accounts influenced by Antonio Gramsci and Raymond Williams, the concept of culture often vies with that of ideology for purposes of explaining how beliefs, values, and attitudes supportive of particular social relations come to be established in everyday life and taken for granted.[7] Aside from its influence on academic disciplines, an anthropological notion of culture is a common reference point in both public discourse and private conversation. As Margaret Mead observed over thirty years ago and as is still true today, "the words 'in our culture' slip from the lips of educated men and women almost as effortlessly as do the phrases that refer to period and place."[8]

I contend that the anthropological notion of culture can be profitably employed in theology. As it does in other humanistic disciplines of the academy, an anthropological notion of culture sets new questions and directions for theological research. Indeed, such a notion has already infiltrated contemporary theology by way of common sense, affecting how theologians understand such topics as the nature of Christian identity and communal traditions, the relations between social practice on the one hand, and Christian beliefs and symbols on the other, and the character of apologetics and interreligious exchange. This influence on theology often, however, remains implicit and unself-conscious, thereby blunting the capacity of such a notion to establish fruitful new avenues for theological study, and hiding from the theologian's purview a decisive postmodern shift in the anthropological understanding of culture within the academy. It is this postmodern modification of an anthropological notion of culture that holds the greatest promise as a tool for theological study.

In an effort to make theological uses of a notion of culture more self-conscious, the first chapter of this book strips away the familiarity of the modern anthropological notion of culture by sketching the history of its development, from associations with high culture in the eighteenth century through its solidification as a term of art, especially in U.S. cultural anthropology after 1920. Chapter 2 renders all the different aspects of this established anthropological sense of culture explicit, and chapter 3 shows how a number of these aspects have come in for criticism since the late 1970s and early 1980s. After this concentration on the notion of culture itself in the first part of the book, the second part treats topics in theology.

I intend to demonstrate the overall profit of a cultural approach to these topics while cautioning against the influence of those aspects of the classic post-1920 anthropological notion of culture rightfully subject to recent postmodern attack.

Perhaps because I began this book at Yale and completed it at the University of Chicago, I am indebted to an unusual number of people who gave generously of their time and expertise in the effort, which I hope was not in vain, to help me improve it. The following people read the manuscript in part or as a whole and offered valuable suggestions: John Thiel, Bill Werpehowski, David Dawson, Ian McFarland, Nicholas Healy, Serene Jones, Amy Carr, Chuck Mathewes, Mary Fulkerson, Sheila Davaney, Hilda Koster, Rebecca Chopp, Jennifer DeWeerth, Alain Weaver, Delwin Brown, Bill Carrol, Kazi Joshua, and Beryl Satter. Members of the Yale-Washington Group offered much appreciated insights at a later stage in the revision process. Jan Pranger, whose work on ecumenism and missions proceeds along similar lines as my own, has been an invaluable conversation partner since my arrival in Chicago. My editors, Michael West of Fortress Press and Paul Lakeland (my coeditor for the GTI series) kept the book on track, and provided welcome reality checks. It has been a pleasure working with them, and with the rest of the Fortress staff, among them book cover designer Craig Claeys and trusty copy editor and production manager David Lott. Of course, none of these people is likely to be entirely happy with what I have done, but the book is no doubt better for each of them.

PART ONE

The Notion of
Culture

1

The History of "Culture"

A long circuitous route joins the English word *culture* with the modern anthropological sense of the term now current in so many academic disciplines. From that history of "culture" that Raymond Williams has called "one of the two or three most complicated in the English language," an anthropological sense emerged as late as the 1920s and even then primarily only on the American anthropological scene.[1] In many ways (as we will see in chapter 3) the concept remains in process. No time-honored given but a rather recent construct, the anthropological notion of culture is informed almost haphazardly by associations and problematics peculiar to the historical circumstances through which the term *culture* passed. Rehearsing some of this history will help us understand the significance of the aspects of the anthropological notion of culture to be discussed systematically in chapter 2, and will help us gain in chapter 3 some critical perspective on them.

The word *culture* is not new; it has quite old linguistic roots in Latin terms having to do originally with the care and tending of crops or animals. The idea that human societies differ in customs and practices is at least as old. Such an idea presumably appears wherever contacts are made with people in foreign lands and stories are told about them. What *is* relatively new is the association of this idea of different ways of living with the word *culture*. New, too, is an anthropological interpretation of those differences. Only in modern times are differences in culture offered in explanation of the readily perceptible fact that peoples of the world differ from one another in their ways of life. Differences among peoples are no longer attributed, as they were in medieval and Renaissance times, to a God-given order of being like that found in nature.[2] These differences are not the results of racial or genetic variations, or of environmental factors such as climate. They are no longer thought to bespeak differences in origin—Europeans descending perhaps from Adam and Eve, Africans from so-called "pre-Adamites." Differences

3

among peoples have their source in the ongoing life of human beings in groups and are maintained over generations mainly by way of processes of imitation and example. Human beings construct the character of their own lives through group living. Differences in forms of human life therefore reflect nothing more than the distinct histories of bounded groups of people. Gone with this anthropological account of difference is the evaluative component common to previous explanations: ways of life different from one's own represent neither the golden age of one's past nor a heathen diversion from a paradisical innocence originally shared by all human beings; they represent neither states of ignorance or childhood nor less developed stages of living. How does such a distinctively modern understanding of human difference emerge as a sense of the word *culture*?

The Cultured Person

The idea of human culture seems to have originally been a metaphorical extension of the use of the word in agriculture and husbandry. In the same way one could cultivate crops or animals in order to better them, one could cultivate one's person, specifically one's highest capacities or faculties, in order to develop or perfect oneself. Francis Bacon and Samuel Pufendorf in the seventeenth century were among the first to resuscitate Cicero's notion of a *cultura animi*: "a field, though fertile, cannot be productive without cultivation, nor a mind without teaching. The culture of the mind (*cultura animi*) is the business of philosophy. It removes imperfections, roots and all, and prepares minds for seed sowing. It imparts to them, and, as one might say, sows, things which when come to maturity will produce abundant fruit."[3] In Britain, the cultured person pursued self-perfection, as Matthew Arnold said, "by getting to know the best that has been said and thought in the world." "Culture" in the age of Goethe sometimes became a synonym for the more usual German term *Bildung*: a cultured person was a person with education, a member of the then-new German middle class with a claim to political participation and national leadership by virtue of intellectual training and heightened aesthetic sensibilities. Particularly in France, the cultured person was someone civilized, a person of sophistication and refinement who populated the king's court, the aristocrat of delicate manners emulated by the up-and-coming of middle rank.

The cultured or civilized person in France and Britain, the *gebildeter* individual in Germany, was perhaps a secular substitute, as some argue, for a lost or threatened meaning to life expressed in Christian discipline. A *self*-disciplined person replaced the creature of God, reshaped and reformed by saving grace.[4] Matthew Arnold explicitly identified the harmonious perfection of capacities brought about by human self-cultivation with salvation. In an early *Bildungsroman* (or novel of self-education), we read that "man . . . has to develop, to shape himself [*sich ausbilden*], to give himself the last touch of the file that will bathe him in glory and grace—in short, man must therefore be his own second creator."[5] Culture in the sense of spiritual, artistic, and intellectual refinement provided human persons with a model for self-control once the more traditional restraints of social mores and religion could no longer be taken for granted.

Whatever the merits of a secularization hypothesis, claims to culture no doubt represented claims to status among new and emerging elites with the breakdown of feudal hierarchies and the consolidation of sovereign nation states. Those educated at university and those whose sensibilities were trained through exposure to the arts might arguably have achieved a status that peasants and craftsmen or the landed aristocracy lacked. *Bildung* was the means whereby a German middle class solidified its hold on the court administration and supplanted the influence of an older aristocracy with feudal roots. In Britain and France the emergence of a more dualistically framed opposition between high culture and popular practices helped the modern state consolidate its power by devaluing particularistic and local customs. From the viewpoint of a high culture elite, values and customs displayed by the people appeared ignorant and superstitious, bestial and unrefined. A "culture war" like this helped, particularly in France, to prevent particularistic and local customs from coming between the individual and a head of state who was owed absolute loyalty.

In a number of ways this notion of high culture—referring to a process of individual education and refinement, and, by extension, to the products of such processes (works of art and literature)—runs contrary to the anthropological sense of culture. This notion of high culture is similar to an anthropological notion of culture in assuming that the character and shape of cultured life is a human construction. But contrary to an anthropological notion of culture, high culture is an evaluative and exclusivist concept: not all persons are cultured and those who are are better than those who are not. Moreover, unlike the anthropological notion, high culture is not a term highlighting differences among those who display it. General processes of refinement and the basic nature of the results need not vary over time and space. Differences among the cultured are at most quantitative, matters of degree: one can be more or less cultured. The word *culture* when used in a high culture or evaluative sense is therefore found in the singular rather than the plural: there is *a* high culture to be shared in varying degrees by cultured persons, but no high culture*s*. Finally, high culture is something possessed by individuals. Individuals undergo a process of refinement and they separately display the state of being cultured that results. Reference is not primarily to social groups, although high culture as an indicator of status might suggest the development and possession of high culture by a particular social class and perhaps point thereby to a use of the notion in the plural. Class recognition might permit a high culture of elite classes to be opposed to the popular *culture* of lower classes.

Such an attribution to social groups—the idea of a cultured *society*—seems to have been the first step on the road to an *anthropological* sense of the word *culture*. The development of a *social* reference for the word followed different trajectories, however, in France, Germany, and Great Britain.

Cultured Society

France

In France the idea of high culture was intimately connected from the first with issues of social control in an increasingly centralized state.[6] The localized orders of feudal society, comprised of multiple, densely interconnected subgroups—clans, families, corporations, guilds, parishes, and so forth—had started to unravel in the sixteenth century. The growth of a centralized government required the further demise of these localized sites of order to the extent they represented the potential for resistance to centralized government authority. High culture educated elites—the enlightened of France—were to aid this process of social reconstruction (with, in the Ancient Regime, or without, in post-Revolutionary France, an absolute monarch). These elites proposed to manage rationally a society that lacked its own self-regulating feudal mechanisms of order. The method of management involved civilizing the populace; a new order of social relations around a centralized hub could be achieved if the particular and local customs of the masses were disqualified and replaced by a high culture ideal. The manners and values of *individuals* were to be reformed but the objective of the process was directly social: orderly social relations were to be the primary result of efforts to bring individuals up to the desired level of perfection. A single model for human life, which the upper classses of French society exemplified, was to mold the chaotic diversity of local and particular customs into a unitary design. A uniform and universally binding cultural ideal could turn human beings into citizens, wear off their particularistic features and make them essentially identical units under the direct rule of the state.

Culture, as a synonym for civilization, in this way ran counter to the nonevaluative respect for plurality found in a contemporary anthropological notion of culture. Culture or civilization represented the means by which problematic differences in ways of life among the various classes of French society could ultimately be overcome in the interest of social order and unity. A unitary ideal opposed to plural forms of life, civilization was a cosmopolitan notion. Riding above all merely local traditions, and not to be identified with any one of them, it could be found anywhere, among the educated elites of any European state at least. Unlike the anthropological sense of the term, culture was not a particularistic notion; culture in the sense of civilization was not differentiated by social group, and so was not bound by context. Indeed, civilization was the opposite of customary or traditional forms of life. It was to replace them; it represented an escape from the influence of tradition or custom in human life. What anthropology tells us is inevitable—particular and local custom—was that from which Enlightenment civilization wanted to free humanity. Unlike custom or tradition, civilization or culture was a self-conscious construction of human beings, a self-directed form of education, something made rather than found, the product of reason rather than blind habit. Localized traditions or customs were not themselves considered cultures, as an anthropological notion of culture would have it; they were "natural," unformed and un*in*formed, disordered and wild states, requiring the education and discipline that civilization brings.

The basic presupposition of an anthropological notion of culture does come into view here: society is a human construction or, one might say, here the notion of society (in the sense of those immediate relations among individuals that can be opposed to the organizing capacities of the state) emerges for the first time to be the object of human managerial skills.[7] Also, like an anthropological sense of the term, and unlike a high culture preoccupation with only intellectual, spiritual, and artistic achievement, culture refers to a whole body of manners or ruled patterns of social interaction through its associations with "civilization" and its French root *civilité* (a term originally denoting the French upper classes' meticulous observance of rules of conduct befitting their high social status). Finally, culture in the sense of civilization can point in certain circumstances toward a quasi-ethnographic interest in local traditions and customs.

The social task of civilization could itself suggest that the unreformed behaviors and values of the masses were more than merely passive, "natural" objects for management by educated elites. Especially when local traditions and customs resisted processes of civilization, attention might be turned to those traditions and customs as having some significance in themselves, as alternative ways of living with a density and coherence sufficient to block temporarily efforts at reform. They became more than the chaotic and curious ways of a barbarous and superstitious people utterly lacking in what the educated classes alone could offer a state in need of consolidation—some unified pattern for social living. Instead, the very objectification of local traditions and customs in the interest of social control prompted a totalizing vision of them, an effort to comprehend them as a whole. A sort of "functionalism of the erroneous and the abhorrent" sprang up as a backdrop to the possibility of rational progress.[8] How local customs and traditions hang together had to be investigated systematically if they were to be taken apart effectively.[9] The life of the common people was not necessarily unruly and anarchic as the result of unconscious and irrational influences, and thus in need of a civilizing discipline. To the contrary, it might be overly controlled by the rigidities of custom and therefore require enlightened disruption by a tradition-free reason. Once they were made the focus of interest in themselves, local customs and traditions were brought in any case within the compass of a single developmental history. In the so-called universal or conjectural histories of the Enlightenment, they became, not the opposite of the civilizing process that was simply to replace them, but stages on the way toward civilization as an ideal pattern for social living.

Some sort of diversity in forms of life is hereby recognized, and an explanation compatible with a single proper pattern for human life offered. Forms of living that do not presently conform to that ideal pattern—the customs of European peasants or of non-European societies—can muster no ultimate challenge to the value of a civilized order. They simply represent past stages through which cultured or civilized peoples have progressed. They are the childhood of a developmental history of the world whose inevitable end is European civilization, or a memoriam to the archaic should they resist the process of civilization. A hierarchy of oppositional contrast becomes in this way a hierarchy of grades. Like the incremental development of a high culture sensibility on the part of an individual person, the customs and behaviors of different groups can be deemed more or less cultured when positioned along an axis of time that spans the history of the human race. In contrast to an anthropological sense of the term, culture in these world histories remains an evaluative notion, and an insistence on a unity of process and outcome overrides the significance of differences among forms of life. A single line of psychic development from ignorance to enlightenment unifies the peoples of the world whatever their ethnic or national backgrounds or group histories. All that stands in the way of such a natural progression is local or accidental circumstance destined to fall away. A universal law of human psychic development in this way undercuts any incipient recognition in these universal histories of culture as a "constituting medium" of the differences displayed by the peoples of the world.[10]

Germany

Although closely associated with the personal cultivation of one's spiritual and intellectual gifts or *Bildung*, in Germany the word *Kultur* applied primarily to social groups.[11] Used by a non-noble German intelligentsia, *Kultur* commonly referred to the highest achievements of society. Those achievements were not, however, identified with civilization. Civilization referred to external behaviors embodied in political, social, and economic institutions; culture referred to a society's intellectual, artistic, and spiritual achievements. The distinction had nationalistic overtones from the first. Originally used within Germany to elevate the status of a newly emerging intellectual elite over that of the landed aristocracy, the distinction was quickly employed as a marker of German supremacy vis-à-vis other nations, particularly France. The German aristocracy mimicked French manners in the eighteenth century; the French had an outward civilization but no culture. Germany might be backward in its economic and political structures, hardly a unified nation at all, but it could be a nation superior to the French in virtue of its *Kultur*.[12]

In contrast to the cosmopolitan, international mission of civilization, the German sense of culture was particularistic and group-bound. Like an anthropological use of culture, it was a delimiting notion, setting social groups off from one another. Culture was what made the German people in particular distinct, what made them to begin with a unified social body capable of contrast with other nation-states. While no less sure of the supremacy of German culture than the French were of the civilization they hoped would spread across the globe, Germans had first to secure a sense of themselves as a distinct people through the notion of *Kultur*. Culture in German usage reflected

> the situation of a people which, by Western standards, arrived at political unification and consolidation only very late, and from whose boundaries . . . territories have again and again crumbled away or threatened to. . . . Whereas the concept of civilization has the function of giving expression to the continuous expansionist tendency of colonizing groups, the concept of *Kultur* mirrors the self-consciousness of a nation which had constantly to seek out and constitute its boundaries anew, in a political as well as a spiritual sense, and again and again had to ask itself: "What is really our identity?"[13]

For the German intelligentsia, *Kultur* was, indeed, what enabled the Germans to resist the encroachments of an expansionist French nation, the purveyor of a transportable Enlightenment. Intellectual, artistic, and spiritual achievements could be Germany's bulwark against French-dominated internationalism—not simply because they represented a higher form of achievement than an external civilization but because they manifested a spirit that was peculiarly German. The distinctively German character of its *Kultur* interrupted the uniformity of Enlightenment civilization as an ideal for all peoples.

This idea of *Kultur* as the distinctive expression of the German people could be generalized in keeping with a greater respect for diversity of ways of life than that found in Enlightenment paeans to civilization. The result—beginning with the work of Johann Gottfried von Herder—was a plural notion of cultures similar to an anthropological one: every people or nation, not just the Germans, displayed a distinctive culture.[14]

As had happened in the case of Enlightenment universal histories, an analogy was drawn here with cultivated individuals, with the high culture of educated persons. The analogy was not applied, however, to a single developmental process spanning the different societies of world history. It was applied, instead, to each such society individually. The human race considered as a whole did not reproduce the process of enlightenment undergone by individual persons. To the contrary, each of its peoples was like an individual person, displaying in its intellectual, spiritual, and aesthetic achievements a characteristic form. In the same way that every cultivated person had his or her own way of feeling and experiencing the world, so too did every social group.

Aesthetic and organic categories associated with high culture in Germany were hereby applied to societies. As Johann Wolfgang von Goethe maintained, a cultured person achieved a singular style; organizing talents and experiences into one harmonious whole, the cultivated person made of his or her life a work of art. Societies too could be considered personified wholes, each setting forth a unique spirit in organized interactions between its innate capacities and environmental factors.

Aided by this aesthetic holism, the idea of culture as a boundary-setting mechanism was retained in pluralistic usage. Cultures were self-contained complexes whose integrity might be disrupted by untoward external influences; each people should go its own way independent of the rest, neither imitating nor defiled by others. Investigation of cultures should respect this same implication of aesthetic holism. As a self-contained complex, each culture should be taken on its own terms, interpreted with reference simply to its own characteristic form. Moving away from developmental preoccupations of Enlightenment universal histories and toward a more anthropological mode of analysis, understanding a culture was no longer a matter of understanding how some other way of life was that culture's past or future.

The pluralistic sense of culture developing here was not quite, however, the nonevaluative sort found in contemporary anthropology. German culture clearly surpassed that of the French, although perhaps this was not evident by way of a direct comparison. For Herder, contemporary German culture had reached the height *of its type* in the happy adolescence of its life span as a national culture, while the French was suffering its decline in decrepit old age. In general, evaluations of culture were not comparative in Herder's history of humanity. As a particular manifestation, suitable to a particular time and place, of the the diverse ways of being human, each people "bears within itself the standard of its perfection, totally independent of all comparisons with that of others." Herder also ridiculed the ethnocentrism of universal histories that proposed a single line of human development: "Men of all quarters of the Globe . . . ye have not lived and enriched the Earth with your ashes, that at the end of time your prosperity should be made happy by European civilization." But just as individuals could differ in degree of cultivation so too could whole peoples. The evaluative connotations of high culture remain within this pluralistic sense of group or national cultures. All human societies have culture—that is what distinguishes them from animals. "O man, honour thyself: neither the pongo nor the gibbon is thy brother: the [Native] American and the Negro are." But some of these human societies evidently have more of it than others: "The native of California and Terra del Fuego too learned to make and use bow and arrows. He has language and ideas, skills and arts, that he learned as we learned ours. To this extent he was really cultivated and enlightened, *though only in the lowest degree.*"[15]

The German pluralistic use of the word *culture* also approximated an anthropological use in making culture a marker of a society's influence over individuals. The cultured individual is bound by the culture of his or her group, and therefore should be no cosmopolitan figure, haplessly aping the external manners of a French-dominated, European-wide elite. No matter how extraordinary the individual, he or she is shaped decisively by the particular culture in which he or she has been "educated to humanity." Each person "is actually formed in and for society, without which he could neither have received his being, nor have become a man." "No man gives birth to himself, and he is just as little self-born in the use of his intellectual powers. . . . Even eye and ear had to learn to see and hear, and everyone must realize how artificially the supreme tool of our thought, language, was acquired. Clearly nature has arranged our whole makeup . . . to depend on this help of others."[16]

The mechanism of this formation of individuals is an inherited tradition of ways of speaking and thinking, handed down, as Herder says, "from father to son." But the social construction of group differences is not yet, as in anthropological discourse, an alternative to other forms of explanation.

Herder is heavily indebted to Montesquieu's appeal to climactic conditions as an explanation for group differences, and his use of analogies with nature (that is, societies are like plants) prompts a quasi-racialist hypothesis of differences in inner "genetic" disposition among peoples of the world. Group differences, finally, are not contingent developments of social life. Some natural law works itself out with necessity in the peoples of the world, a natural law requiring the greatest possible diversity of human cultures compatible with their harmonious integration into one organic whole: whatever can be will be, Herder is fond of saying, and "mankind, both . . . as a whole, and in its particular[s] . . . is a permanent natural system of the most multifarious living powers."[17]

Britain

Great Britain, and in particular Scotland, has its own Enlightenment tradition in which culture is identified with civilization, but a social sense for the word *culture* really comes to the fore there with anti-modernist, anti-Enlightenment movements of the late eighteenth and nineteenth centuries.[18] High culture as a principle of social reform and national rejuvenation might save the nation from the mechanistic and leveling effects of industrialization and democracy. "The best that has been said and thought in the world" provides a standard of excellence by which to judge and rework the values of the marketplace and the society it had produced.

High culture has a socially expansive sense in this usage, for example in the writings of Matthew Arnold: "The great men of culture . . . have had a passion for diffusing, for making prevail, for carrying from one end of society to the other, the best knowledge, the best ideas of their time." The individual cannot reach the personal perfection of a cultured life unless he "carries others along with him in his march towards perfection . . . continually doing all he can to enlarge and increase the volume of the human stream sweeping thitherward." Thereby, "culture, instead of being . . . frivolous and useless . . . has a very important function to fulfil for mankind."[19]

Besides having social effects, the cultivation of individuals was thought to require social means. Against the optimistic belief of the Enlightenment that human perfection might be achieved by simply tearing away the hindrances of custom and prejudice, these British social critics believed certain social institutions were necessary to the same end—for instance, a strong state government dedicated to the cultivation of its citizens, a national system of education, some institutionalized body of national leaders to direct public taste. Culture would not prevail in society as the natural result of some spontaneous development; social planning was required—the engineering of new institutions or at least active efforts to resist industrialization and democracy and reinstate previously existing forms of economic and social relations.

Like what happened in Germany in the eighteenth and early nineteenth centuries (and in great part as a result of German intellectual influence in Britain), "internal" achievements of an intellectual, artistic, and spiritual sort were here set against the mere "externals" of social and economic relations, but now the terms *internal* and *external*, *culture* and *civilization*, had a different application. External civilization was identified with the newly emerging character of *British* life that was to be reformed by a healthy dose of high culture. The distinction between internal and external was therefore not, as it was in Germany, primarily a way of maintaining national independence and nationalistic pride. It was a means to national *self*-criticism, a way of making clear the "diseased spirit" of the times.[20] In this respect a social sense of high culture in British usage perhaps approached a function of the contemporary anthropological notion of culture: it enabled the British to step back from the life they were living and contemplate alternatives to it.

A similar alteration in the application of culture and civilization, with a similar effect, was also common in late nineteenth- and twentieth-century German social theory. The internal culture of the educated and aesthetically sensitive could be opposed to the French manners of the aristocracy but it could also be opposed to the practically oriented, work-a-day lives of the common people and a nonintelligentsia bourgeoisie. It was so applied after the German intelligentsia became part of the fabric of government and began to feel their status threatened from below.[21]

Also like the contemporary anthropological notion of culture, high culture when used in Britain as a principle of social reform suggested the primacy of social influences on the lives of individuals. Revolutionary democracy and laissez-faire industrialism were often viewed as nothing more than the breakdown of social controls. Enlightenment ideals of equality, fraternity, and freedom for individuals produced an anarchic display of impulse and passion where they disparaged the importance of custom and social institutions as disciplinary forces. High culture with its social implications and social conditions was to make something human out of the raw capacities, animal passions, and natural self-will that modern life had unleashed. Society made the man and high culture was to be its standard.

The anthropological idea that culture is the *constitutive* medium of individual experience, rather than a high culture overlay or refinement of an already formed human person, is approached here. But the high culture origins of this usage continue to pull in a contrary direction. Culture in an anthropological sense is an originary formative influence on individual persons and as such must be exercised primarily through unconscious means.

Apart from any reflective choice or training, one simply finds oneself exhibiting the linguistic skills, tastes, and thought patterns of the people among whom one has been brought up. High culture activities, however, are specialized, even marginalized activities, in modern industrialized societies, and they are exercised in any case through essentially reflective processes of "reading, observing, and thinking." One would expect such activities to have a formative influence, if at all, only relatively late in an individual's life. Unlike the unconsciously pervasive influence of custom, if their influence on society is to be extensive it must be promoted according to these British social critics by conscious social planning. Finally, as disciplining agents, high culture activities seem more like repressive forces than constitutive ones. The desires and impulses upon which they work already have a shape and character of their own. These desires and impulses may be called "raw" and "rude" in order to contrast them with the high culture refinement that is to discipline them, but only by the most extreme hyperbole can they be terms of contrast with culture understood in an anthropological fashion as the prerequisite for any defined or formed human living at all.

The characterization of modern society as an anarchic play of impulse and desire suggests, too, that culture is not susceptible here to use in the plural. The only alternative to a society disciplined by high culture standards is anarchy. "The best that has been said and thought" should therefore have universal sway. "Our best self," our ordinary self perfected through reading, observing, and thinking, "is not manifold, and vulgar and unstable, and contentious, and ever-varying, but one, and noble, and secure, and peaceful, and *the same for all mankind.*"[22] High culture is not the expression of some class or group of people; it is the expression of our *humanity* and as such should be found everywhere in the same form. High culture is not context-bound like the cultures that anthropologists talk about; it is not some particular way of taking things that one can set alongside of others, but a way of taking the whole of what has been commonly been said and thought, a way of critically subjecting that whole to standards of excellence. Those standards, Arnold seemed to presume, are universally authoritative.

Implicit within this English-language idea of a cultured society lie, however, the germs of a plural usage. Sometimes the problem with modern society is not diagnosed as its inability to control, through strong state institutions, the anarchic play of desire. Modern social life is as organized, as controlled, as any way of living that preceded it; it is simply organized along the wrong lines to produce willful, self-interested, and materialistic persons. So both a radical like Robert Owen and a Tory like Robert Southey can claim that the fault lies with the way modern society is put together. As Owen remarks: "Any general character, from the best to the worst, may be

given to any community . . . by the application of proper [social] means."
The problem with modern society is that "under this system . . . all are
trained civilly to oppose and often to destroy one another by their created
opposition of interests. . . . No general and substantial improvement can
arise until it shall be superseded by a superior mode of forming character
and creating wealth."[23] Modern Britain has a national character and therefore its own system of education and *culture*, one might say.[24] It just shapes
its citizens to their detriment: "Consider these people, then, their way of
life, their habits, their manners, the very tones of their voice . . . the words
which come forth out of their mouths, the thoughts which make the furni-
ture of their minds; would any amount of wealth be worth having with the
condition that one was to become just like one of these. . . ?"[25] In criticizing
what had become of Britain one form of life is therefore opposed to another. A *particular form* of human society—commonly identified with feudal-
ism, monastic discipline, or a rural way of life—is elevated over another—
modern urban industrialism—instead of organized social life per se being
opposed to modern anarchy.

A less evaluative recognition of plural cultures can emerge from an anti-
modernist English-language usage if one interprets the culture that is to be
society's standard of excellence in formal rather than material terms.[26] Arnold,
for example, never bothers to specify what "the best that has been said and
thought" is. Perhaps he fails to specify this because he takes what "the best
that has been said and thought" is for granted. It is also possible, however,
that the content of the standard is irrelevant to the point he wants to make.
What matters is that *all* the stock notions of society be subjected to *some* standards of excellence. Against the fragmenting, narrowing, and leveling effects
of modern society, one must simply counterpose a harmonious, organically
organized totality. The elements to be organized and the particular principles
used in the process are not very important. Any number of materially different societies formally united by the ideal of harmonious perfection can therefore ward off the anarchy that modern life represents, and no single ideal of a
cultured society need homogenize the peoples of the world. If this sort of
organic holism, typical of both British romantic and German uses of culture,
can be attributed to many social groups, Arnold might be approaching here a
modern anthropological idea of culture*s* as whole ways of life.

A plural usage remains implicit, however, in British anti-modernism.
Even if an anthropological idea of culture is approached, the word *culture* is
not commonly used to refer to it. When British anti-modernists say that all
peoples of the world have culture, by "culture" they do not mean the whole
ways of life of such peoples but the exceptional individual in every one of
them who transcends his or her social context in an expression of pure

humanity. British anti-modernists exhibit very little interest, moreover, in the differences in intellectual, moral, and aesthetic standards found among peoples of the world. Cultural evolutionism in late nineteenth-century Britain—the dominant precursor to modern anthropology in the English-speaking world at the turn of the century—made these contributions.

Cultural Evolutionism

British cultural evolutionists, notably E. B. Tyler, fit an Arnoldian notion of high culture within a developmental world history with roots in the eighteenth-century Enlightenment perspective discussed earlier.[27] As in the world histories of the eighteenth century, one could talk of the culture or civilization displayed to some degree by all human societies including the most primitive—Tyler's most famous book was entitled *Primitive Culture*. But culture did not primarily mean the refinement of manners displayed in interpersonal relations—the typical French Enlightenment sense of civilization as a distinct way of life. It meant instead the high culture achievements promoted and sustained by discrete social institutions—morality, science, the arts, law, religion—a list much the same as Arnold's (although Tyler, who was much less critical than Arnold of modern British life, would also often include technological and industrial arts). The culture of any society was that society's best ideas, its accumulated knowledge.

Thus, culture in British evolutionism approached the modern anthropological notion by being used explicitly to refer to the institutions of many different social groups. Since those institutions varied, this account of culture was bound up, too, with an understanding of differences among those groups. British evolutionism, however, seemed to move away from modern anthropology by losing culture's high culture associations with organic holism.

The understanding of culture in British evolutionism fragmented the holism of high culture by focusing on discrete institutions or intellectual forms. It placed those intellectual forms or institutions into some developmental sequence—for instance, magic precedes religion and religion gives way to science—or offered a developmental history of particular intellectual forms or social institutions considered separately—for instance, the modern British institution of marriage developed from a primitive or savage rite of capture. The different intellectual forms and institutions of a single society were not often understood in their interrelations. Instead, at least some of those forms and institutions were associated with prior developments of culture typical of other more primitive social groups. Some forms and institutions of modern British life, for instance, religion, might be understood as holdovers or survivors from a previous stage of intellectual development and be considered more appropriate, therefore, to Britain's past or to contemporary societies of a less developed nature. Some intellectual forms and social institutions, those deemed survivals, had much more to do with the past and with primitives than they did with the society in which they were found.

Nineteenth-century British evolutionists could talk of the plural stages or developmental levels through which a particular form or institution of culture passed; they could talk of different societies as being more or less cultured in the sort of intellectual activities and social practices they exhibited. But they did not speak of plural culture*s* in the way a modern anthropologist would. Indeed, they were perhaps less likely to talk of cultures in the plural than their eighteenth-century Enlightenment counterparts who offered similarly conjectural histories of world civilizations. They did not focus directly on whole ways of living—on the part of upper or lower classes, the educated or uneducated, savages or modern Frenchmen—but on general types of intellectual activity or social institution that they thought they could find in much the same form, or at least in some recognizable stage of development, from one society to the next. The different aspects or elements of culture were not context-bound and therefore relative to particular social groups. The fact that they were not was what allowed nineteenth-century evolutionists to scour the practices of the globe looking for different versions of the same type of intellectual activity or social institution to set within a single developmental sequence.

This lack of a plural usage of "culture" was connected with a nonanthropological evaluative notion of culture as a single unitary ideal. There was only one ideal form for each of the different aspects of culture and one ideal way in which they might be interrelated—an ideal that British evolutionists, unlike Arnold and the degenerationists of the time, equated with the cultural life of modernized Britain. That single ideal allowed different cultural practices, and the different societies with which they were associated, to be developmentally ordered in ethnocentric fashion:

> The educated world of Europe and America practically settles a standard by simply placing its own nation at one end of the social series and savage tribes at the other, arranging the rest of mankind between the limits according as they correspond more closely to savage or to cultured life. The principle criteria of classification are the absence or presence, high or low development of the industrial arts . . . the extent of scientific knowledge, the definiteness of moral principle, the condition of religious belief and ceremony, the degree of social and political organization, and so forth. Thus, on the definite basis of compared facts, ethnographers are able to set up at least a rough scale of civilization.[28]

The recognition of a diversity of cultural forms was also undercut in British evolutionism by the idea that the human intellect proceeded in the same way, for the same ends, everywhere. Upholders of an associationist and utilitarian psychology, British evolutionists believed that from an otherwise blank slate people formed ideas through contact with the external world in pursuing the ends of greater material happiness and greater control over nature. Similar types of cultural forms were therefore to be expected in different societies as the result of independent invention: apart from any historical contact, like minds would come up with like ideas in similar circumstances. Differences in cultural forms resulted when the reasoning processes common to human beings started from false premises or inadequate experience. Human beings everywhere were after the conclusions of modern British science and technology but sometimes they only came up with magic or religion.[29]

This intellectualist orientation, which viewed cultural development as a progress toward better ideas, was unlike a modern anthropological notion of culture too in that it held out an ideal of escape from unconscious custom through habit-free reflection. Besides reasoning upon false premises or inadequate experience, what held the development of culture back was the inertia of custom or habit that produced irrational survivals, the continuation of forms of culture among a people who were at a stage of intellectual reflection to know better. Contemporary practices were not criticized, as in modern anthropology, with reference to the customs of other peoples; contemporary practices were not subject to criticism as one form of customary practice among other possible forms. Contemporary practices were criticized instead as the irrational holdovers of custom or habit from the perspective of a better knowledge proceeding free from such conservative constraints.

An epistemological difference with modern anthropology appears here. The British evolutionist view of cultural advance presupposes an understanding of the relation between culture and intellect that is different from that found in modern anthropology. British evolutionists think of forms of culture (and their subsequent survival in irrational custom or habit) as *consequences* of human intellection; modern anthropologists think of culture as the necessary *precondition* for any productive exercise of the intellect.

Transition to an Anthropological Sense

The English word *culture* seems to take on an anthropological sense the more that the German meaning of *Kultur* influences the way the English word is used in studies of other peoples. Tyler may have popularized the term *culture* in such studies and opened the way for a greater German influence by allowing the term to take on the German-influenced Arnoldian sense of high culture. But the crucial turning point toward a contemporary anthropological sense came when German-trained scholars arrived in America and substituted the German meaning of the word *culture*—the customs of particular peoples viewed as distinct self-contained wholes—for the one in English language use. Franz Boas becomes the transitional figure in this account. There are also, however, internal tensions within British evolutionism and the circumstances of its employment that led in a similar direction.

For example, an implicit contextualism (or effort to interpret particulars in terms of their context) figures in an evolutionist account of survivals. Certain intellectual forms or social institutions are explained as survivals of preceding stages in cultural development because they do not fit the level of development displayed by other aspects of a society's culture. Ideally, then, all the various aspects of a society's culture should fit together, in much the way a modern anthropologist would expect; the various aspects of a culture should make sense with reference to one another, as manifestations of the same stage. The stages of cultural evolution from primitive to modern become, then, hypothetical reconstructions of the various types of society in which all aspects of culture do fit together in that way.

A preoccupation with functionalism is also at work in nineteenth-century British evolutionism, as a foreshadowing of the kind displayed in classical post-1920s anthropology, where one expects to understand every aspect of culture in terms of its contribution or role within an integrated cultural whole. In British evolutionism the various aspects of culture are at least thought to have a function within a generally utilitarian understanding of the ends of human life; they are rendered intelligible with reference to such a function. If some aspects of a society's culture do not presently appear to promote an interest in material happiness or advance the goal of controlling nature, the evolutionist must suppose that they did fulfill such a function in the past.

These implicit forms of contextualism and functionalism remain in tension with the absolutist implications of a single ideal of development in British evolutionism; they suggest a nonevaluative relativism. If certain intellectual forms or social institutions seem irrational now, they were once in a different time and circumstance expressions of the highest ideas that the mind could offer. They made sense, then, at that level of cultural development, even if from our more advanced intellectual vantage point they do not make sense now. For instance, science might be a much better way of achieving control over nature, but magic can be considered in the same breath with science insofar as it represents an alternative way of pursuing the same ends. Magic is the functional equivalent of science for an earlier age. Morals clearly advanced over time but the primitive values of other peoples might be "adaptive" given different environmental circumstances and a different level of technological capacity.

If combined with a less optimistic Arnoldian outlook, this relativistic side of evolutionism might set the stage for the type of social self-criticism promoted by modern anthropology. According to British evolutionism, contemporary Britishers have no monopoly on culture; other forms of culture exist alongside those that British people display. Among theorists more inclined to dissatisfaction with contemporary British life than progressivist evolutionists, these cultural forms of past times and other peoples might present hope of change, might represent a challenge to the complacent self-satisfaction of the settled and prosperous of Victorian times. The present practices of respectable British society cannot be taken for granted as a priori standards for the good and the true; they have competition from the beliefs and values of other peoples that cannot be ruled out of court from the start by the supposition that they are not themselves forms of culture. In this way the ethnocentrism implicit in developmental histories of culture might be contested; British science and social mores could no longer be the presumed telos of world history.

Crucial for the realization of possibilities like these within British evolutionism was a greater sensitivity to history. Evolutionists had generally opposed more historically inclined diffusionists, that is, "ethnologists" who used the hypothesis of historical contact, rather than the hypothesis of similar but independent processes of invention, to explain the existence of similar cultural phenomena among different peoples. Moreover, although they maintained that cultural forms developed over time, evolutionists often had little interest in the historical accuracy of the developmental sequences they proposed. Such sequences were thought to reflect necessary laws of intellectual development and so a great deal of direct documentary evidence for them was usually not required.[30]

Students of other peoples with a greater sensitivity to history, Franz Boas for one, could push evolutionism toward modern anthropology by deflating, first of all, the evolutionist penchant for classifying cultural forms across social lines. One could argue on historical grounds for the superficiality of the similarities of cultural forms across social lines of which an evolutionist mode of analysis made so much. Apparently similar cultural phenomena were actually the product of quite specific and complex historical processes that varied from case to case.[31] The fragmenting comparative analysis of evolutionists, evolutionist analysis that lifted cultural forms out of context and immediately classified them along with cultural phenomena in other societies into general types, was therefore illegitimate. Cultural forms had to be studied in terms of their own historical context before any wider generalizations about commonalities in culture could responsibly be made. According to some commentators, a German historicism that goes back at least as far as Herder was making itself felt here.[32]

If the mistakes of evolutionism were not to be repeated all over again in the study of context-specific historical processes and influences, empirical investigation had to displace here too the conjectural reconstruction of history from apparently similar cultural phenomena in different times and places. One could not simply presume, as earlier diffusionists had, that historical contact accounted for similar-appearing cultural phenomena in different social groups. Instead, one was required to make "careful and slow detailed study" of particular cases, to do intensive empirical research into the actual practices of people.[33] Study of contemporary peoples would therefore require fieldwork.

This focus on empirical description of historical contexts promoted a modern anthropological kind of contextualism. That is, focusing on a particular historical context forced one to study the cultural forms of a group of people primarily in relation to one another. The practices of people in other times and places were of no immediate relevance to such study. Cultural forms that the incipient contextualism of evolutionism understood in relation to a stage of culture crossing many different social groups were now understood in relation to other practices of the same group of people with which one started.

Especially when combined with a native German speaker's associations of culture with aesthetic holism, this contextualism led Boas to the first plural use of the English word *culture* in an anthropological sense.[34] The cultural forms of a group of people were tied together for purposes of analysis. Considered all together in this way they constituted the culture of a particular social group, unified, one would suppose in line with German aesthetic holism, as expressions of a single distinctive character. The boundaries of the cultural whole followed the small scope and limited geographical area of field work that were necessary to produce intensive empirical description.

In ways reminiscent of its use in German nationalism and French efforts at internal social control, such a sense of bounded cultural wholes fit the situation of Western colonial rule that facilitated fieldwork in foreign lands. Anthropologists set out to describe the whole that the culture of native peoples formed prior to Western intervention, even as that same Western expansion made possible their own field-based enterprises. On the one hand, anthropologists could argue thereby on behalf of native peoples: the integrity of their cultures demanded they be left alone. On the other hand, colonial administrators, with or without the conscious collaboration of anthropologists, could conceive of native peoples as some manageable whole, and try to predict the repercussions of colonialist interventions on their ways of life. Once understood as an integral whole, native practices could either be enlisted as they stood for colonial administrative purposes, or taken apart to foster assimilation to a Western way of life.

Ironically, given its roots in a preoccupation with historical process, the contextualism that was produced here fostered a synchronic analysis typical of modern anthropology. Investigation of particular historical contexts via fieldwork limited the time frame of analysis. One was forced to consider the practices of a people primarily as they appeared in the present. Focus on the vagaries of specific historical contexts knocked out, moreover, the developmental sequences of evolutionism, its wide swings over various time periods. Without the ability to presume a developmental past or future, one was left with evolutionism's stages, each now viewed as historically contained within a particular place and time.

The same attention to vagaries of historical context undercut evolutionism's confidence in universal psychic processes, thereby opening up a greater appreciation for diversity among cultural forms. Differences in culture had to be taken with greater seriousness once they could not be placed along a single line of progressive intellectual achievement. If cultural forms were the product of local historical context, no single explanation in terms of universal psychic laws could be offered for the multiplicity of cultural forms found within and across societies. The specifics of historical context had destroyed the grounds evolutionists gave for universal laws of cultural development—the idea that similar cultural phenomena always have the same causes. A single set of principles therefore could no longer provide a uniform touchstone for explaining differences in cultural phenomena.

Without a single standard of explanation there could be no single standard of evaluation either.[35] Cultural forms could not be assessed for their relative adequacy in achieving the same ends, defined prior to investigation of social groups and therefore according to an ethnocentric understanding of utility or happiness. Instead of being subject to such external standards of assessment, cultural forms might have functions specific to the particular social group to which they belonged. Ends served would therefore not push beyond a social group's practices to require assessment with reference to the practices of other groups. Ends served by cultural forms might be as local as the contextual accounts of cultural forms that were to replace evolutionary comparisons. (Indeed, as we will see in chapter 2, in post-1920s anthropology the purpose of cultural forms is so local and internal as to be identified simply with maintaining the characteristic shape of the social group in which they figure.) The functionalism of evolutionism in this way becomes relativistic and nonevaluative.

Differences in the values and customs of different societies were now given a distinctively anthropological interpretation. They were not, first of all, the result of differences in biological capacity. Boas proposed his ideas about culture in direct opposition to racialist hypotheses. Behavioral differences among peoples were not due to differences in racial stock but were attributed to differences in culture. Cultural differences did not, moreover, become biologically encoded over time. Boas directly attacked racialist ideas that had entered evolutionism by way of Lamarckianism—the theory that adaptations to environmental circumstances could be biologically inherited. Cultural evolutionism, with its claim of universal laws of intellectual development, presented an alternative at least to polygenesist racialism—the idea of original differences in hereditary stock; such differences were not the explanation for the differences among various peoples' ways of life. But without an attack on Lamarckianism, evolutionism could still explain the failure of certain groups of people to progress further than they had by claiming that the customs and accumulated life experiences of such peoples, whatever their origins, had become biologically encoded.

Differences in values and customs were not, in the second place, explained in more typical evolutionist fashion in terms of the different circumstances in which the same intellectual processes common to humanity set to work. Differences in custom, values, and beliefs became, instead, one might say, their own principles of interpretation; there was no secondary mechanism of biology or universal psychic law working in, through, or behind them. They sustained *themselves*, simply by being repeated and by the force of habit and traditional authority that such repetition generated. They sustained themselves, in other words, mainly through unconscious processes of habitual repetition that conditioned the behaviors of every individual growing up with them. The specific historical context of a people's practice was itself therefore the primary explanation for differences among peoples' customs, values, or worldviews. In keeping with the Germanic associations of *Kultur* with the inherited traditions of particular locales, these different historical contexts were termed cultures.

If cultural context was now the explanation for differences among peoples, biological capacities would have to be uniform and insufficient of themselves to determine values, customs, and beliefs. Innate intellectual capacities would also have to be much the same among every people but the direction and results of their exercise fundamentally conditioned by particular cultures. A nonempiricist, German-influenced epistemology enters anthropology here; the human intellect is conditioned from the very start, not by some ahistorical Kantian set of categories or structural principles, but by the concepts, values, and worldview of the particular culture in which human beings begin to think.

This ends our overview of the way the English word *culture* gains its anthropological sense as a group-differentiating, holistic, nonevaluative, and context-relative notion. Using what we now know about the complexities of this process, let us explore systematically in the next chapter the various aspects of this anthropological notion of culture as it solidified after 1920 in U.S. anthropological circles and established its wide influence in so many fields over the last half-century.

2

The Modern Meaning of Culture

We now turn to exploring various aspects of the notion of culture in the form in which it solidified in cultural anthropology, particularly in the United States after the 1920s. I will describe the kind of appeal to culture that eventually became a dominant paradigm within the discipline of anthropology—how the notion was used, the sort of object it specified, the kind of analysis it implied—in terms general enough to encompass, without too much distortion, most major schools in U.S. anthropology up through the 1960s—for instance, students of Franz Boas such as Ruth Benedict, functionalists, structuralist followers of Claude Lévi-Strauss, and symbolic or interpretive anthropologists.[1] Starting from a rather narrow base in U.S. cultural anthropology and initially opposed in Britain by the influential social anthropology of A. R. Radcliffe-Brown, this general understanding of culture gradually fanned out so as arguably to become the central focus of the discipline of anthropology as a whole.[2] As we will see in chapter 3, it is also the notion of culture that has come in for concerted criticism after the 1970s by, among others, post-Geertzian anthropologists (such as James Clifford), and poststructuralist cultural critics. It is the foil over against which a new paradigm for the study of culture has begun to emerge.

Basic Elements

Making up the anthropological understanding of culture during this period of its heyday is the following loose congerie of ideas. There are connections among the various aspects, but also tensions, the product no doubt of the mutiple lines feeding into the complex prehistory of an anthropological understanding of culture.

1. First, and perhaps most basically, *culture is understood as a human universal*. All (and only) human beings have culture. Culture is the defining mark of human life.

"Culture" has "nature," therefore, as its contrast term. What is not cultural is natural, in the sense of being merely "physio-biological" or "animal." What is not cultural is, in short, subhuman. The "animal" and "biological" are quite closely associated to form this contrast with culture. Animals are biologically determined in their behaviors. Human beings, because they lack biologically based blueprints for behavior, are formless and aimless, hardly human at all, without culture:

> The behavior patterns of . . . animals are, . . . to a much greater extent, given them with their physical structure. . . . For man, what are innately given are extremely general response capacities. . . . Undirected by culture . . . man's behavior would be virtually ungovernable, a mere chaos of pointless acts and exploding emotions, his experiences virtually shapeless. Culture . . . is not just an ornament of human existence but . . . an essential condition for it.[3]

2. Though culture is universal in the sense that all people have one, the anthropological use of the term *highlights human diversity*. All people have culture but they do not all have the same one. What culture amounts to varies widely with time and place. "The fact of 'culture' is common to all; the *particular pattern* of culture differs among all."[4] Culture therefore comes in the plural; the anthropologist speaks of cultur*es*.

The search for commonalities in culture has had its ups and downs in anthropology, but the recognition of marked differences in human behavior is the prior founding intuition of the discipline generally. Anthropology's object is to come to terms with significant differences in human behavior worldwide. It justifies its existence as a discipline by a distinctive account of such differences—they are cultural, and not products, say, of biology or climate. Indeed, the primary indicator of culture for the anthropologist is diversity. Forms of human behavior are usually discussed in terms of culture precisely when it is clear such forms may be absent elsewhere. That human beings eat is not attributable to culture; all people do so as a function of somatic needs. That some humans never eat domesticated pigs and cows can be attributed to culture just because it is known that others do.

3. *Culture varies with social group*. The differences that break culture into a plurality of forms follow differences between such groups. If cultures differ from one another, that is because they are the cultures of different societies. "'A Culture': the specific pattern of behaviors which distinguishes any society from all others."[5]

A culture is the attribute, then, of a particular social group. A society, for instance, an African tribe or a European nation, has a culture. Individuals may differ from one another, but these differences are not termed differences of culture unless they can be associated with membership in different networks of social interaction. When they cannot be so associated, differences between individuals are assigned a physiological basis or a basis in the idiosyncrasies of personal experience.

The boundaries of a particular culture become in this way the boundaries of a particular society. Where a society breaks off so does its culture. Cultures tend therefore to be discussed as isolatable units in geographical space.

4. Insofar as it is specific to a particular group of people, *a culture tends to be conceived as their entire way of life,* everything about the group that distinguishes it from others, including social habits and institutions, rituals, artifacts, categorial schemes, beliefs and values. Thus, "culture is essentially a construct that describes the total body of belief, behaviors, knowledge, sanctions, values and goals that mark the way of life of a people. . . . In the final analysis it comprises the things that people have, the things they do, and what they think."[6]

5. Moreover, because cultures are group-specific they are *associated with social consensus.* If it is the culture of a group, a culture is evidently what every member of the group more or less shares. "We may . . . identify 'culture' with the extent to which the conventionalized behavior of members of the society is for all the same."[7] A culture spreads itself equally over all the members of the group to which its ascribed.

If cultures are group-specific, then cultural differences must fall between such groups and not within them. A society may have its own divisions—divisions by class or by status and occupational affiliations—but these divisions do not alter the consensus character of culture. A distinct culture may be attributed to each of these subgroups, if they have sufficient institutional isolation to approximate a difference between societies. But once again the culture of the subgroup is spread evenly throughout its membership. Social subdivisions, moreover, are not thought to conflict with the homogeneity of the wider-society culture: the distinct behaviors of subgroups seem merely to add onto a culture that continues to be shared by all members of the widest social group. The culture of upper-class Americans, for example, may be significantly different from that of lower-class ones, but both classes presumably still share the culture of the United States, for instance, a fondness for democratic government and respect for personal freedoms.

6. In keeping with its suggestions of all-inclusiveness and its use to define the human, *culture is understood to constitute or construct human nature.* Culture does not function to regulate or repress it. Indeed, there is nothing to human life with any definite form or shape of its own that might exist outside culture so as to be so regulated or repressed. Culture makes human life from the first; it is in that sense its constitutive medium and not some secondary influence on it. Human beings get from culture all the

shape, form, and definiteness their actions manifest. Culture is therefore not talked about as redirecting or constraining already-established behaviors, with clearly defined goals and underlying interests—not talked about as redirecting or constraining, say, the rapacious and willful inclinations of the profligate and unrefined. If culture works *on* anything, it works on bare animal or bodily based capacities with an extensive and indefinite range of possible outcomes. Those capacities, of themselves and without the guidance of culture, might lead in any number of different directions and take any number of different forms.

7. Human beings may be made by culture but they also make it. *Cultures are conventions in the sense that they are human constructions.* "Everything . . . created by man, in the process of living, comes within the concept of culture."[8] Human beings may be nothing without culture but they are responsible for what culture amounts to in any particular place and time, that is, for the particular shapes cultures take, and for their maintenance. An anthropologist in the field observes a culture only insofar as it is already formed and up and running in the lives of human beings, but he or she nevertheless presumes its emergence as the cumulative effect of past human interactions that have become habitual or routine over time, and he or she has direct observational knowledge in any case of the ongoing educative efforts necessary to transmit it to future generations. A culture is viewed by the anthropologist, in short, as "the accumulated transmissible results of past behaviors in association."[9] Culture in this way becomes another name for traditional inheritance, for the customary behaviors that result from and are handed down by way of human historical processes. "Culture means . . . traditional behavior which has been developed by the human race and is successfully learned by each generation."[10]

8. The plastic character of human biological equipment, the fact of cultural diversity, and the purported origin of that diversity in the vagaries of human history, combine to suggest strongly the *contingency of cultures*. However longstanding and uncontested by those participating in it, a culture could have been otherwise; the existence of other cultures is proof of that. Sharing the contingency of the processes of human interaction that gave it definition and now sustain it, a particular culture can never claim inevitability.

9. Because culture is constitutive of humanity and cultures are aligned with social groups, *the notion of culture suggests social determinism: society decisively shapes the character of its members.* The character of one's culture is contingent but one's conformity to it is not. Individuals may influence the culture of their society through their activities—altering its constitution, furthering or hampering its continuation over time. Their capacity to do so

is implied by the conventional character of culture. But this agency on the part of individuals is always subsequent to, and predicated upon, their prior formation by the culture into which they were born. They first became the people they are by being formed by the culture of their society, by internalizing as children, in the process of being socialized, an already existing culture, a culture of which they simply found themselves a part and could have done nothing themselves to produce. At least initially, individuals are almost the "passive porters" of a culture: "they are born into different . . . ways of life, and these they must follow because they have no [other] choice."[11]

Methods of Study and the Object They Construct

These basic elements of the modern anthropological understanding of culture suggest that certain ways of studying culture would be appropriate. These procedures of analysis bring with them, in turn, certain further presumptions about the nature of cultures, presumptions that develop implications of the basic features of the modern anthropological idea of culture.

Holism

Because a culture characterizes a whole group of people, the anthropologist does not take up the various elements of a group's way of living one by one, in a disjointed fashion; nor does he or she view them together as a mere aggregate. Instead, the anthropologist considers them as *forming some sort of whole*. The anthropologist, when identifying a culture, views it from above, so to speak, as a single, albeit very complex, unit.

The distinctiveness of a culture—what makes it different from another and therefore definable *as* one culture among others—cannot be captured by considering its discrete elements or any enumerative set of these. It can be captured only by getting a sense for what sets apart this group of behaviors and artifacts as a whole, a sense for the distinctive *manner* or *way* of living that runs through all its isolatable parts. Thus, an anthropologist may say that a culture exhibits a distinctive "pattern or configuration," "theme," "style," or "mentality," the choice of phrasing depending in great part upon the analogy drawn, for instance, to a work of art or to the life of an individual person. A culture may be "a personality writ large," as Ruth Benedict was fond of saying, bound up to form a discrete unit by characteristic purposes, goals, or preoccupations, or a culture may be comparable to a style of art or architecture, exhibiting its distinctiveness in and through a certain canon of taste.[12]

In short, if the behaviors of a particular group of people are to be talked about as a culture, they must be somehow all of a piece. The character of those behaviors can therefore be *summed up by generalizations* about the qualities that such behaviors always exemplify. The distinctiveness of a culture is captured by efforts to typify it.

Cultures tend to become in this way *qualitatively distinct incommensurables*. "Between two wholes there is a discontinuity of kind."[13] "Cultures differ like so many species . . . and their common basis is lost forever. It seems impossible . . . to bring cultures into any continuous series."[14] Efforts to understand their different respective natures therefore take precedence over efforts to see them together in terms of any similar elements they may have in common.

Getting a sense for a culture therefore involves no direct comparison with similar seeming beliefs or behaviors in other groups. Two groups of people may both engage, for example, in marriage rituals but in the one case the ritual expresses the characteristic concern of members of the group to accumulate wealth; in the other, the customary value placed on exorbitant expenditure. A simple comparison of behaviors in different groups, made possible with reference to cross-cultural types of human action (for instance, marriage ceremonies), therefore tells the anthropologist very little of what he or she wants to know. Comparative cross-cultural discussion of behaviors will become fruitful only after the anthropologist has gained a sense for the qualitative differences between cultures as wholes.

Analysis in Relation to Social Behavior

As the above examples of cultural difference suggest, what makes a culture a unitary whole, what typifies it as a distinct unit, is often identified in ideational or mental terms, for instance, as a characteristic set of norms, values, beliefs, concepts, dispositions, or preoccupations. Culture has the progressive tendency, indeed, to become identified with what people think and feel, and not with the behaviors, artifacts, technological processes, and so forth, from which the anthropologist starts in the field.[15] Culture is a subset of what is observed—for instance, a people's conceptions of and attitudes toward the pots they make and not the pots themselves or the technological processes used to make them. Or culture comprises the anthropologist's own abstract generalizations or ideas about the character of the activities observed—for instance, not so much what the Azande believe or feel in making witchcraft accusations as what those practices show about the general preoccupation with questions of responsibility and blame among the Azande. In any case, culture is now *distinguishable from social behaviors*.

This mental or ideational conception of culture, dominant among cultural anthropologists in particular, mirrors a high culture contrast with material civilization. But it is far more inclusive. Culture, especially when it is understood as the informing spirit of a whole way of life, may be most obvious in high culture productions, but culture cannot simply be identified with such high culture forms, or with articulate, formal expressions of belief and value. It encompasses as well the taken-for-granted, tacit background of beliefs, concepts, values, attitudes, and so forth, that are the constant accompaniment of everyday activities. Culture includes beliefs and values that, like language, are in unreflective use as well as those that are made the explicit focus of literature, song, or ritual activity.

By including such a tacit or background dimension, culture can retain the all-inclusive character mentioned above. The anthropologist who studies culture can discuss every aspect of what is said and done by a particular group of people; culture retains its reference therefore to a whole way of life. But the anthropologist studies all this with reference to its cultural aspect, its meaning dimension. Even the most trivial "material" details of social life can come within the anthropologist's purview—say, the arrangement of chairs in a school room—because they signify the values, beliefs, and so forth, that constitute a culture; in a lecture hall, for example, that arrangement signifies the difference in status and authority between students and teacher.

Culture as *the meaning dimension of social life* is, then, autonomous of social behaviors to a certain degree, sufficiently autonomous to justify the anthropologist's distinction between culture and social behaviors, and sufficiently autonomous to justify thereby the existence of cultural anthropology as a discipline. At the extreme, culture can be discussed (for example, in cognitive anthropology) without explicit reference to social activities—as categorial schemes inside the heads of the individual members of a social group. But, more usually, culture is discussed in direct relation to social activities, as a public feature of social behaviors and their consequences. By discussing culture in this way, the anthropologist respects the fact that, particularly when understood as a taken-for-granted background of meaning, culture is an abstraction drawn by the anthropologist from the concrete facts of socially significant behaviors.[16]

This knowledge that culture and society are inseparable in fact and only analytically distinguishable does not prevent the cultural anthropologist, however, from discussing the relation betwen culture and society in basically causal terms. *Culture is related to social behaviors as their ordering principle.* Culture is a control mechanism, a sort of blueprint for action, guiding social behaviors. Even interpretive anthropologists, who generally eschew causal analysis (culture is social action's interpretive frame and not its cause), are still led to affirm that culture is a control mechanism governing behavior by the idea that human beings would otherwise be formless without it.[17]

Culture also seems a force directing action because the whole of a culture is viewed as a norm. All that a culture includes—not just explicit norms or values, but beliefs, attitudes, dispositions, sentiments, and so forth—constitute what a people values, what they honor and reward, and therefore enforce against violation by formal and informal sanctions. The particular manner or way of living, the pattern or design that makes a culture distinct, becomes in this way more than a descriptive generalization— that is, an account of what commonly occurs. The notions of pattern or design take on the meaning of directives for action.

Finally, culture is viewed as an action-governing mechanism because social order is thought to require what culture represents—a group consensus on beliefs, attitudes, appropriate dispositions, and so forth. "What . . . binds men together is their culture, the ideas and standards they have in common."[18] Social order, coordinated action among the many members of a society, requires a willingness on the part of each to do as others expect, and that ultimately requires everyone to share the same body of beliefs, values, and attitudes. A community of action is predicated upon—indeed, almost equated with—a community of meaning. "It is only because people know the kind of behavior expected of them, and what kind of behaviors to expect from others, in the various situations of life, and coordinate their activities in submission to rules and under the guidance of values that each and all are able to go about their affairs."[19] This understanding of culture as a force for social order is clearly bound up with the idea of social determinism. Individuals must have effectively internalized the culture into which they were born so as to become social actors who believe and feel in more or less the same way about the activities in which they engage.

Integration of Cultural Elements

If the various elements of a culture are to be considered as a whole, they must have some internal organization. One must be able to specify the manner and degree to which the various elements are interrelated or intertwined, what exactly their connections are. At the minimum, they must all be consistent with one another; at the maximum, they might cohere as a system.

Showing their interrelations establishes that the boundaries that form them all into a discrete cultural unit are not simply artificial ones of geography; those boundaries do not simply reflect the spatial limits of a culture's social group. A culture's own internal order or organization establishes its boundaries as an integral sum total.

This *insistence on the interrelation of the elements of a culture* is also a consequence of viewing culture as a principle of social order. If a culture is to integrate or hold a society together, it must itself be integrated or hang together. Social coherence implies cultural coherence. The elements of culture must be somehow coordinated if they are to produce coordinated social action.

Cultural anthropologists offer various accounts of the manner in which cultural elements are interrelated. Sometimes the principle of integration is an *expressive* one. Cultural elements hang together with one another because one dominant motif, style, purpose, or theme presides over the entirety of cultural and social life. All cultural (and social) dimensions of life "express" the same purpose, style, or theme. The analogy here is aesthetic or personalistic. The constitutive elements of a culture hang together in the way the different parts of a work of art or the various contributors to a school of art do—by exhibiting a single style throughout. In the same way that everything a single person feels and believes may be dominated by a particular drive or preoccupation—say, by an interest in material success—so may a whole culture.

A culture can also be integrated on a *semantic* or logical level. The beliefs and values that make up a culture are consistent with or imply one another. In this way the Azande's beliefs about human motivations, about the misfortunes that spring from witchcraft, and about the workings of magic "fit" with one another, "every bit of belief . . . with every other bit in a general mosaic of mystical thought."[20] As Clifford Geertz explains the same logico-semantic sort of connections between a culture's notions of reality and its typical attitudes and values:

> For the Navaho, an ethic prizing calm deliberateness, untiring persistence, and dignified caution complements an image of nature as tremendously powerful, mechanically regular, and highly dangerous. For the French, a logical legalism is a response to the notion that reality is rationally structured, that first principles are clear, precise, and unalterable and so need only be discerned, memorized, and deductively applied to concrete cases.[21]

On a logico-semantic level—on the level of meaning—cultural elements hang together in the way a text, or a narrative does. Or they are generally consistent and interrelated with one another in the way that the contents of an individual person's mind and emotions tend toward consistency and coherence.[22]

The anthropologist can also discuss the interrelatedness of cultural elements in terms of formal laws or *structures*. In so doing, beliefs, values, and so forth, are related syntactically rather than semantically. Analogous to the way linguistic elements are organized according to grammatical rules, cultural elements become values in quasi-mathematical, abstract codes. For example, the ideational elements of a myth might be organized this way: the idea that men spring from the earth is to the underrating of blood relations as the idea that men are born of women is to their overrating. In formalized terms: $x : ~y :: ~x : y.$[23]

Finally, cultural elements can be interrelated with reference to their social function of maintaining order. They are *functionally* integrated. Cultural elements are connected with one another to the extent that each does its bit to further the end of a nonconflictual and stable social order. Cultural elements are not related directly, either semantically or syntactically, but by way of their (socially useful) effects on action. Thus, a religious belief in life after death is related to a culture's socially useful attitudes of solidarity with one's fellows and confidence and courage in the face of difficulties, by shoring these attitudes up in a crisis situation, the loss of a loved one, that might otherwise break them down.[24] The analogy here is to a machine or organism: the elements of a culture work interdependently, like gears or bodily organs, for the sake of the whole, in order to sustain its smooth functioning.

Contextual Focus

If the particulars of a culture are interconnected in such ways, they cannot be understood in isolation from one another. *Understanding any particular requires one to view it in its context;* anthropological investigation becomes a form of contextual analysis. The oddity or apparent nonsensicality of a particular belief or value is dispelled when the anthropologist considers it in relation to the rest of the culture and, usually also, with reference to the context of group behaviors in which it is situated. Thus, "to make intelligible a number of beliefs, all of which are foreign to the mentality of a modern [person]," one shows how "they form a comprehensible system of thought and how this system of thought is related to social activities, social structure, and the life of the individual." Such beliefs make sense "only when they are seen as interdependent parts of a whole."[25] Anthropologists "render obscure matters intelligible by providing them with an informing context." The anthropologist restores the whole "imaginative universe" without which the particulars of a culture can only seem obscure.[26] Like a sentence in a text, or an organ of a body, or a phonetic element in a system of semantically significant sounds, an element of a culture, according to the anthropologist, has no meaning, significance, or point independent of the whole wider context in which it figures.

This penchant for contextual analysis also promotes a localized one. *The relevant context for understanding particulars becomes a clearly restricted geographical space.* The frame of analysis of particulars is a local one extending no further than the boundaries of the social group to which the culture under investigation is attributed. The relevant social groups, moreover, are usually quite small in scale. Large communities make it difficult for the anthropologist to get a sense for a culture as a whole, especially when this must be achieved by way of firsthand fieldwork.

It is true that anthropologists make implicit comparisons with other cultures since the distinctiveness of a culture is defined by contrast with others (that is, a culture is definable *as a culture* only in distinction from others that it is not). At least implicit comparison is also made with the anthropologist's own culture, since an anthropologist cannot help understanding a foreign culture in the terms of his or her native land and in the terms of the anthropological discipline of which he or she is a part. But none of this takes away from the fact that the primary agenda of the anthropologist is to understand the import of cultural elements—their meaning or functioning—precisely for the social group in which they are found.

Synchronic Emphasis

The time frame of contextual analysis is also quite restricted. The elements of the context exist at the same time; anthropological analysis itself is therefore a synchronic rather than diachronic one viewing matters across time. The past cultural or social history of a group is of no immediate relevance for the anthropologist; it forms no part of the context analyzed. The genesis or development of a particular belief or norm—where it came from, how it arose—is of no special import when determining its meaning or point now. Social or cultural contexts that existed in the past do not, moreover, help the anthropologist understand present ones. If a particular behavior or belief exists now, it does so because it has a meaning or point in terms of the rest of what is said and done at the present time. Past cultural elements are not carried over into the present by sheer force of inertia; if they continue in circulation, the present context gives them some reason for being.

The anthropologist's attention to context is like historical analysis in that it pays close attention to the particular time and place in which cultural phenomena occur. Unlike most historical analysis, however, the anthropologist's has very little, if any, temporal sweep. Anthropological investigation is, so to speak, "synchronically historical," analyzing a particular slice of the historical sweep of things in such a way that *everything relevant to the analysis takes place more or less at the same time*. The anthropologist is like the historian who "may pause in his narrative for the depiction of a cross-sectional moment," thereby the better to delineate relations among the historical phenomena studied by abstracting from their temporal relations.[27] Indeed, the more abstract the account of those relations—the more they depart from a simple descriptive rendering of what people say and do—the more atemporal they appear.

Besides a synchronic understanding of cultural context, the anthropologist understands comparative, cross-cultural analysis synchronically. Different cultural contexts are usually not brought together for purposes of analysis in virtue of their historical relations—for instance, because one culture had an historical influence on another or because one culture is the past form of a present one. Cultures are instead *related taxonomically or structurally*. Their differences from one another are laid out spatially rather than temporally.

Change within a culture does enter the anthropological picture but only as a secondary matter to be understood from the baseline of an ordinarily static system. On an organic analogy, cultures may have their own internal principles of change: they eventually tire, grow old, and die. Like natural systems, cohesive interdependence among their constituent parts is an internal goal; cultures move of their own accord in that direction.

Generally, however, the source of cultural change is external. Should outside influences diminish or add to a culture, the relations among its constitutive elements shift in order to remain in balance, in order to retain the culture's characteristic pattern or shape. If cultural elements are systematically related, any change in one requires change to the others. Boundary maintenance is crucial to the life of a culture; influences from outside are always potentially disruptive.

Finally, change can be understood as failure to abide by cultural codes. Change may occur when not all the individuals of a society are effectively socialized, their biologically based aptitudes proving recalcitrant perhaps. Or change can occur when cultural expectations are not able to be acted upon because of altered social circumstances. For example, cultural expectations appropriate to rural life may no longer work, and may therefore suffer change, when brought by dispossessed farmers to the city.[28]

Aims of Analysis

One point of an anthropological idea of culture is *to promote a nonevaluative alternative to ethnocentrism*. Evaluation may come later but it is not built into the category of analysis that enables others to be described. Everyone has a culture; no people has any more culture than any other. The notion of culture is therefore not itself a means by which others are evaluated; it cannot be itself a source of invidious distinctions between good or bad, high or low.

Culture, to be sure, highlights the differences among peoples. But the idea of culture as a human universal binds those different ways of life together as common objects of a disinterested attention or even as common objects of human sympathy. Cultural differences appear within the framework of a presumed common humanity. The appreciation of cultures as complex wholes is, moreover, a distanced one of almost aesthetic equanimity. Following a metaphor of high culture, the anthropologist can regard different cultures as if they were all finely rendered works of art, literature, or music. The contextual preoccupation of anthropological accounts of culture also disengages, at least for a time, the anthropologist's own culture-specific standards of truth, beauty, and goodness. In order to render a fair account of the workings of another culture, the anthropologist must attend immediately to that culture's understandings of truth, beauty, and goodness, and not his or her own. The notion of culture in this way fosters a disinterested suspension of judgment in the interest of fair description. Value-laden notions of truth, beauty, and goodness have no absolute standing in such processes of description—an absolute standing that would in effect identify those notions with the anthropologist's prior understanding of them. Instead, such categories are distributed relativistically at the start, that is, according to particular social contexts, their meaning having become a matter of local circumstance. For all these reasons, the anthropological notion of culture discourages the snap judgments of a complacent ethnocentrism. Difference from the characteristic sentiments, beliefs, and values of one's own social group is not, as it has so often been in the course of human history, the source of instant repugnance.

Finally, by recognizing the contingency of culture, the anthropologist widens the scope of human possibility by suggesting that no one culture, however taken for granted it might be by its participants, is necessary. He or she thereby *furthers a humanistic project of social criticism.* The different behaviors of others give the anthropologist a way of assessing the costs and benefits of human behaviors with which he or she is more intimately familiar. If the Polynesians on Margaret Mead's telling lead happier lives as the result of freer sexual relations, why not take our cue from them? Criticism of one's own culture is promoted by viewing it from the distanced perspective of some other.

By such means the anthropologist approximates in a new idiom the Enlightenment project of freeing human society from the dead weight of tradition or custom—be that tradition one's own or that of others. There is no escape from the social inheritance of culture; culture is an inevitability, a human universal. But no particular culture has a similar inevitability; any culture can conceivably be escaped—into some other. Reflection on cultural differences hereby replaces culture-free reflection as a means to social change. "A very little acquaintance with other conventions, and a knowledge of how various these may be, . . . [does] much to promote a rational social order."[29]

3

Criticism and Reconstruction

A number of the central aspects of the anthropological notion of culture discussed in chapter 2 have come in for increasing criticism in recent years. It seems less and less plausible to presume that cultures are self-contained and clearly bounded units, internally consistent and unified wholes of beliefs and values simply transmitted to every member of their respective groups as principles of social order. What we might call a postmodern stress on interactive process and negotiation, indeterminacy, fragmentation, conflict, and porosity replaces these aspects of the modern, post-1920s understanding of culture, or, more properly as we will see, forms a new basis for their reinterpretation.

Fueling this postmodern refiguring of the notion of culture are arguments impugning both the accuracy and ethics of the prior notion. Anthropologists espousing a modern understanding of culture have been misled by the analogies they draw—to texts, organisms, or works of art. They have mistakenly read the presuppositions of their methods of approach into what they study. They have ignored or grossly underestimated evidence conflicting with presumptions of stasis and consensus. Their understanding of culture has been vitiated by associations with nationalism, colonialism, and the power plays of intellectual elites, alluded to in chapter 2.

In part these criticisms and the resulting postmodern shift in the notion of culture represent an internal movement within anthropology. I attempted in chapter 2 to present the various features of the modern notion of culture in an intelligible order that brought out their interconnections. But tensions riddle the account—tensions, for example, between the material and ideational dimensions of social life, between historical process and stasis, between the agency of persons in social interactions and social determinism, and between the hope for new human possibilities and the importance of social stability—tensions due in great part to the lingering traces of the tortuous history of the notion recounted in chapter 1. Anthropologists such as James Clifford would purify the notion of culture of this history, ridding it, for example, of the remains of high culture aestheticism. Or they would bring such tensions to the surface in order to resolve them in favor of previously slighted features of the notion, for instance, in favor of historical process, submerged in the modern account of culture within a static synchronic analysis. They would have anthropology be true to its ethical intentions, true, for one, to its tolerant, nonevaluative impulse jeopardized by associations of the discipline with colonialism and the influence of nationalism on its understanding of culture. Those anthropologists who view culture, with primarily descriptive intent, as part and parcel of public social action (for instance, symbolic anthropologists with a dominant influence on the field after the 1960s), may be prone to attend to the messy details of culture in action, the conflict-ridden, confused twists and turns of real-life situations, downplayed in an understanding of cultures as unified wholes. The self-consciousness about the anthropologist's process that is cultivated by the same school of anthropology may prompt, as well, critical reflection on the metaphors employed by anthropologists and reassessment of the way anthropologists help to construct, in a possibly self-deceiving fashion, the objects of their study.

Challenges to the modern understanding of culture and the resulting postmodern shift are also products, however, of a cross-fertilization with other disciplines. Disciplines such as history, literary theory, "conflict" sociology, and political science begin to employ an anthropological notion of culture and in so doing bring their own perspectives to it. Once historians recognize that events are culturally mediated for both historians and the people they study, once historians engaged in long-term studies make it part of their task to reconstruct the "mentalities" of the past, the anthropological notion of culture they employ is historicized: if history is a matter of culture, then culture is a matter of history.[1] Scholars of the global economy (Marxists, world-systems theorists) have an interest in the way, say, international corporate capitalism is played out culturally in local contexts; they thereby alter the merely local, closed sytem analysis of culture commonly employed by anthropologists.[2] In great part because of the social constructionism that the anthropological idea of culture highlights, literary theorists begin to put popular and high culture on a continuum, thereby modifying the traditional associations of high culture that anthropologists tend to employ unthinkingly as analogies. Deconstruction and poststructuralist discourse theory suggest that determinacy, closure, and consistency are no more to be expected in the tacit cultural forms of everyday life than they are in formalized and explicit ones. "Conflict" sociologies, which follow Max Weber or Karl Marx rather than Emile Durkheim or Talcott Parsons in conceiving of society in terms of conflict among different groups or forces, increasingly give the meaning of behaviors and situations for human actors a central place in their study, and thereby contest assumptions of consensus in cultural analysis. Neo-Marxists influenced by Antonio Gramsci and Michel Foucault modify their understanding of ideology to bring it into line with an anthropological notion of culture. Discussion of ideology shifts from legal, religious, and political discourse to the common sense of everyday life, to the experiential meaning of common human affairs. The struggles for power in which ideology figures become in this way dimensions of all human activity, and are highlighted in importance since, according to these theorists, power cannot be consolidated effectively through coercion alone but requires consent. Political struggle is therefore not focused on control of the state, and its military or policing apparatuses; political struggle is waged over the meaning of situations and culturally valorized terms (for instance, family, freedom, patriotism). Politics becomes a matter of culture, and culture as a result is politicized. Especially given these associations with ideology, an ideology critique can be launched against the anthropologist's understanding of culture: the way an anthropologist describes a culture is ideological in the sense that it disguises the unequal workings of power both within the society studied and between the anthropologist and his or her subjects.

In this chapter I sketch these converging challenges to the modern notion of culture, by detailing the various kinds of arguments now being lodged against it from a basically postmodern standpoint. This critical reflection sets up, by the end of the chapter, a constructive discussion of how the notion of culture might be reformulated from a postmodern perspective.

Criticisms

The Charge of Inattention to Historical Process

Underlying a number of criticisms of the modern notion of culture is an attack on its dehistoricized character. In the modern approach, culture appears at the start as a given, as something already formed and finished. Assuming a culture is already there on the ground, the anthropologist's task is simply to describe its shape and workings, and/or its transformative effects on individuals, its mode and efficacy of transmission. Left out of the account is how culture came to have this character, how it came to have the shape that is now transmitted, with whatever degree of success. The modern anthropologist does affirm that human beings produce culture in and through their social interactions; every culture is a human construction. But he or she fails to give sufficient attention to this activity of production itself. Culture therefore appears as a product apart from the historical processes in and through which it emerges. The agency of human actors, their ability to determine their own lives, is also disparaged, and, contrary to the founding intentions of the discipline, particular cultures begin to seem like facts of nature—givens of human life that human beings can do very little about, what they must simply work with and from, rather than exceed imaginatively in light of the alternative possibilities for living represented by other cultures.

This dehistoricizing turn is partly the effect of expediency: the shape of a culture and how it hangs together are perhaps more easily described if one brackets questions of historical process, especially given the time constraints of field-based observation.[3] The relevance of issues of genesis for description of culture is also disputed in modern anthropology: what matters is how something works and not where it comes from. But such a judgment of irrelevance is based on a too-narrow identification of questions of genesis with either accounts of diffusion or cultural evolutionism. Questions of genesis need not lead, as they did in those cases, to an atomistic isolation of particular forms of culture and a decontextualized reading of their significance. In contrast to cultural evolutionism, the historical processes at work can be identified with those of the society under investigation. And rather than stop analysis of a particular cultural form with the claim of diffusion—the claim that a cultural form is derived from contact with other people—the anthropologist can go on to discuss how that cultural form has been made to fit within the rest of what a people says and does.

The dehistoricizing of culture may also simply be a residue within modern anthropology of how non-Western peoples were viewed within cultural evolutionism. Like cultural evolutionists, the modern anthropologist is not interested in the past of the people he or she studies because those people are, or represent, the West's own past. The culture from which the anthropologist speaks is in historical process; it has a past. But non-Western cultures do not have a past in the same way: they *are* the past—relics of a vanished age, ruins, petrified fossils, the living dead.[4] Nothing precedes the childhood of the human race and it has no future but the West.[5] Freeing anthropology from *its* intellectual past would therefore mean, to the contrary, attributing historical process equally to both the culture under anthropological investigation and the culture from which such investigation proceeds.

An emphasis on products apart from process may also be due to the continuing influence in modern anthropology of a high culture understanding of culture. When one focuses on the material advances of civilization or the intellectual and spiritual heights of cultured society, one focuses on achievements, the amassed material and spiritual wealth of a society, its valued possessions. Historical processes of emergence recede in significance behind their productions. Historical processes of concern are primarily those relating to simple accumulation and preservation of what has already been achieved—historical processes concerned with keeping and adding onto what one has.[6] When high culture notions are employed explicitly as metaphors or analogies in anthropology they have a similar effect. Attending to a work of art usually means attending to it as is, in its completed form, apart from any reference to the processes by which it was produced, apart from the course of its production. Like a text that has a sense independent of its author, his or her intentions, and the process by which it was written and published, the public culture of social action can be given an interpretation that is not bound tightly to the way it is produced by specific actors. The sense of culture is then one thing; actual social interactions and the intentions of the participants in them are another.[7]

Against Cultures as Internally Consistent Wholes

The tendency to see cultures as wholes is criticized for being a hypothetical construction of the discipline that unself-consciously distorts the realities of lived practice. The modern anthropologist, by observing disparate events and talking with multiple informants at different times and places, is able to sum up a culture as a whole. But in reality, so the criticism runs, culture never appears as a whole for the participants in it. No one is likely to know it all and the whole of it is never mobilized on any particular occasion.[8] Only bits of culture appear at any one time according to the dictates of a situation and the various interests of the actors in it.[9]

The anthropologist's own needs, and not the needs of practice, are behind the idea of culture as a whole. The whole is the screen against which the anthropologist's efforts of understanding can be projected. With the presumption that a culture is a whole, every cultural element becomes readable, decipherable; the anthropologist's project becomes a significant intellectual exercise. Without it, the anthropologist seems "condemned to the intellectually sterile activity of endlessly cataloguing haphazard data."[10] As Ruth Benedict maintained, to renounce the idea of culture as a whole is "to renounce the possibility of intelligent interpretation."[11]

Since a culture does not figure as a whole in the practice of participants, the perception of it as a whole becomes the exclusive privilege of the anthropologist's superior perspective. This superiority of perspective runs contrary to the fundamental egalitarianism of the anthropological impulse, and mirrors, moreover, the superiority of Western power in the colonial situation in which anthropologists, especially prior to 1945, did their fieldwork. The administration of colonized peoples requires a totalizing vision of them; it helps if they can be seen as manageable wholes.

The effort to typify such wholes, to sum up their character by qualitative generalizations, is criticized as a residue of relations with the biological sciences (for instance, evolutionism) that figured in the complex prehistory of the anthropological notion of culture. Arising in contradistinction to biological explanation, culture was to replace biology as an explanation for differences in human practice. Native Americans behaved differently from Europeans not because they were biologically different from them but because they were culturally different. This opposition to biological accounts of differences in human practice did not prevent, however, the use in modern anthropology of biological analogies for cultural differences, with certain invidious consequences for anthropological description. Despite the opposition to biological forms of explanation, differences among cultures still seem in significant respects like the natural differences that distinguish species. Thus, in the biological sciences of that prehistory, differences among natural kinds are typified so that a single animal can stand in for the whole of the species, and the whole of the species is treated as if it were a single animal with particular characteristics. One can speak of "the dog" as a loyal animal and mean thereby both the species as a whole and any single dog of one's acquaintance. Every dog is a typical example; and the species is viewed as if it were an individual and not a collection of different individuals about whom one can form only statistically reliable generalizations. In the same way, any Trobiander can stand in for any other and for the whole culture in modern anthropology. One talks about Trobriander culture by talking about "the" Trobriander. Confirming the anthropologist's seduction by biological accounts of the essential natures of things is the fact that, like discourse about species differences, amalgams are understood in anthropology to be corruptions of the purity of a culture's nature. A Westernized non-Western culture often seems something like a sterile half-breed. Moreover, like what happens in efforts to describe the nature of an animal species, characteristics of human behaviors are deemed proper to the culture itself and not a matter of environmental factors or a mattter of a culture's relations with others. Thus, in these early biological sciences one might say that the dog is a loyal animal—loyalty is a species marker—and not just that the dog displays loyalty in its relations with beneficent human owners. In the same way, the anthropologist might say that the culture of the Feloops is characterized by generosity—generosity is its defining nature—and not just that the Feloops displayed generosity in helping the British against their French colonial rivals.[12]

In a charge very much like that lodged against the idea of cultural wholes, the idea of coherence or consistency among the elements of those wholes is criticized, too, for being a product of the distorted optics of anthropology as a discipline. The anthropologist extracts from social practices cultural elements—characteristic beliefs, values, and so forth—and goes on to organize them into some coherent or consistent framework. But in use these cultural elements are unlikely to demonstrate those same logical or structural properties. Cultural elements as part of the public domain of social practices come to be interrelated in and through social interactions. Their interrelations are not intrinsic to them, not formal or syllogistic relations, but social ones, arising within social life by way of interconnections among the practices in which cultural forms are involved. Given such a mode of production, interrelations among cultural elements tend to be far messier in fact than they appear to be in abstract theory. In contrast to the tight connections found in a machine or a deductive system, cultural elements in the form in which they are mobilized in practice have the partly integrated, partly discontinous character of an octopus, its "tentacles . . . in large part separately integrated, [and] neurally quite poorly connected with one another . . . who nevertheless manages both to get around and to preserve himself for a while any way, as a viable if ungainly entity."[13]

The people under study may themselves theorize their culture, bringing what they believe and value into some systematic connection, showing their logical relations, smoothing over contradictions that do not appear significant in practice. But unless the anthropologist mistakenly associates the anthropological notion of culture with a high culture stress on intellectual achievement, he or she has no reason simply to identify such theorizing with the culture of a society per se.[14] The anthropologist should be aware of the way in which his or her own questioning induces native informants to take a semi-theoretical disposition toward beliefs and values, and should therefore not allow the results of such questioning to reinforce an intellectualist bias in anthropological investigation.[15]

The demand for cultural consistency seems almost an aesthetic demand, more appropriate in a high culture context than an anthropological one. Expectations of coherence are part of the appreciation of aesthetic forms. The merits of literary productions, for instance, are gauged from Aristotle to modernist criticism according to a criterion of unified consistency.[16] The text itself, the object it represents, or the author's intentions, form some self-consistent unity.

If the text does not exhibit the appropriate degree of coherence on its surface, the task of the good interpreter is to discover it by some sort of metalevel reading; the interpreter superimposes a more coherent text upon the one from which he or she began.[17] The anthropologist does this as well, moving beyond the messy details of everyday life to construct an otherwise hidden unity. Much interpretive digging is necessary to bring out the structural, functional, or hermeneutic depths that prove the coherence of a given cultural surface. By such interpretive efforts, both literary critics and anthropologists justify their own significance. The need for such efforts establishes their unique privilege and authority. The discrepancy between the levels of surface confusion and hidden unity translates in this way into a difference of power. Just as a text must passively await the critic's illumination, so the people studied by an anthropologist seem powerless to give a unified sense to their lives apart from the anthropologist's own explanations and interpretations of them.

Anthropologists who wish to purify the anthropological notion of culture of its high culture associations should therefore be wary of these demands for consistency. If anthropologists continue to use aesthetic analogies, recent poststructuralist literary theory suggests they might better remain on the surface of things and eschew expectations of unity in what they study.[18] Finally, the egalitarian impulse of anthropology should prompt them to repudiate a hierarchy of surface and depth that would make the superior knowledge of the anthropologist part of the very fabric of the anthropologist's method.

Against Consensus

If a culture is not a consistently unified whole it is difficult to see what sense it can make to say that it is upheld by every member of a social group. Culture, when so understood, does not seem a possible focus for common agreement. Abiding by a culture that is disconnected and fragmented in use, group members can hardly be said to believe or feel the same things in any strong sense.

There are additional, more direct reasons, however, for disputing the idea of cultural consensus. Again, anthropology can be charged with perpetrating a kind of optical illusion. Without adequate proof, the anthropologist simply assumes universality of belief by generalizing from the small sample of individuals with whom he or she is acquainted to conclusions about the whole.[19] The anthropological practice of summarizing a statistically common or lowest common denominator viewpoint also disguises the fact of genuine diversity of opinion among the anthropologist's informants. A similar effect is produced by the anthropologist's penchant for hypostasizing a single native subject: "the native point of view," "the Trobrianders," "the Nuer," and so forth.[20] Searching for consensus, the anthropologist often identifies with those native authorities on the life of their people with the power to suppress diverging opinions. The anthropologist accepts the official definition of social reality and ignores other native accounts of it, thereby reproducing within his or her discourse the false universality that is one mark of ideology, the false universality by which the powerful in the society under study disguise the particularity of their own interests.[21] The anthropologist's own discourse assumes, consequently, a similar monological power, the power to write with a single voice and silence the discrepant voices of others.[22]

Coming at a society as an outsider, the anthropologist is deceived by the surface appearance of consensus. Every member of a society may declare the same beliefs, prominently display in their discourse the same fundamental categories, hold high the same values; it is highly unlikely, however, that they will all mean the same thing by them. A consensus on the meaning of fundamental culture values is no more likely in other societies than in our own, where, for example, people of both left- and right-wing political sensibilities are likely to espouse the value of patriotism while interpreting its implications quite differently for questions of internal dissent and foreign policy. Shared elements of a culture are prone to be vague and unelaborated in and of themselves, more a matter of form than of substance, more a matter of vocabulary and manner of expression than articulated belief or clearly defined sentiment. This very lack of definition is what enables them to be shared, to be the focus of interactions among a whole group of differently situated people.[23]

In getting beyond the appearance of consensus to more detailed description of differing accounts of cultural elements, the postmodern anthropologist would be taking his or her cue from a poststructuralist understanding of meaning and leaving behind a referentialist one. The sense of a cultural form, like the sense of any sign or symbol, is not fixed by a transparent reference to reality. It is plural and shifting, always different and deferred, in keeping with the ever-changing, multivalent circumstances of its historical production.[24]

Should the anthropologist find—incredible as it may seem—a genuine consensus in meaning among members of a social group, the anthropologist should not be fooled, either, into presuming shared consent. At least some members of society may be simply going along with and acting in accordance with dominant beliefs or values for lack of other options, without giving them much credence or believing in their legitimacy. The failure to produce alternative interpretations of cultural elements may hide degrees of consent far short of full commitment.[25]

The expectation of consensus hides not only the way different senses are given to cultural elements; it hides outright conflict. Even anthropologists sensitive to the variety of interpretations of cultural forms (for instance, symbolic anthropologists) seem curiously blind to culture as a site of struggle and contention, perhaps because they fail to see what might be at stake. Once again, anthropologists have the tendency to aestheticize and/or intellectualize culture, to see it as a sphere of only formal structure or meaning and not power. The anthropologist represses the reality of conflict by describing culture in terms of categories and analogies that appear to have nothing to do with power—culture is a set of conventions or norms, a code; culture is like a game or a drama or a text.[26] An Aztec priest tearing out the heart of a captive becomes nothing more than a religious communion in which, it is believed, the deceased passes on to become a hummingbird.[27] Commoners crawling prostrate before Trobriander leaders are merely engaging in the co-construction of meaning. Bali is "not a structure of power . . . but a structure of ceremony. The taxation, the bloody instability, the apparently drugged state of much of the population, . . . |the| control exercised by Chinese merchants, all this is no more than artistic elaboration on the wonderful text that is the Balinese social formation."[28] Murder, robbery, and imprisonment surrounding a Jewish merchant named Cohen and the five hundred sheep he collected as indemnity in French-controlled Morocco are a mere series of cultural misunderstandings, having little to do, apparently, with the brutalities of colonialism.[29] A spectacle to the anthropologist who views it from an observer's distance, culture according to the anthropologist becomes a spectacle even for the actors in it: "Objectivism constitutes the social world as a spectacle presented to an observor who takes up a 'point of view' on the action, who stands back so as to observe it and, transferring into the object the principles of his relation to the object, conceives of it as a totality intended for cognition alone, in which all interactions are reduced to symbolic exchanges."[30] What anthropologists thereby miss is the power dimension of meaning. How situations and the actors in them are understood makes a difference in what it is those actors can conceive of doing. Power is therefore at stake in the interpretation of beliefs, values, or notions with a cultural currency. Struggles over power come to be enacted in struggles over meaning. In that space that poststructuralism opens up between a cultural form and the multiple possible meanings of it, contests over power are engaged.[31] Culture, like a text, "produces meaning through the struggle over the definition of signifying forms—a struggle that conveys the sense people make of history in their desires to preserve, alter, or revolt against the terms in which it appears to them."[32]

Against Culture as a Principle of Social Order

If participants in the same culture do not hold genuinely common beliefs and sentiments, the idea of culture as a principle of social order becomes tenuous. The priority placed on order within anthropology seems to become, indeed, a mere holdover from the culture or anarchy problematic of Matthew Arnold's day. In the modern account, the form-giving function attributed to culture is elided with order in a narrower sense. But if culture is constitutive of an otherwise amorphous humanity, human action in both conflict-ridden and harmonious groups must have a culture-given shape; the possession of culture clearly should not be identified with the second sort of group exclusively.

Especially when culture is discussed in ideational terms, the anthropologist who stresses the importance of cultural consensus for social order reproduces, unwittingly or not, the gambit by which high culture was used by intellectual elites in the eighteenth and nineteenth centuries to justify their own social and political importance. The dissemination of culture is the way to maintain social order and therefore educated elites have a sociopolitical importance that traditional elites (for instance, the old aristocracy) and moneyed elites (for instance, the new bourgeoisie) do not. A grab for status leads intellectual elites to downplay other principles of social order—say, system integration (the meshing of institutional forms) or integration by way of formal procedures or nonnormative media such as money, or social harmony arising out of the widespread satisfaction of needs. Since the modern anthropologist believes cultural consensus is a prerequisite for social order, whenever social order persists the anthropologist attributes it to consent, to a common conviction about the legitimacy of established practices, thereby dismissing the possibility that social order might be heavily buttressed by such factors as techniques of surveillance and the systematic use of terror, the distractions of consumerism, or the inability of the general populace to figure out what is going on and mobilize action accordingly through existing organizations. When meaning in this way simply replaces power in the explanation of social order, the anthropologist becomes, unwittingly or not, a champion for the status quo.

The equation of social order with community of meaning is only one error that the anthropologist makes in proposing culture as a principle of social order. In addition the anthropologist moves without sufficient warrant from the fact of ideas, values, and sentiments in common circulation to the claim that they operate as principles directing action. The *anthropologist* may require these generalizations about culture in order to understand what the people he or she is studying are doing but that is not a reason for thinking the people studied direct their own action according to the same principles. Trading often on the ambiguity of the word *rule*, which can mean either a statistical regularity ("Trobrianders as a rule do this") or a directing mechanism or principle ("Trobrianders act according to a rule that prescribes this form of action"), anthropologists "slip from the model of reality to the reality of the model." "A rule which fits the observed regularity in a descriptive way" becomes "a rule which guides behavior," either consciously, according to the usual prerequisites for behavior directed by rules, or, since behavior based on conscious rule following is hard to confirm empiricially, more often unconsciously.[33]

Norms for action may be part of a culture: most cultures include explicitly formulated customs, laws, rules, and regulations. These norms are not necessarily, however, the constitutive principles of social action. Rather than orchestrating such action to begin with, they more usually enter the social picture as secondary regulative principles, helping out when the usual course of action misfires.[34] The anthropologist, in assuming such norms are responsible for social order commits, moreover, the fallacy of normative determinism: because norms are meant to control behavior, it does not follow that they actually or successfully do so.[35] The efficacy of norms depends on any number of intervening sociopolitical variables, for instance, whether such norms are pushed within educational institutions and communication media, whether they are backed up by sanctions, and so forth.

In criticizing the modern understanding of culture as a social-ordering principle one need not deny that the beliefs, values, and so forth of a culture influence the sort of action that participants find appropriate; affirming such an influence is part of the postmodern proposal of a politics of culture we have just been discussing. What is wrong with the modern idea of culture as an action-governing principle is the suggestion that culture has certain social effects on its own, apart from the specific uses made of it by historical agents. Anthropologists commit the fallacy of internalism.[36] The social effects of a cultural form cannot simply be read off of it; in between the cultural forms and their influence on action come historical agents and what they make of those cultural forms in particular situations. Social context as much as cultural forms themselves determine the manner in which those cultural forms direct action. What is reactionary in one context may be subversive in another. Thus, the idea that a woman's place is in the home might simply reinforce the status quo where increased economic opportunities for women are becoming a reality. One could also imagine, however, how the same ideal could be used to subvert the status quo where women have traditionally been forced into degrading lines of outside employment (for instance, prostitution). A domestic ideal for women might be used to keep women in the home; or, it might be used to argue for a general change in business ethics now that women have been integrated into the workforce.

> Rather than assuming that a particular set of values and beliefs serves ipso facto to bind individuals of all strata to the social order, a more satisfactory approach must examine the ways in which individuals differentially situated in the social order respond to and make sense of particular symbolic forms, and how these symbolic forms, when analyzed in relation to the contexts in which they are produced, received and understood, serve (or do not serve) to establish and sustain [that social order].[37]

To put the point another way: Society can hardly be organized *by* a set of values and beliefs if they are themselves part of what is at stake in disagreements over the course that society should take.[38] Culture does not have an automatic purchase on action the way a language, perhaps, has an automatic purchase on the strings of sentences produced by the human beings who speak it. Cultural forms have the force of social directives only by way of human agents struggling over their meaning and social import. Followers of the modern notion of culture overlook, in short, the "how," the mechanism of culture's translation into social directives, perhaps because, once again, their viewpoint on culture is an aesthetic or intellectualist one.

What makes the modern notion of culture wrong is not the bare claim that culture is an ordering principle. What is wrong is the *way* culture is talked about as an ordering principle: the idea that culture is an already constituted force for social order simply waiting to be imposed upon or transmitted externally to human beings who passively internalize or mechanically reproduce it. Culture becomes a force for social order by isolating culture from the ongoing social processes that produce it and by rendering thereby the human agents involved in such processes mere passive receptors.

By making the case for culture as a principle for social order in this way, the anthropologist seems to reify an abstraction. The cultural dimension *of* social interactions becomes a thing on its own, really preceding human agents and their social interactions as their cause.[39] The anthropologist may be overly influenced here by the analogies he or she draws; thinking of culture, for example, as a language, the anthropologist may take over unself-consciously the reification of language as an atemporal system independent of language use that is typically found in structuralism.[40] Or, the anthropologist may be misled by the high culture roots of the anthropological notion in which culture is contrasted with the material processes of civilization: spiritual processes of art and literature are clearly distinct from the external processes of society according to this understanding of high culture.[41]

If, more in keeping with the anthropological drift of the notion, culture is viewed instead as something created and recreated in the "material" social interactions of which it is an integral part, then the account of culture as an external order imposed on passively socialized recipients makes little sense. Culture may have an established shape prior to the social interactions of human beings in the present. In this sense culture could be discussed as a prior determinant of social action, setting a baseline, a starting point, for any modifications or reworkings of it over time.[42] But the same active processes of social interaction that gave rise to cultural forms and their interconnections remain continuously at work, in the present as much as in the past. Cultural forms cannot therefore be artificially frozen, separated off from changes they might undergo at the hands of social actors.

Suggestions of a deterministic transmission of cultural forms are thereby lost. Human beings may understand themselves and the situation of their actions in terms of an already established culture; but that culture has no continuing influence into the present apart from the active efforts of these people to interpret and use it anew. This active agency should be extended, moreover (at least potentially), to all members of society, to all persons engaged in social interactions. Active agency cannot be limited to those persons (for instance, teacher, parents, authorities) who are socially empowered to convey or transmit culture to others. The idea that these others would passively assimilate the culture conveyed seems a holdover from an Enlightenment context: the idea provides support for an elite class's contention that it can successfully transfigure the whole of society through education.[43]

Against the Primacy of Cultural Stability

In this new account of culture and social action, change is no secondary matter, as the modern understanding of culture would have it. Historical processes that bring with them the constant possibility of change are the baseline against which stable, established cultural forms are measured, and not the reverse. What is stable is viewed as the temporary precipitate of an ongoing process that puts it in jeopardy, instead of change and genuine historical process being considered deviations from a norm of static stability.

Nor is change primarily externally generated. To be put off its regular, orderly functioning, culture does not require outside influences—those of another culture or those lodged within some acultural biological dimension of individuals. Culture has its own internal principles of change—fluid forms susceptible of varying interpretations, loosely connected elements that can therefore be ordered and reordered to support or contest various social arrangements, perhaps logically incompatible beliefs or values that might be pushed and pulled, one against the other, by politically opposed factions, or the potentially subversive remains and traces of alternatives to now-dominant cultural forms, interpretations, or arrangements. Cultural changes are not, then, the result of a failure to follow culture; they are the product of efforts to conform with a culture that has its own indeterminacies and internal strains and conflicts.

Change is possible because culture and society no longer form, as in the modern understanding of culture, an expressive totality, every aspect reinforcing all the others by virtue of their following the same structures or principles. Culture is never independent of social processes, and social interactions never occur apart from cultural interpretations; but culture and social interactions fall out of sync with one another, at the very least because of a time lag. The very materiality of the social processes that produce cultural changes—the fact that these processes take time and involve genuine historical struggle—means that social interactions and cultural productions never perfectly correspond. Cultural forms cannot be made to mean just anything: should cultural forms be already on the ground with a particular meaning and organization, their own semantic potentials act as drags on the interpretations and uses to which they may now be put by social actors. Reinterpretation and reapplication of cultural forms in and through social processes cannot occur instantaneously, and are unlikely to be easy for all actors in every social circumstance. For all these reasons, cultural production lags behind social action.[44]

Innovation is a possibility even in cases where determinate cultural forms function as rules directing action. These rules do not resemble rules of a game or the formulae of mathematics; they do not, like them, require mechanical execution but the tact, dexterity, and artfulness to act appropriately in unpredictable and highly complex social circumstances. Following cultural rules may therefore mean "necessary improvisation."[45] What the anthropologist's penchant for formalization disguises as the routine execution of a rule "emerge(s) in practice as a flow of tugs and pulls, requests and counterrequests, where tempo and grace are of the essence."[46] Moreover, a cultural rule need not always require one form of response in a certain circumstance; when following a cultural rule in a given situation there may be many different ways of responding appropriately.[47] Thus, abiding by the cultural counsel, to "act like a man" might mean, when confronted by another man's hostility, coolly ignoring or outwitting him or heatedly challenging him to fight—without this difference in response reflecting any real difference in how masculinity is understood. Given such a flexibility of proper application, changing one's responses, innovating, need not involve breaking the rules, moving outside the parameters of cultural codes. It is the enculturated individual who may be innovative; innovation need not require an individual to draw primarily upon acultural somatic reserves or desires, aspects of his or her life that might purportedly be free of or transcend culture.

Against Cultures as Sharply Bounded, Self-Contained Units

Because change, conflict, and contradiction are now admitted *within* culture, the anthropologist has no reason to insist on a culture's sharp boundaries. Sharp boundaries are no longer needed to protect a homogeneous, stable, and unified whole from outside dissension and disruption.[48] Sharp boundaries no longer establish the place where disagreements lie or change arises—beyond the sphere of a culture itself.

Since the anthropologist does not have this particular investment in boundary maintenance, he or she can move away from an identification of culture with social units localized in geographical space. The more or less objective boundaries of a social group—where social interactions break off or become less dense—need no longer be used to define the limits of a culture. The assumption that boundaries of a social group establish boundaries of a culture can be understood as a holdover from the nationalistic prehistory of the anthropological notion of culture evident in our discussion of Germany in chapter 1. Nations insist on the correspondence between culture and social unit; such correspondence is the way they legitimate a right to separate statehood.[49] Even if a correspondence between culture and society is true for the case of modern nation-states (and not merely a tactic of legitimation), there is no reason to expect it to be a universal phenomenon. For example, in sharply stratified agro-literate societies, educated governing elites and peasant farmers may have very little to do with each other culturally, yet form interdependent links of the same sociopolitical order.[50] Cultures may also cross social boundaries—nothing could be clearer in a world united by electronic media. Finally, in today's world "social and cultural boundaries coincide less and less closely [because] there are Japanese in Brazil, Turks on the Main, and West Indian meets East in the streets of Birmingham—a shuffling process which has of course been going on for quite some time . . . but which is, by now, approaching extreme and near universal proportions."[51]

Cultures are simply not distributed in space as the possessions of different social groups. Each social group does not have its very own culture affixed to it like a license plate.[52] According to a postmodern reading of them, cultural forms, or sets of them, bear no one-to-one relationships with particular groups of people.[53] Cultural forms are associated with a particular group only after an effort of interpretation and alignment with their social practices. The same cultural forms of themselves are therefore available for a different use by other groups. An anthropology that focuses on the differential distribution of cultural objects must give way before an anthropology interested in their differential workings, in the different uses to which they may be put by different groups of people.[54]

By not championing sharp boundaries for a culture, the anthropologist is freed, moreover, from the sort of closed-system analysis characteristic of followers of the modern notion of culture. The anthropologist need not yank cultures, and the societies with which they are associated, out of the wider stream of global history, and reify them so as to produce apparently self-contained, self-referential units.[55] By not doing so, the anthropologist avoids being misled by the prehistory of the anthropological notion in which plural cultures were understood on an analogy with self-contained individual persons. Contrary to such an understanding of individual persons, anthropology refuses to see individuals in isolation from society and views the idea of their self-contained identities as a fiction. If cultures are like persons, then they too should be understood in their wider context—a global one.[56]

Cultures should be set back within the wider historical field from which they are abstracted. The anthropologist's interests may continue to be local but local manifestations of intersections and exchanges with this wider global context now become part of them. Such intersections and exchanges need not seem foreign to cultural analysis once culture itself loses its connotations of homogeneous unity. These relations with the outside, relations at the boundary, are not qualitatively different from relations inside.

Although this may be more apparent now in the age of global world-systems, the cultures that anthropologists study are never likely to have been closed systems in fact. The assumption of closed systems was simply one of disciplinary expediency.[57] It was one that also served to hide from the anthropologist and his or her audience the realities of colonialism. Ironically, the anthropologist affirmed cultures were closed systems just as they were coming under the influence of Western imperialisms.[58]

By setting cultures within a global historical context, cross-cultural analysis loses its static, taxonomic character. Connections between cultures are not made with reference to "stable internal architecture" but with reference to historical processes of exchange and interconnection. Cultures are not turned into static, disconnected things through processes of abstraction and reification; they are seen instead as dynamic, interactive phenomena.[59]

The modern idea of cultures as self-contained units in relations of indifferent exteriority with one another seems increasingly incompatible, moreover, with the founding intentions of anthropology to avoid ethnocentrism.[60] The idea of self-contained cultures is useful when combating aggressive ethnocentrism, the sort of ethnocentrism that would impose its culture on others and destroy their distinctiveness. The very notion of self-containment spawns, however, a more complacent form of ethnocentrism. Cultures are shut up in their own little boxes, they become windowless monads, lacking all capacity for mutual influence. Each proceeds on its separate way, unchallenged by others. If one had been born into another culture, one would think and feel differently; but since one was born into this culture rather than that one, nothing is to be done but relax and enjoy it.[61] Other cultures are merely different—neither inferior nor superior to mine—and therefore indifference replaces critical engagement with them.

However well-intentioned, the separate-but-equal view of self-contained cultures expresses tolerance by ignoring the political realities of inequality.[62] The anthropologist may present native peoples and Western nations as if they were on a level playing field, the one in principle equal to the other as alternative and independent cultural sets. But occluded thereby are the actual unequal political and economic relations between them, political and economic relations that would have to be attended to in the interest of genuine cultural equality.

These real inequalities that the anthropologist fails to admit into his or her analysis surface, ironically, in the superiority the anthropologist claims as an opponent of ethnocentrism. Others are imprisoned within their cultures unable to see alternatives to them. The anthropologist secretly condescends by assuming a standpoint above cultures, from which he or she can see his or her own—or any—culture as just one among others.[63]

The modern strategy of using other cultures as a foil for cultural self-criticism fuels, moreover, a dichotomous typification of other cultures that is problematic. We are all one way; they are all another. Other cultures are turned into static stereotypes to produce a clear difference from one's own.[64] Because a contrast with the United States or Europe is to be the fulcrum for self-criticism, the modern anthropologist is uninterested in those aspects of a culture that might have been diluted by or mixed with some other: cultures must be pure. Differences within a culture become unimportant, too. All such differences become alike in their differentness from the anthropologist's culture. The anthropologist ignores diversity within a culture in order to concentrate on those respects in which it is *not* what some other culture—particularly his or her own—is.[65] This disrespect for difference and complexity runs contrary to the founding motives of anthropology; it represents a failure to follow through on the interest in difference and complexity that is characteristic of anthropology as a discipline.[66] It also shows disrespect for the cultures so described, a disrespect buoyed by power differences between anthropologist and native peoples. The anthropologist may be using other cultures as a means to self-criticism, but they are still being worked over as mere tools for the anthropologist's own projects. The anthropologist cannot be fully true to the discipline's egalitarian motives by taking over the very procedures of dichotomous typification that once justified an ethnocentric imperialism and colonialism. Whether the point is to buttress or undermine its own cultural perspective, the politically stronger group gets to impose its essentializing definition on others, a definition that disparages their inventiveness and historical agency.[67] With this final criticism of the modern notion of culture, the very characterization of different cultures by way of qualitative contrasts becomes questionable.

Reconstruction

After all these criticisms, what remains of the modern understanding of culture? Very few of the aspects of that understanding have actually been discarded. Most are retained with more or less their modern senses; they have just been decentered or reinscribed within a more primary attention to historical processes. Thus, the postmodern anthropologist does not deny that cultures may be made up of taken-for-granted meanings, or may be given shape by stable configurations of cultural elements. Nor does he or she deny that such taken-for-granted meanings and configurations may be shared by all persons affiliated with a particular culture and thereby serve to solidify their social relations. A drive toward these features of culture is, indeed, what one would expect if culture is a stake in historical struggles. Human actors are struggling over cultural elements precisely in order to imbue them with established meanings and fixed interrelations and to bring them to bear in definite ways so as to support certain forms of social organization. The struggle is being won when all people have been convinced or induced to believe and act accordingly.[68] Such successes, however, are more the exception than the rule. Just because they are the products of historical processes, none of these features of cultures can be simply presumed. Homogeneity, consistency, order, are no longer unempirical, a priori presumptions; sometimes they occur, sometimes they do not. They are temporary and provisional results, moreover, of historical processes that continue unabated. Historical struggles precede any clearly defined meaning or organization of cultural elements; and these definitions are never so firm as to stop their flow.[69] Interconnections among cultural elements, for example, are never so fixed that they cannot be broken apart and rearranged in the ongoing course of cultural process.

Some aspects of the modern notion are substantially revised; the functions of most of these remain, however, much the same. For example, the anthropologist might still consider cultures as wholes; but they are now considered contradictory and internally fissured wholes. Even successful struggles of cultural consolidation are likely to contain internal inconsistencies. The social relations in and through which such cultural consolidation occurs are usually too messy and complicated to permit anything else. Such cultural consolidation (temporarily) contains or neutralizes contradictions to make them work for a particular social purpose; but they are not eradicated.[70] No effort of cultural consolidation, moreover, ever has the field of culture as an historical process to itself. Every form of cultural consolidation generates its own characteristic sites of resistance and contradiction; and around it swirl opposed meanings and ways of articulating cultural elements that have not been forced finally from the field. Cultures as wholes remain contradictory because the power of culture, unlike the power of coercion or brute force, can never be concentrated solely in any one party's hands.[71]

The postmodern anthropologist can still consider culture an essentially consensus-building feature of group living. That consensus becomes, however, extremely minimalistic: it forms the basis for conflict as much as it forms the basis for shared beliefs and sentiments. Whether or not culture is a common focus of *agreement*, culture binds people together as a common focus for *engagement*.[72] The struggle over culture, whether and to whatever extent it produces true commonality of beliefs and sentiments, presumes culture as common stakes: all parties at least agree on the importance of the cultural items that they struggle to define and connect up with one another.[73] Participants are bound together by a common attachment to or investment in such cultural items, and not necesarily by any common understanding of what they mean.[74] Such cultural items constitute common reference points for making sense of social action, but they need not produce a genuinely common understanding of what is happening: one person's oppression is another person's justice though both may feel the need to appeal to "the American Way" in making their judgments.

The differentiating function of the modern notion of culture is also retained in the postmodern version, but the account of cultural difference is modified substantially. Differences are not marked by boundaries separating self-contained cultures. On a postmodern understanding, cultural elements may cross such boundaries without jeopardizing the distinctiveness of different cultures. What establishes the distinctive identities of cultures in that case is the way in which such common elements are used, how they are handled and transformed.[75] The distinctiveness of cultural identity is therefore not a product of isolation; it is not a matter of a culture's being simply self-generated, pure and unmixed; it is not a matter of "us" vs. "them." Cultural identity becomes, instead, a hybrid, relational affair, something that lives between as much as within cultures.[76] What is important for cultural identity is the novel way cultural elements from elsewhere are now put to work, by means of such complex and ad hoc relational processes as resistance, appropriation, subversion, and compromise. There may be patterns to such uses that help characterize a particular culture, and style might remain a possible metaphor for cultural identity so defined. The concept of style would in that case, however, shed its past connotations with autonomous self-determination, and refer, instead, to secondary processes of taking over and making one's own what one finds—what comes to one from who knows where, what is imposed upon one, what one meets up with in one's travels to a new place.[77] Creoles and exiles, colonized peoples who "write back" to colonizing nations using those nation's own literary forms, ethnic or racial minorities who revel in their own mixed heritage, become models for this interrelational notion of identity.[78]

Finally, the postmodern understanding of culture retains the self-critical function of the modern notion but now the internal diversity of cultures is as much the fulcrum of self-criticism as any external cultural "others."[79] The anthropologist relativizes his or her own culture not just by showing that there are alternatives to it among the ways of life of different people. This strategy of self-criticism, we said before, is compatible with a complacent, albeit somewhat self-distanced and ironic, ethnocentrism. The anthropologist completes the attack on ethnocentrism by pointing out as well the complexity and diversity that exist within any one culture—the anthropologist's own or that of others. A culture includes its own alternatives and these more clearly represent unavoidable challenges to one another. The anthropologist promotes self-criticism, in short, by uncovering and giving sense to the internal contestations of a culture, by disputing the homogeneity and consistency of a culture, by resisting the temptation to assume unified cultural totalities. Differences among cultures are in this way matched by differences within cultures; and therefore cultural critique is not pursued at the expense of respect for the complicated details of other people's lives.

PART TWO

Culture and
Theology

4

The Nature and Tasks of Theology

Beginning with this chapter, the agenda of Part Two is to use a chastened, postmodern view of culture to explore some basic issues in Christian theology. The overall task is a genuinely exploratory one: How might some fundamental theological topics appear differently, what new directions for their investigation might arise, were one to experiment in theology with a postmodern view of culture?

This postmodern view has no sacrosanct status within such an exploratory project. It forms no uncriticizable basis for a simple unilateral reevaluation of theology. This view of culture may turn out to be theologically unserviceable or in insurmountable tension with commitments of a religious nature that many Christian theologians would be loathe to compromise. Indeed, the new directions that a postmodern understanding of culture suggests for theological research are not theologically neutral. Christian theologies come in many different stripes and, as we will see, not all of them would find these recommendations congenial, either to their understanding of the theological task or to their substantive opinions on matters such as sin and salvation. For the reasons outlined in chapter 3, the postmodern view does, however, have this going for it: it seems a more plausible cf. Stenmark account of culture than the modern view current since the 1920s. To the extent that a wide range of Christian theologians show the influence of that modern view, they may want to reassess its influence in light of these postmodern developments.

Whether or not the word *culture* is employed, something like the modern anthropological understanding of culture crops up repeatedly in contemporary discussion of a surprisingly large range of theological questions. For example, "culture" in the influential typology of theological positions offered by H. Richard Neibuhr stands in for "the world." What Christian theologians make of the world, of the practices and beliefs of the wider society, is viewed by Niebuhr as a judgment about culture. Theological evaluations of those practices and beliefs run along a continuum from "Christ against culture" to "the Christ of culture."[1]

Modern theologians such as Niebuhr, who favor a position to the "against culture" end of the spectrum, worry about Christianity's simple submersion in the culture of the day and about the loss thereby of the distinctiveness of its message. Modern theologians such as Ernst Troeltsch, who (according to Niebuhr at least) fall closer to the "Christ of culture" end of the spectrum, worry about the continued relevance of Christianity to the Western culture whose fortunes have become so closely wrapped up with it. For Troeltsch, Christianity is the religion of Western culture: Western culture has been decisively shaped by Christianity even as Christianity has been decisively shaped by it. A major task of the theologian is therefore to determine the shape theology should take in light of historical developments in the modern West so as to further Christianity's positive contributions to the future of Western culture.[2]

"Culture" in contemporary theology also becomes a way of talking about the historical particularity of Christianity itself, an issue of prime importance in theological discussion at least since the nineteenth century. Cultural diversity as a human universal—the fact that one is always speaking from somewhere, from a position of cultural specificity in action, thought, and feeling—suggests to theologians the propriety of their speaking from where they are, out of the particularities of Christian communal practice. Theologians as diverse as Friedrich Schleiermacher, H. Richard Niebuhr, Karl Rahner, and a host of postliberal theologians, hold this view.[3]

Theologians, moreover, typically account for differences in Christian belief across time and space by attributing those differences to the influence of culture. Christians in the fourteenth century did not believe what Christians believed in the fourth century, nor do African Christians believe what European Christians believe because of differences in their respective ways of life. Theological description of missions, the spread of Christianity by evangelization, becomes in this way the study of "enculturations." Theological discussion of what people across all such differences in time and place might have in common as Christians often avails itself, too, of ideas that are associated, as we saw in chapter 2, with a modern anthropological understanding of culture: some sort of social transmission of heritage, characteristic spiritual affinity, or ruled patterns of behavior.

The anthropological understanding of culture bridges, then, a surprising range of theological schools of thought, as well as theological topics. The idea of culture as a human construct not only bridges the neo-orthodox and liberal wings of contemporary Christian theology; it is also the basis upon which Gordon Kaufman and his followers argue for their understanding of theology as a creative enterprise.[4] Moreover, theologians who make it their mission to reinterpret the Christian tradition in light of the contemporary situation, or to correlate situation and Christian message, often understand the situation at issue in explicitly cultural terms.[5] Finally, the distinction between theory and practice commonly employed in liberation theology has a history tightly interwoven with the modern—and now postmodern—development of ideas of culture found in the social sciences.[6]

Examples like these of the infiltration of modern theology by an anthropological idea of culture could be multiplied—and will be in the chapters to follow. These chapters organize such examples according to three topics broad enough to cover the wide range of theological issues to which ideas about culture are relevant. This chapter treats the nature of theology and its tasks. Chapters 5 and 6 tackle the question of Christian identity, both as a boundary issue that concerns the relation between what is and is not Christian, and as an issue that concerns what positively unifies Christian ways of life. A final chapter investigates how theologians explain and evaluate diversity among theological viewpoints and how they account for theological creativity.

All of Part Two has to do, then, with issues of theological method—this chapter explicitly so, but the other chapters, too, in that they concern the most basic kinds of issues that theologians discuss, issues that reflect back on the character of theology's own procedures. Methodological questions in theology are never finally independent, however, of more substantive theological commitments. The four chapters will also show how the plausibility of theological recommendations made in light of postmodern understandings of culture depends on what one believes about God, humanity, and their relationship.

Theology as a Part of Culture

The most basic contribution that an anthropological understanding of culture—postmodern or not—makes to theology is to suggest that theology be viewed as a part of culture, as a form of cultural activity. Most contemporary theologians would admit as much. Theology is something that human beings produce. Like all human activities, it is historically and socially conditioned; it cannot be understood in isolation from the rest of human sociocultural practices. In short, to say that theology is a part of culture is just to say in a contemporary idiom that it is a human activity.

Saying so may raise the question of how to understand God's influence on the process of human cultural construction. Where is God's influence felt if theology is a human work? Such a question is, however, no harder (or easier) to answer when expressed in cultural terms than it is when expressed, as it has been for the last several centuries, in terms of a modern Western historical consciousness. The task of figuring out theology's connection to God's influence on human life is much the same whether theology is viewed as a part of human history or of human culture.

If contemporary theologians agree that theology is a part of culture, they do not all understand this claim in the same way. Most of the disagreements are over the level of cultural specificity that is of primary importance when understanding Christian theology as a cultural activity: How wide is the cultural frame within which Christian theology should be set? Is Christian theology best viewed as a culture-specific activity, something that takes place within *a* culture, a specifically Christian one presumably? Or is it best viewed within the very general frame of culture as a distinguishing mark of the human? According to an anthropological understanding of culture, both viewpoints are appropriate, but which should take priority? In this chapter I argue for the priority of the former view and then draw out some implications for theological method.[7] If theology takes place within a culture and is therefore a culture-specific activity, what does this suggest about the nature of theological operations, about what theologians do? What kind of activities might be considered theological and how are they related? Are some of these activities, as postliberal theologians suggest, analogous to those of cultural anthropologists?

Gordon Kaufman is one prominent theologian who uses the idea of theology as a part of culture to situate theology within the widest possible frame of reference.[8] Saying that theology is a part of culture becomes a way of talking about theology in terms of what it means to be human. Kaufman and his many followers therefore focus attention on the anthropological idea that culture is a human universal, a defining feature of human life. As a result, the meaning and significance of theology are primarily assessed with reference to the general features of some universal cultural enterprise, one that proceeds along much the same lines in all times and places. Thus, according to Kaufman, human beings always face the task of constructing a life-orienting worldview for themselves. Theology is a particular version of this search for meaning, for a pattern of fundamental categories that will, as cultures do, orient, guide, and order human life. The adequacy of theology can therefore be judged by how well it performs these general cultural tasks. Does it, for example, help people successfully navigate their world and cope effectively with life's vicissitudes?

The cultural specificity of theology is not lost on Kaufman. Theology is a specific version of the general cultural quest in that it seeks some ultimate point of reference that helps people come to terms with the mysteriousness of life. Theology also exhibits the particularities that distinguish specific cultures: the categories that form its answers to the search for meaning—say, the category "God"—are not shared by all human beings. Ideas about God and Christ are admittedly only part of the life-orientations of cultures influenced by Christianity—both the Christian culture of churches and Western cultures in which Christianity has been a major formative influence. But the very point of this understanding of theology as a part of culture is to widen the context for interpreting Christian theology beyond such culture-specific locales.

In sum, Kaufman identifies theology as a part of culture simply in order to situate it within a general understanding of the basic tasks and questions that define human life as a quest for meaning. Such an approach thereby conforms with a rather traditional understanding of philosophical theology. Theology becomes a kind of philosophical enterprise in which answers to perennial issues of importance to human beings the world over are sought. The universal search for answers to life's general questions, according to Kaufman's understanding of it, seems very much like this sort of philosophical theology, although now different cultures, rather than different philosophical schools, vie with one another for the right to claim to have done so successfully. The major difference seems to be the practical context and consequences of the worldviews generated. These worldviews, unlike the more theoretical or speculative conclusions of much philosophical theology, arise out of efforts to gain orientation in the face of life's mysteries; their primary point is to help one live.

Kaufman's use of the idea of theology as a part of culture also brings his work into line with theologies that try to correlate the Christian message with the human situation in order to show the meaningfulness and plausibility of Christianity in general cultural terms. To the extent that these correlationist theologies use the anthropological idea of culture to discuss the human situation, the idea functions much the way it does for Kaufman, as a way of talking about the human as such. The culture or human situation with which the Christian message is to be correlated is discussed in terms of a general structure of human processes that takes much the same shape whatever the context. All human processes show the same tensions and polarities between drives for individuation and participation, or open out onto a transcendent horizon, or eventuate in some limit-situation or limit-experience, a sense of their own boundedness and finitude along with an intimation of that by which they are bounded or contained.[9] Approaching Christian theology as a part of culture means, then, correlating the Christian message with human universals, with general structures that are at the bedrock of all human knowing and doing.

Theologians who follow a method of correlation also see the importance of understanding Christian theology as a part of more specific cultural contexts. To a perhaps greater degree than Kaufman, theologians like David Tracy are attentive to the particularity of Christian theological traditions. The point in making the Christian message one pole of the correlation is, indeed, to do justice to that particularity. Christian theology should be appropriate for a Christian context; what Christian theologians say should reflect the particularities of a specific religion. Showing the meaningfulness and plausibility of a theology that properly reflects the cultural specificity of Christianity requires, however, viewing that theology as a part of culture in a wider sense. It requires, in short, the method of correlation itself, a procedure that demonstrates such a theology's connections with certain general characteristics of culture understood as a human universal. Interpretations of symbols and categories specific to Christianity are existentially meaningful and have a claim on truth only to the extent they disclose and are adequate to common human experience, that is, basic structures of human thought and action fundamental to human life at all times and places. One could say then that, despite the interest in Christian specificity, the whole raison d'être of a method of correlation hinges on assumptions about culture as a summary of human universals. One can argue, moreover, that the conditions for making such correlations hamper an interest in Christian specificity. The results of context-specific investigations into the Christian pole of the correlation have to be expressed in terms of the cultural universals of the other pole (the human situation) in order for correlation to be possible. The Christian message must also concern limit experiences, the character of universal structures of human consciousness, or the fundamental polarities of existence. Undercutting the particularities of the Christian pole are cultural universals that span both sides of the correlation.

The interpretations of theology as a part of culture found in the work of Kaufman, in traditional philosophical theologies, and in theologies of correlation, all slight anthropology's interest in cultures in the plural. They overlook anthropology's primary interest in the differences and distinctive qualities of cultures, and its use of each such cultural context as the primary framework for the interpretation of what is to be found within it. Anthropology insists cultures only come in specific shapes; there is no culture in general. The point of anthropology's generalizations about culture as a human universal is therefore simply to enable a preoccupation with the particular. Common cultural processes there may be, but generalizations about them are constructed out of a comparison of particulars. Unlike what Kaufman seems to assume, what is built into the anthropological method itself—the idea of culture as a human universal—does not serve as a description of such commonalities.

An anthropological approach to theology will not, then, naturally encourage the formulation of human universals into which the practice of theology can be fit. To the contrary, anthropology tends to deflate claims about human universals made by other disciplines. An anthropological idea of culture encourages theologians to develop a primary interest in the particular. Like the nineteenth-century theologian Friedrich Schleiermacher, they should not expend much interest in general ideas about culture in their own right but use those ideas, as Schleiermacher used the human sciences of his day, to locate theology in a very particular place on the cultural map. Theology from an anthropological point of view would be something like what nineteenth-century scholars called a "positive science." Thinking about theology as a part of culture would mean thinking about theology as a part of some specific, communally shaped way of life, with all the full-bodied and concrete comprehensiveness that the expression "way of life" conveys from an anthropological point of view.

But of what specific culture is theology a part? Training one's eye, as an anthropologist might, on the most particular and local cultural contexts that seem pertinent, one might easily respond "religious communities"—churches, in the Christian case. As we will see in the next chapter, however, defining a Christian communal culture is difficult. It is far from clear, for example, that one can use "way of life" in its full anthropological sense to talk about Christian churches apart from the wider cultural contexts in which they are set. Nor is it evident that Christian communal practices are self-contained in the way their identification with the church might suggest: Christians' primary sociocultural relations are not easily confined to their relations with other Christians. But for the purposes of this chapter, we can identify the cultural context with Christian communal practices. Christian communal practices are the ones most pertinent to, and most directly responsible for, Christian theology as a specific cultural production in its own right. To say that Christian theology is a part of culture is to say that theology itself is a cultural production; theology is something shaped *by* concrete social practices, and those social practices must be at least, and in their most important respects for these purposes, Christian ones.

Even at this early stage, without being developed any further, the proposal to view Christian theology within a Christian cultural context might seem worrisome. Kaufman fears that abiding by such a proposal means dulling the theologian's capacity for critical thought, stifling creative theological construction, and giving Christian culture some unwarranted privilege within a pluralistic religious scene. Correlationist theologians fear such a proposal conflicts with the universal nature of Christian claims by turning Christian theology in on itself. Replies to objections like these—indeed, to many more of them that are typically lodged against postliberal theology—will be found in this and the chapters to come. The objections are good ones for the most part and will require rethinking what it means to say that Christian theology is culture-specific in light of postmodern developments. But even at this stage, the objections of Kaufman and correlationist theology can be addressed in a preliminary way.

Both objections prejudge the nature of the Christian social practices within which theology is lodged. Kaufman assumes that if theology operates from within a Christian cultural context it must work rather passively with an already given worldview that Christianity supplies.[10] Rather than simply take over such a worldview from a Christian cultural context, Kaufman proposes a magisterial effort, availing itself of the widest range of human learning, to *construct* a worldview in which the category "God" figures centrally. It is an open question, however, whether a Christian cultural context is ever really able to provide what Kaufman is concerned to repudiate; a postmodern understanding of culture suggests, instead, that a given worldview is unlikely to be a constitutive feature of any communal practice.

Kaufman also suggests that the distancing effect of an anthropological approach to Christianity as just one orienting outlook on life among others combines with Christian worries about idolatry to make Christian culture too narrow a context within which to do theology. For both religious and anthropological reasons, it seems illegitimate for a theologian to give a Christian perspective on life the benefit of the doubt and simply work from there. Focusing exclusively in that way on a single, admittedly human tradition of religious discussion shows undue arrogance and threatens to make an absolute out of historically and culturally conditioned categories and concepts.[11] Knowing that what Christians say about God cannot do full justice to the finally mysterious character of ultimate reality and knowing that Christianity is just one attempt among others to orient life, the theologian should resist the temptation to operate solely from within a Christian context and rise instead to a more expansive, holistic, and global outlook. "The simple and direct commitment" that so often characterizes ordinary participation in a Christian cultural context seems, in short, to be incompatible with the required critical distance on Christian practices.[12] This argument by Kaufman again, however, prejudges the character of Christian practices, in particular the degree to which they allow for or encourage their own critical revision. As we will see, a postmodern understanding of culture suggests any culture will have a hard time ruling out the kind of critical reflection that Kaufman's understanding of theology demands.

For similar reasons, there is no reason to think that theology's being set in a Christian cultural context rules out theological claims that are universal in scope. Because theology operates within a Christian context is no reason to think theologians are discussing matters that only concern Christians. Theologians can proclaim truths with profound ramifications for the whole of human existence; that they do so from within a Christian cultural context simply means that the claims they make are shaped by that context and are put forward from a Christian point of view. Indeed, if, as an anthropologist would insist, assertions always show the influence of some cultural context or other, following a procedure like that is the only way that universal claims are ever made. Arguably, in some theologies of correlation—say, that of Karl Rahner—universal claims are being made on just such a particular basis. Universals are being generated from a Christian point of view; philosophizing is done from within theology.[13]

The concerns about the universal scope of theological affirmations that lie behind a method of correlation can be understood in another way, however. For Rahner, for instance, correlation with common features of human experience is a way of showing that what theologians discuss has a claim on the whole person. Its correlation with features of the human as such makes clear that theology is of deep and direct concern to people in their day-to-day lives, that it speaks to them in a way that informs their total existence. Theology is no arcane body of abstractions; instead, it refers to matters that the concrete self-understanding of persons cannot ignore. Without depending on claims about the commonality of human experience, an anthropological approach to theology as a context-specific activity suggests a new way of making the same point.

Theology in Everyday Life and as a Specialized Activity

Theology is often identified with the productions of educated elites such as clergy and academics. When that identification is made, theology is equated with writings in which conceptual precision and logical coherence are at a premium. These writings are produced in primary conversation with other writings of a similar sort, and they tend to be read only by people with the same educational background and institutional support for sustained intellectual pursuits as their authors. As such a highly specialized intellectual activity, theology seems irrelevant to the common concerns of most people. Putting theology into the cultural context of a Christian way of life challenges this view of theology; it makes theology much more an integral part of daily life.

Such a revised understanding of theology follows the anthropological shift in the understanding of culture away from associations with high culture. Culture is not primarily located in the intellectual or spiritual achievements of the community—its great works of art, philosophy, or literature. Instead, culture refers to the whole social practice of meaningful action, and more specifically to the meaning dimension of such action—the beliefs, values, and orienting symbols that suffuse a whole way of life. This meaning dimension of social action cannot be localized in some separate sphere specifically devoted to intellectual or spiritual concerns. It accompanies all social action as a constitutive aspect of it; it is what makes action socially meaningful and not a mere biologically based reflex (say, a twitch) or purely personal idiosyncrasy (say, an aversion to peas).

Thinking of theology in cultural terms does not, therefore, suggest the primary placement of theology in a high culture realm, as, say, a religious form of literature or philosophy. Christian theology has to do, instead, with the meaning dimension of Christian practices, the theological aspect of all socially significant Christian action. Christian theology in this primary sense would, accordingly, be found embedded in such matters as the way altar and pews are arranged. Their placement usually has a meaning, a theological aspect, in that it embodies a sense of the difference between minister and laity, and between God and human beings. All Christian activities would have a meaning or theological dimension in this sense—going to church, protesting poverty, praying, and helping one's neighbor. They are socially significant Christian actions in virtue of being constituted by a sense of what Christians believe and how they should lead their lives. They are all, then, theologically informed actions in a most fundamental sense.

As a matter of day-to-day practice, the beliefs, values, and orienting symbols of Christian life can, of course, also be directly expressed. They do not remain a merely implicit dimension of social action. Christian social practice essentially involves making theological affirmations about God and Jesus and about human life in their light. One does that, for example, when one prays, confesses one's beliefs, exhorts oneself or others to properly Christian forms of behavior, preaches, or laments the injustices of life before God. In the ordinary course of Christian life, there is also occasion for engaging in theological investigation of those beliefs, values, and symbols. One does that when one's beliefs are directly challenged, or when it simply becomes clear that others do not agree. Why does the church down the street refuse to hold joint communion services with us? One is prompted to engage in theological investigation when situations seem difficult to reconcile with one's beliefs, or when trying to interpret novel circumstances in light of one's Christian commitments. How can my Christian beliefs help me cope with situations of injustice? What does God's love mean if it is compatible with the early death of my child? How can one preach the good news to someone living in poverty? Occasions for theological reflection arise, too, when the theological statements or theological dimension of social practices in different areas of Christian life seem to conflict, or when one considers whether changes to Christian practice are justified. How is the offer of God's gracious love and forgiveness in the eucharist compatible with the condemnation of homosexuals that my pastor preaches? Should altar and pews be rearranged so that the minister is surrounded by the congregation? Does it make sense for Christians to kill others in defense of their country?

Theology as a specialized intellectual activity raises the same sort of questions but often in a more general and abstract way. It investigates them, moreover, in a sustained fashion according to criteria less attuned to the urgencies of everyday life; criteria, for example, that put a premium on clarity, systematicity, and consistency of expression. Meeting such criteria is a luxury that the needs of everyday life cannot often afford. The effort often requires, too, a level of intellectual training and institutional support unavailable to most people. Despite these differences, an approach to theology as a part of Christian culture suggests that specialized theological investigation should be placed on a continuum with theological activity elsewhere, as something that arises in an "organic" way out of Christian practice.[14]

Academic Theology in Relation to the Everyday

If academic theology incorporated this idea of a theological continuum, what difference would it make? Presumably, academic theology would try to lessen the gap between itself and theological activity elsewhere. An academic theology could do this by being more concerned about its connection to everyday Christian practice and less obsessed with its standing relative to philosophy or other intellectual enterprises espousing similar criteria of excellence. This might make a difference in how it tries to meet the criteria at issue. For example, creating a system of Christian beliefs by way of logical deduction might not be worth the effort if it produced a theology irrelevant to the wider concerns of Christian practice. Friedrich Schleiermacher in *The Christian Faith* makes an objection to a theology of logical deduction for much this reason; it marks a difference between theology and the philosophy of religion.[15] One might also try to meet criteria of intellectual excellence without forfeiting a nonacademic audience, through, say, an accommodation to styles of expression found in more popular literature.

Given the importance of Bible reading in Christian social practices generally, the use of biblical images and rhetorical cadences might help.

Academic theology could also show that it has an organic connection to
Christian social practices by making these practices its subject matter.
While associated with postliberal theology on the contemporary scene, a
suggestion like this is not unusual in modern academic theology; only the
explicitly cultural terms for its expression are. For Schleiermacher, academic theology is about Christian communal piety. More directly, it concerns
the public expressions in speech of a Christian piety shaped in community
with others.[16] For the famous twentieth-century theologian Karl Barth, it
concerns the language about God peculiar to the church.[17] For liberation
theologians, it has to do, more specifically, with the theological dimension
of Christian practices of political engagement on the side of the poor and
oppressed.[18] For many feminist theologies, it means giving expression to
the theology of women's lives.[19] Using the idea of theology as a part of
Christian culture as a guide, let us explore what is implied about the character of the relationship between the two if academic theology has for its
subject matter the theology of Christian social practices. What sort of relationship is being set up between academic theology and a theology of
Christian social practice that does not take a specialized form?

How Not to Understand the Relationship

The anthropological idea of culture suggests it is best not to discuss that
relationship in terms of a distinction between theoretical reflection and its
material object or between second- and first-order theology. Discussing the
relationship in those ways makes too sharp a distinction between the two,
as if they operated on substantially different planes or levels. It thereby
threatens to reinstate the separation between theory and practice that an
anthropological understanding of culture disputes, by suggesting that academic theology is a purely intellectual activity and not one kind of material
social practice among others. Practice always has its own theoretical dimension, as these two views see. But it is equally important to see the degree to
which theory—no matter how high-flown—has its own practices. Unlike
the general run of social practices, which produce meaning as a matter of
course simply insofar as a meaning dimension of beliefs and values is a constitutive feature of them, academic theology (like other culture industries)
is a material social practice that specializes in meaning production. Academic theology is itself a material social process, a kind of Christian social
practice in its own right with material means (for instance, libraries, school
rooms, powerful institutions for its dissemination), a specific type of product (for instance, books, lectures, learned discussions), and production val-

ues (for instance, clarity, consistency of affirmation). It is not mere theoretical reflection on material social practices. As a form of theoretical reflection, academic theology may, it is true, be prompted by or brought into subsequent connection with the lived realities of Christian practice in a way that either legitimizes or undermines them by argumentative means; liberation theologians are the ones who insist on such connections most strongly. But this general approach easily loses sight of the material and social processes of theological reflection itself as a form of meaning production. Academic theology, on this approach, does not appear to engage in Christian social practice in the full-bodied sense of, say, first-order theology where affirmations are made and life is actually experienced in Christian terms. In its capacity as a second-order exercise, academic theology seems merely to talk about such practices—about those affirmations, about that way of living. Existing in some sort of derealized sphere, it seems to have no affirmations or life of its own.

The language of reflection and of first order/second order also tends to deflect attention from the constructive interpretive activity of the academic theologian and thereby to deflect attention from the contestable character of any particular proposal for giving clarity and systematic coherence to the theological aspects of Christian practice. The language of reflection and of first order/second order suggests that the academic theologian simply follows the dictates of the object studied as he or she goes about clarifying and ordering beliefs and values that circulate in Christian practice. It implies that those beliefs and values already exist as some consistent whole on the level of practice and that the academic theologian is doing nothing more than laying out the elements of that whole in the proper order they already have with one another. Thus, postliberal theologians might say that on their understanding of academic theology the theologian is simply describing (or redescribing in technical language not characteristic of Christian practice generally) the internal logic of Christian practice.

This postliberal claim that second-order theology describes the internal logic of first-order theology does, it is true, have its ambiguities. Sometimes it sounds as if the theologian actively constructs a logic for everyday or first-order Christian practices in the process of performing his or her second-order duties. Theologians could therefore be expected to come up with different accounts of the logic of Christian practices, and would have to engage in extended arguments with one another if the merits of any one such account over its competitors were to be demonstrated.[20] Postliberals also suggest the constructive character of their second-order work when they make clear that, by talking of second-order theology as a description of the internal logic of Christian practice, they mean to eschew the application of external norms to Christian practice (say, norms provided by some independent metaphysics or analysis of universal structure of human experience).[21] The second-order treatment of first-order practice is not merely descriptive, then; it has a normative component whereby some first-order Christian practices, and some second-order ways of making sense of the logic of those practices, are criticized. The norms employed are internal in the sense that they do not come from outside the Christian context itself. Most of the time, however, postliberal talk of describing the internal logic of first-order practices strongly suggests that second-order theology does nothing more than uncover a logic internal to those practices themselves; the task of second-order theology is simply to make explicit what is already present there in an implicit, unformulized manner.[22] Presumably only one logic is implicit in the practices, to which the second-order theologian is merely to conform. The critical or normative capacities of the second-order theologian are therefore not exercised in the process of articulating the logic of Christian practice; he or she criticizes and recommends changes in only those particular Christian practices that deviate from "the" logic or grammar of the faith, a logic or grammar that second-order theology seems simply to be tracing according to its already-established outlines.[23]

As a postmodern understanding of culture makes especially clear, however, the cultural dimension of a whole way of life never offers of itself the sort of clarity and consistency that academic theology pursues. Every academic theologian is therefore producing his or her account of the way the theology of practice should be understood and arranged, and every such account is in potential competition with a host of others. Indeed, contrary to the idea of any sharp separation of levels, the academic theologian's construal is in potential competition with many nonspecialists' understandings of Christian beliefs and values and of how they hang together, understandings that develop as a matter of course in efforts to lead a Christian life.

Postmodern anthropologists offer a number of reasons why the beliefs and values that circulate in the everyday social practices of a Christian way of life are unlikely to exhibit the definite meanings and theoretical consistency that academic theologians pursue in their own work. First, if the beliefs and values at issue are really part and parcel of social practices, every one of them is liable to be pushed and pulled this way and that by a variety of situation-specific forces that are unlikely at any one time to produce similar outcomes across the board. For example, in an uncoordinated fashion each belief or value is subject to a variety of social forces (such as the interest of church leaders in maintaining an uncorrupted faith versus the difficulties that some recommendations made on that basis might pose for rank-and-file Christians in their daily lives). The meaning of Christian beliefs and values, what does or does not follow from them, is also subject to outright political conflict in a general sense, conflicts over the shape that Christian practice should take. Since they form the cultural dimension of social practices, what Christian beliefs and values mean has a lot to do with which social practices seem meaningful—the Christian thing to do. Does, for example, the equality of persons before God make enslaving others an un-Christian practice? According to what understanding of Christian equality would it do so?

Matters like this come up in a piecemeal fashion. Not every belief or value is pertinent to every social practice that makes up a way of life, or to the same sort of practice every time. The needs of everyday social practice rarely involve, therefore, a thorough consideration of Christian beliefs or values as a whole. The issue of consistency is not often forced, then, by day-to-day social practice, and when it does come up—as it surely does—it rarely carries very far across the complexity of beliefs and values that have a general circulation in a way of life. Indeed, the distribution of beliefs and values across social practices is often segmented in a way that keeps the question of consistency from arising. Thus, a belief in God's initiatives might suffuse one's practices in church, and recede before a sense of one's own responsibility for Christian service to neighbor the rest of the week, without any possible incompatibility between these ideas coming to mind.

Finally, academic theologians will not find what they are looking for already instantiated in Christian social practices of everyday life because those social practices do not often require the beliefs that constitute them to have very definite senses. As a rule, participants in social practices hold beliefs whose meanings they have not fully unpacked. Children or newcomers are not the issue here; it is simply that full participation in the practice does not require detailed understanding. American citizens, for example, might heartily affirm the values of liberty and justice for all, and engage happily in practices in which those values are instantiated, without, however, being able to say very exactly what those values mean, nor need they do so in order to do the sorts of things that good Americans do. The cultural dimension of social practices is typically, moreover, so undefined that it leaves room for quite a number of possible interpretations. Thus, recitation of a creed is part of many church services but church practices rarely enforce any highly specific interpretation of what its elements mean. Commentary on aspects of the creed in sermons or even rigorous catechetical training is never sufficient to exclude a range of possible interpretations. Christian beliefs about the ultimately mysterious character of faith—its reference to an ultimately incomprehensible God—run contrary, indeed, to any effort to pin down the meaning of Christian beliefs too definitively. If participants in the social practices that constitute a way of life do not fully understand the meaning of the beliefs they hold, and if what they do believe is generally rather vague, there is no easy way to ascertain the consistency of such beliefs, or to test one belief for its consistency with another.

Theologians who use the language of theoretical reflection or of first- and second-order theology are aware of the fragmentary and conflicting character of beliefs and values in Christian practice. Indeed, for Schleiermacher this is one reason why a "scientific" theology is needed: to clean things up. Rather than fully accept responsibility for the creative character of their own constructions, these theologians, however, try to dig underneath the messy surface of Christian practice to something that will make their decisions about meaning and order for them. In Schleiermacher's case, that something is the Christian experience of redemption which all these fragmentary and conflicting statements of Christian practice are expressing, trying to give speech to. For postliberals, that something is some underlying body of rules or patterned order to which the theology of practice conforms despite its messiness. This body of rules or patterned order is not explicit in the day-to-day practice of Christians; they have the know-how but are incapable of telling academic theology what their know-how is. Its expression is reserved for the specialized theological investigation of clerics or educated elites; for instance, such rules are formulated in the creeds of church councils.

Especially in the postliberal case, this hermeneutical exercise of digging below the surface of Christian practice seems to mimic the procedures of anthropologists that postmodern developments criticize. Postliberal theologians in fact compare their procedures to anthropological ones. Like its anthropological counterpart, however, postliberal theology seems to make the following mistake. Theology projects onto the object studied what its own procedures of investigation requires—a coherent whole. The method of study itself thereby validates the conclusions of the theologian while disqualifying the people and practices it studies from posing a challenge to those conclusions. The theologian is only uncovering a force for coherence that is already a part of practice, but whatever this is is only apparent once the theologian points it out.

One can say, then, that no internal logic of Christian practice already exists to dictate and thereby validate all by itself the constructions of postliberal theologians. Nor does Christian piety, the experience of redemption in Christ in all its life-shaping implications, exist as some already complete whole to be simply explicated or unpacked. It does not exist as something to which the theologian can always refer back, something on which the theologian can thereby always count, to establish of itself what it is proper to say about God, the world, and the self, and those statements' relations to one another.[24] By denying this I do not also mean to deny the propriety of making sense of Christian beliefs and values in terms of a Christian way of life. As the following remarks indicate, doing so is basic to the very idea of viewing Christian theology as part of a Christian cultural context.

The meaning of Christian beliefs and values becomes apparent with reference to other beliefs and values that Christians hold, and with reference to the way those beliefs and values figure in further Christian statements and actions. One does not know what Christians mean by God without also knowing what they mean by Christ or by human existence lived religiously. What Christians mean by God is made clear by what they go on to do with the notion—whether it figures, for example, in actions characterized by anxiety-ridded fear, or joyful risks for the sake of others; whether, say, statements using the notion are confident of their capacity to refer to God or signal their own inadequacy. Similarly, in the course of daily life or in theological argument, a particular belief or value will seem right according to how well that belief or value hangs together with others and with the rest of Christian social practices. The determination of rightness is a matter of fit. For example, if Christians worship Jesus, then they should talk of him as divine (and the reverse). If the celebration of the eucharist brings about their fellowship in Christ, then relations with others in church should make that fellowship evident—by singing and witnessing in common, by passing the peace, by sharing a meal in common of their own devising after the service, by communal acts of service to neighbors. Like anthropological investigation, then, judgments about the meaning and propriety of theological particulars are contextual in those ways.

One cannot, however, presume from this contextualism that contexts for assessing meaning and propriety are already set up and not a matter of controversy. One cannot assume that the employment and fit in Christian practice of any particular belief or value have already been established and take a single form. How ideas about God are used in the course of Christian social practice may determine their meaning but they need not always be used in the same way. Propriety may be a matter of fit but that need not mean that all Christians agree on whether a particular idea or value fits, or on what would have to give in order to establish it. If white Christians treat their black neighbors with scorn outside of church, is it fit for these whites to make their black neighbors sit in the back of church? If their sense for all persons as children of God means that white Christians treat their black neighbors kindly in church, should not their concern for them extend outside it as well? If one believes women are equal in the economic and political spheres of life, with what right does one deny them equality within the church?

A Christian way of life is no doubt constituted by some degree of general agreement about what theological particulars mean and whether they fit with the rest of what Christians say, do, and value. Without some established patterns of approbation and disapprobation, there would be no recognizable way of life at all. Thus, Christians certainly show respect for the things of God in church. They profess love of God and neighbor, even if they are not sure exactly what is or is not compatible with that. They try to make Jesus as important as they can, short of enormous damage to the rest of what they believe to be true and right. Contrary behaviors are liable to meet with general disapproval. Without agreement in approvals and disapprovals at some level or on some things, no pattern of social practices could exist.

Most matters taken up for specialized theological investigation are not, however, of this sort. There would not be much point to the effort if they were; the theologian by arcane logic would simply return to beliefs and values that no Christian ever doubted anyway. Instead, the issues taken up by theologians tend to be matters of controversy.

Academic theologians might try to suggest that established patterns of practice are enough to resolve matters of controversy—maybe that is what it means to follow the internal logic of Christian practice or be guided by what the Christian experience of redemption in Christ implies. A comparison with established patterns of Christian practice will sort things out, make clear whether a controversial matter is really an appropriate thing for Christians to say and do. This suggestion threatens, however, to reify such patterns of practice by lifting them out of the social processes that formed and continue to form them. Contrary to such a view, and in keeping with a postmodern emphasis on the primacy of process, established patterns of action are not fixed but are themselves susceptible to change in the course of further Christian action. New practice is never simply repetitive. The novelty that is part of the continued use of notions or symbols like redemption in Christ always, therefore, brings with it additions, alterations, and unexpected twists to preestablished meanings.

The meaning of a Christian belief may have a fairly definite sense in an established context of uses to which it is put, but that meaning presents no absolute standard that predetermines future uses. No given context can control the meaning of a particular belief or value; that belief or value can always be inserted in some other context, the given context itself being perhaps revised or rearranged. The context of usages that establishes meaning is itself ultimately unanchored, in other words. The regular patterns of use that give a belief or value meaning are not themselves ruled by anything. Usage may determine meaning but the patterns of such usages are not fixed or inelastic.

Moreover, one cannot appeal to something underlying or behind the surface of these changing patterns of actual uses that will sort out in advance which new uses of Christian notions will turn out to be right or wrong. It is not possible, for such purposes, to appeal to something that controls the play on the surface of Christian practices—say, the rules or depth of grammar those practices follow, competency in the performance of a Christian way of life, or the experience of redemption. New uses that will meet eventually with general agreement are not already contained somehow in those rules or that competency or that experience. Proper future practice cannot therefore be figured out ahead of time by capturing what someone fully competent in the ways of Christian practice already knows or what a full experience of redemption in Christ already implies, or by laying out the rules that Christian practice abides by. There exists no a priori set of appropriate possible uses to be contained in that experience or competency, or in those rules. Appropriate uses are not, for example, already present in germ within the depths of Christian experience of redemption in Christ, awaiting their simple expression. New uses are not the simple expression of any transcendent standard of correctness; they are instead produced through a kind of experimental, inherently controversial work. The propriety of a new use, in short, is not apparent before it actually emerges and there has been some public effort to establish whether it works.[25] Is it possible that noncelibate gay people should now be ministers in the church despite the common condemnation of that practice in the past? What would this new practice signal for Christian morals, what changes would it suggest in the meaning of God's love? Does it suggest a Christian can disapprove of the behaviors of a minister and still take spiritual direction from him or her? What would it mean for the relationship between church practice and developments in the wider political and social arenas in which Christians participate? Not knowing immediately what to make of a suggested revision to Christian practice, like gay ordination, is not helpfully discussed in terms of a failure of competency, or lack of full exposure to redemption in Christ, or improper socialization in the rules of Christian life—as if someone really competent or having a full experience, or well-versed in the rules should automatically know. Instead, not knowing immediately is part of the hard process by which that competence, experience, or ruled use is formed and tested in community.

A Better Way to Understand the Relationship

We are now in a position to go back to the original question: What does it mean to say that specialized theological investigation is about Christian social practices? We apparently do not mean that academic theology is

directly governed by social practices themselves as if those practices constituted some object to which academic theology tries merely to conform or at
most to decipher. We mean that the problems that academic theology tackles are prompted by social practice. We mean that academic theology is
about what day-to-day Christian social practices are also often about; for
instance, the propriety of new proposals for Christian belief and action,
how to deal with conflicting strands of Christian social practice, what to do
when previously established Christian practices are challenged by new situations. Academic theology is therefore about Christian social practices in
the sense that it asks critical and evaluative questions of them. It is, finally,
governed by those practices in the sense that it employs a strategy of criticism and evaluation similar to that used in everyday Christian life. Academic theologians ask how well the practices at issue hang together with other
things that Christians believe and value. The materials that academic theology gathers together to show whether something fits or not are also often,
then, found in everyday Christian social practices. Academic theology is
about everyday Christian practice in that the beliefs, symbols, and values
that academic theologians work with have their primary locus or circulation there.

The Distinctiveness of Their Operations. Even though academic theology engages in much the same sort of theological investigation that one can
find in everyday Christian life, it has its own distinctive shape. Even when
academic theology tries to be a transparent vehicle for the voices of the
nonelite, academic theology cannot be collapsed into the theological investigation found in everyday life because it is a form of social practice in its
own right, with goals and standards specifically suited to it.[26] Specialized
theological investigation reflects a division of labor and therefore a difference in processes of production. When problems of practice are raised in
academic theology they therefore suffer some transformation in character;
practical answers to practical problems become intellectual answers to intellectual problems.[27]

How do the processes of producing everyday theology and academic
theology differ? As we have already mentioned, theological investigation in
everyday Christian life tends to be haphazard and attuned to the needs of
the immediate situation. Investigation tends to extend no further than is
necessary to meet the immediate practical need. The object seems to be to
produce a continuation of action in which theological investigation is
stilled; the point is either to return to social action in which beliefs and values are the cultural dimension of that action but are not explicitly stated, or
to practices in which they are affirmed without needing to be queried.

Investigation is designed, in short, to enable one to go on without hesitation or indecision. Once that objective is reached, theological investigation itself is renounced until further practical difficulties call for it again.

Everyday theological investigation, moreover, is not often directed by the entertainment of general principles. Making a decision about proper action or belief seems less a matter of application of explicit precept and more a matter of tact and good timing—knowing when and where a certain affirmation or deed is called for, knowing what affirmation or action to add to a situation so that its various elements form some sort of agreeable balance or harmony. It means employing something like a sense for the game, a feel for the possibilities of Christian living. Using that sort of sense or feel for the game, one figures out, for example, that talk of God's love is better than talk of God's wrath when conversing with others about their infirmity. Or, that it is better to draw initially on a religious repertory of lament rather than songs of praise for God when confronted with grave injustice and its perpetrators—on the one and then the other, in a proper order and timed well to meet the situation specific responses of one's adversaries in ways that highlight the unacceptability of injustice in God's eyes.

The processes of specialized theological investigation, by contrast, aim at their own self-continuance. Their goal is to enable further investigation of the cultural dimension of Christian social practices in the same explicit terms. Specialized theological investigations therefore tend to be less episodic than their everyday counterparts, and seem more cumulative, theological investigation building on theological investigation. These processes of production tend, moreover, to issue in artifacts of meaning—for instance, books or other written documents—products with a permanence that, unlike oral statements and actual deeds, can be distributed and form objects for reference far beyond the situation of their immediate issuance. Finally, in virtue of a division of labor between clergy and laity, between educated "meaning" specialists and the untrained, these processes of production have a relative autonomy from processes of theological investigation in everyday life. That means they develop their own field-specific values, interests, and investments. Every social practice depends for its viability on the generation of a belief in the value of its own productions, a belief in the value of those characteristics that distinguish its productions from others—in this case, the very matters of conceptual thoroughness, clear definition, comprehensiveness, and coherence that make specialized intellectual activity distinct from its untrained counterpart. Investment in such values, taking an interest in them, is a condition for participation in the social practice. Those values also set the norms for excellence relative to the field. The more a specialized theology can show its investment in and conformity to those values the better it is. Different specialized theologies compete among themselves for the legitimacy so conveyed.[28]

Invested in those values, conforming to them as its criteria of legitimacy, specialized theological investigation constructs a theoretical logic that is quite different from the cultural logic of everyday practice. The character of the well-running meaningful social action that everyday theological investigation tries to serve has very little to do with the character of the well-ordered body of beliefs and values that specialized theological investigation produces. So long as the routines of social action are not disrupted and social strife does not break out along its cultural fissures, everyday theological investigation need not find anything problematic in the inconsistency, indefiniteness, or conflicting interpretations of the beliefs and values that figure in everyday social practices. While everyday theological investigation will not arise at all in such cultural circumstances, specialized theological investigation, in keeping with the distinctive norms and values that shape its own social practice, finds these same features of Christian culture a prime impetus for its own work; they show, indeed, exactly why specialized theological activity is necessary.

Similarities in Their Operations. The process of specialized theological investigation is not, however, entirely unlike that of the everyday. The processes have more in common than the differences in their respective norms and interests might suggest.[29] This is so for two major reasons.

Specialized theology behaves much like everyday theology because, first of all, it is also a form of social action. On its own level, with reference to its own internal goods, it therefore reproduces the practical tensions that surround beliefs and values in everyday life. Engaged in potential competition with every other specialized theology over the values that are the stakes of its field, each specialized theology constructs its version of how to articulate and organize Christian beliefs and values in the course of situation-specific contests. It may be after clarity, comprehensiveness, and consistency, but a specialized theology is prompted to pursue such matters by the needs of the moment, needs established in great part by its immediate situation vis-à-vis other specialized theologies. For example, it clarifies what its chief theological competitor seems to leave vague. Or, the problems of consistency that it tackles are those that arise within some situation-specific alignment with theological predecessors—say, problems of consistency that arise within the specialized theologies of one's denomination or the academic institution where one trained. The process of systematizing often has, then, an ad hoc point—the defense of a certain ally or opposition to a particular enemy— and the force of conformity to a value of that sort need not last beyond the same situation-specific variables that prompted its pursuit. An adequate system for one place and time is not for another.

The fact that it is a full-bodied social practice in its own right means that specialized theological investigation is also directed by situational forces in the process of conforming to field-specific values. It may strive for comprehensiveness but it is pushed toward selectivity by the needs of the moment, by a sense for what it is most important to say in a particular situation. As Luther remarked, to be steady on all fronts is no theological virtue if the faith is under assault at a particular point. Theological systems are not generated by following the principle of logical consistency where it leads but by seeing what works against particular opponents and problems. Abiding by the value of systematicity is, then, more opportunistic than principled. Processes of system construction, moreover, are more disassembling and eclectically disruptive than they are strictly cumulative. Instead of building seamlessly on previous theologies in a regular manner, new systematic constructions often proceed by trying to take them apart, by sensing their vulnerabilities at a particular time, and adding, deleting, or emphasizing elements piecemeal so as to put a new spin on the whole. This is what Luther's emphasis on justification by faith did to the way Christian beliefs, values, and religious affections were ordered by his Catholic opponents. Or, in a less oppositional mode, this is what Calvin's view of the third use of the law did to Lutheran theology, in light of new needs for Christian discipline in churches independent of Rome. Finally, an interest in clarity can be deflated by the very effort to seek distinction on the terms of a specialized theological field. One proves one's distinction in those terms by writing in ways that are ambiguous or meaningless apart from strenuous efforts of decipherment, of which only one's peers among specialized theologians are capable. Even if one avoids such inconsistent snobbery—making clear one's investment in intellectual values by becoming virtually incomprehensible—efforts to generate widespread support for one's theological position often have a similar effect. Like what happens in everyday theological practice, the more people one manages to bring on board, the less likely it is that the beliefs and values at issue will have clearly defined senses. Thus, the early ecumenical creeds (for instance, those of Nicaea and Chalcedon) were interpreted very differently by the opposed theological factions that initially accepted them—as became clear in the theological controversies that raged after their promulgation.

The second reason its operations tend to be like those of everyday life is that specialized theology rarely operates in full independence of everyday theology. Academic theology's relative autonomy from everyday theological activity in virtue of its own norms and interests is not absolute autonomy. It is true that its own field-specific interests make it possible for academic theology to try to distance itself from the theology of everyday life and to dismiss the relevance of everyday theology for its own enterprise. In so doing, academic theology would become a simply self-referential and self-contained field. Other theologies with the same production values would be its sole concern. For most of Christian history, however, specialized theology has not sought this sort of absolute autonomy. The simple reason is that the concern of everyday theological investigation is part of its own concerns: What is it proper for Christians to say and do?

While some forms of specialized theoretical activity ignore the concerns of everyday life, theology is not one of them. Specialized theological activity has proper Christian belief and action in mind. It is, indeed, in most times and places part of the effort made by religious elites to control or discipline such belief and action. In virtue of special intellectual expertise and/or church leadership positions, its practitioners are authorized to raise such issues in an explicitly normative fashion. The opinions it ventures move in the direction of the codification or official formulation of such norms. The recommendations it issues are, accordingly, made to all Christians and not simply to the specialist. Christians have generally rejected a division between esoteric and exoteric theologies: intellectuals and church leaders are not to hold one set of beliefs about what Christians properly say and do, and the masses another. Like theological investigation in everyday life, then, specialized theology aims to affect everyday Christian practice.

Specialized theology cannot, however, realistically hope to influence everyday Christian life if it sticks simply to the values specific to its own field. It offers a way of life that is systematically principled and organized according to clear and logically consistent ideas. But to the extent that academic theology abides by values that make the specificities of audience and situation irrelevant, it is not clear how this offer meets the immediate needs of everyday practice. Because of its interest in generalities and in abstract claims with a multicontextual pertinence, its offer may not obviously speak to such situation-specific, practical needs at all—to the shock of world war or genocide, to emerging religious conflict, or attacks on the viability of Christian norms of neighbor-love that spring from economic or political developments. Its offer of a way of life integrated according to theoretical values will also appear superfluous—even dangerous—in situations where, as we have said they usually do, Christian social practices already run reasonably well without it. Indeed, Christian social practices, like most social practices, often run well just to the extent theoretical issues of clarity and consistency are not broached. Religious services, for example, become liable to disruption when differences in the interpretation of a ritual are raised, and often run well when such issues are submerged in a kind of practical social integration around the rite itself. As we have seen, the theological questions that arise in everyday life are specific to situations of conflict, crisis, or indecision. What makes Christian practice well-ordered as a whole—the potential contribution of academic theology—is not generally of concern at all unless talking about that would help solve particular problems. But this sort of relevance to particulars is just what academic theology ignores when it attends simply to field-specific norms of clarity, logical order, and systematicity.

These problems of relevance to Christian practice might presumably be remedied by some secondary effort of application. In that case, the situational and ad hoc logic of everyday theological investigation need not infiltrate academic theology's primary tasks of clarifying and arranging Christian matters into some logically coherent whole. The task of influencing Christian practice is, however, more complicated. If it hopes to influence Christian practice, academic theology does not have the luxury, or indeed the power, to keep initially to itself in that way.

It would have that luxury if it possessed a monopoly on the construction of theological ideas, or could simply tell people, from some unchallenged position of authority, what it is they should say and do. Neither is the case, however. Theological ideas with implications for how Christians are to live are already found on the level of the day to day. In most historical circumstances, specialized theology does not have the sort of institutional backing to encourage efforts to wipe those ideas out and substitute its own specialized theological constructions. The institutions that support the influence of theological specialists do not have the disciplinary reach to police the theological activity of ordinary Christians in the course of their day-to-day lives. Christian social practices, moreover, are often genuinely voluntary. People participate of their own free will and usually suffer no grievous penalties, besides religious ones, should their theologies be opposed by church authorities. The ability of specialized theology to influence everyday Christian life is therefore dependent on the consent of regular rank-and-file Christians.

For these reasons, no academic theology stands a chance of influencing the direction of everyday Christian life unless it makes some sense to people from their own theological outlooks. There is no point in academic theology's making a proposal for change if it does not address people where they already are theologically. From the very start, then, academic theology has to be engaged in negotiations with popular theologies. In its primary tasks of articulating and making a coherent system of Christian matters, it must attend to what people already think, meeting at least some of their theological concerns, talking in much the same terms, correcting popular theological opinion where necessary and in ways that will seem defensible to this broader audience. If their results are to influence everyday life, the primary investigations of specialized theologians must weigh the desire to alter and correct what Christians say and do against the need to gain widespread popular appeal.

In the process, academic theology will have to compete with theologies of everyday life in great part on those theologies' own terms. In this way, the practical requirements for an effective theology on the level of everyday life—the ability, for example, to respond appropriately to the day-to-day needs of a particular situation and make the best use of the opportunities it affords—become part of specialized theology's own field-specific norms. Reined in by a competing set of interests, the logic of theory is kept from drifting too far from the logic of everyday cultural practices.

Moreover, the same ambiguities and opportunistic ripostes that characterize competition among specialized theologies return here in relations between academic theologies and popular ones. Gathering the support of popular theologies means compromising the clarity of any particular academic theological position. Despite the intention to meet theoretical aims of coherence, clarity, and completion, specialized theologies are pulled toward polyvalent ambiguities by the need to find agreement with everyday theologians. The more interpretive leeway an academic theology leaves for its own constructions, the more likely their appeal to a greater number of nonspecialists. Thus, an academic may mean something quite technical by God's parental love, but unless the idea also permits a variety of interpretations that hug ordinary life more closely, it is unlikely to have any widespread practical force. Moreover, like what happens in its competition with other academic theologies, an academic theology has to be concerned about which theological maneuvers—which clarification, emphasis, or logical arrangement—will work best vis-à-vis popular theologies in a particular situation. Academic theology has to be concerned about which theological maneuvers will work best to enlist the support or counteract the influence of the most significant popular theologies at a particular place and time. Once again, then, we see academic theologies internalizing the operations characteristic of everyday theological production. The two are not so different after all.

The Basic Operations of Both

We can conclude that the operations of academic theology, for all their peculiarities, are versions of the operations found in everyday theological investigation. Academic theology continues the same sort of operations found there; it just extends them into a new theoretical field.[30] Indeed, the basic operations at issue—say, a sense of timing and a feel for what is fitting in a particular situation—characterize any social practice. They can be more readily identified with everyday theology than with academic theology, not beause the former is somehow more a social practice than the latter, but because the latter (unlike the former) is invested in certain values like clarity, coherence, and comprehensiveness that apparently run contrary to the character of these operations. We have seen, however, how an interest in such values is qualified even in academic theology. Without the kind of tact and artful attention to circumstances and effective mobilization of situation-specific forces found in full-bodied material social practices, investment in those values is not enough to generate academic theologies—or at any rate, not enough to generate good ones according to the internal standards of the field. Not just any clarification or deductive scheme for organizing a theology will do: only those that can make an opportunity out of the difficulties of one's opponents, or mobilize support from potential competitors in a particular time and place, or utilize the possibilities that a certain sociocultural context affords to convince others of the way of life one believes proper.

The basic operations that theologians perform have a twofold character. First, theologians show an artisanlike inventiveness in the way they work on a variety of materials that do not dictate of themselves what theologians should do with them. Second, theologians exhibit a tactical cleverness with respect to other interpretations and organizations of such materials that are already on the ground.

The materials with which theologians work are incredibly diverse. They include, potentially at least, the whole of the beliefs and values that have ever circulated in Christian social practices—in Scripture, ritual activity, and all the other activities, be they economic or political, in which Christian engage. These beliefs and values of Christian practice cannot be limited, moreover, to explicitly religious ones—what is religious is a slippery matter in any case—but include the meaning dimension of social practices that Christians pursue in virtue of their other social commitments—say, as scientists or U.S. citizens. The materials also include the Christian practices themselves, the shapes they have taken over time—say, as urban household churches, monastic communities or isolated desert ascetics, as engagement with or withdrawal from political life, missionary work, heresy hunts, charitable enterprises, and so forth.

Theologians take responsibility for interpreting and organizing some selection of these materials. They attempt to show how some body of these materials hang together well or cohere according to a certain interpretation of them. Materials are selected and rejected, and their senses mutually modified, in light of one another. What is God's wrath in light of God's mercy? Or God's omnipresence in light of the Holocaust? Or God's providence in light of evolutionary theory? Or Christian commitment to neighbor-love in light of the profit motive that runs industry? The theologian's understanding of the materials selected for use is often a matter of figuring out what follows from them, and that means figuring out their compatibility with the rest of what one believes. Does God's love suggest we will never die? If so, how is that compatible with our ordinary experience of the corruption of all things? Could the conflict be resolved by saying that God's love just means we will never be separated from God as long as we live?

Where one starts in these processes is literally a matter of where one is concretely—socially, politically, practically. It is a matter of one's very particular historical and social locations. Realistic possiblities for selection (what can be taken seriously or what is out of the question), the possible meanings of these selected materials, and what they initially seem to have to do with one another, are established in great part by the the schools, churches, occupations, theological movements, and political organizations of which one is a part.

Meanings and organizations of the materials with which they work are already available in virtue of the social allegiances that theologians have. The materials are not the mute ones, so to speak, of ordinary artisans. They generally come already interpreted and at least partially organized. Most of the materials with which theologians work are already, in other words, theological to one degree or other—say, an already relatively well-defined idea of God's compassion found in an African American spiritual, or the schematic organization of biblical stories summarized in a creed, or the full-blown systematic theology of John Calvin's *Institutes*.[31]

We have seen, however, that this does not relieve a theologian from his or her own constructive responsibilities. This is in part because of novelties of circumstance; something new is always being added to the equation. In part it is because there is always some vagueness or disorganization to be pushed further. There is also always already too much on the ground to make theological decision easy. There are too many potentially conflicting ideas about Christ's death, too many versions of how God's mercy and God's justice can be reconciled with one another, too many disagreements about the political implications of equality before God. In theory at least—tempered by the theologian's initial commitments and an eventual evaluation of whether those commitments can withstand critical scrutiny—the theologian has the whole extraordinarily diverse history of Christian theology (both academic and everyday, present and past) with which to work.

That diversity makes clear that every theologian's judgment is her or his own. There are always other theological possibilities besides the ones from which one starts, and other available resources for reinterpreting and reorganizing the theological materials that are afforded by the social practices with which one initially associates. The materials with which the theologian works are always then "raw" materials in that the shape that they will take in the future awaits the theologian's hands.

The academic theologian, ideally, has greater resources—a wider range of materials—for such a constructive task than does the nonspecialist. Though firmly situated in particular social practices, the academic theologian should know about the variety of what Christians have said and done across differences of time and place. Academic theology, too, can use as its materials other academic theologies and similarly specialized theoretical productions, for instance, the products of scientific and philosophical investigation. This wide range of materials is the great strength of academic theology, its competitive edge, so to speak, in the task of figuring out how Christian beliefs, values, and practice hold together. While clay and a stick can create things of beauty, who has the more options as an artisan? Someone whose work is limited by those materials, or someone with clay, iron, mortar, paints, smelting pots, saws, and welding tools?

Academic theology should not squander its advantages, as it does, when tempted by its relative autonomy as a field, it artificially reduces the scope of its materials. Focusing only on other specialized intellectual productions, academic theology sometimes turns away from all it can use. It blinds itself to everyday theologies, past and present, and to the immediate practical problems that pose difficulties for Christian social practices in the particular historical context in which it works. Ignoring everyday theology, it loses one rich resource for reworking the academic theologies from which it tends to draw its materials. Ignoring the historical context in which they are set, its productions lose their efficacy and appeal as influences on proper Christian action and belief. Concentrating on theoretical productions in the past and present, it may, indeed, fail to include talk about everyday Christian social practices at all, so that these social practices fall out of the elements that it constructs into a coherent whole. Academic theology refuses, thereby, its own mandate to be comprehensive. It leaves its implications for anything but its own social practice, including its implications for everyday Christian social practices, undeveloped.

Academic theology should, instead, take its cue from everyday theology. While everyday theology does not have as much to use, it tends to use everything it can; anything that might work is at least considered. Impelled by immediate practical needs, moreover, this attention to everything serviceable never blunts its focus: What is a Christian to say and do in these circumstances?

Working with materials that are already theological, materials that have already been interpreted and put together in some fashion, requires the theologian to operate in ways that somehow bridge those of artistic taste, good gamesmenship, practical craftiness, and military tactics. The theologian senses the faultlines in the past and present theological productions with which it competes, vulnerabilities it hopes either to patch or to capitalize upon. It knows how to seize the moment, or, better, to create the moment in which a given theology is brought to crisis by a new historical or social development. It sees how the terrain is changed and how possibilities for theological movement arise, with the addition of materials that are out of the theologian's control—say, the loss of state backing for a national church, or new medical technologies (for instance, birth control), or the development of a permanent capitalist underclass. And it knows how making an addition of its own—how bringing something up from the past or from the lives of presently marginalized Christian communities, or how giving some new twist to an element that is already part of the theological materials one works with—can make all the difference theologically. Such a difference might be made, for example, by proclaiming "Jesus is the only Lord" in a Christian empire that institutionalizes theological parallels between divine and human sovereignty. In the same way, adding just the right musical note at the right time or just that dab of color in the right place changes everything, disrupts what came before and forces its elements into rearrangement, toward a new harmony or balance.

Moreover, the skillful theologian knows what the theological materials with which one works will let one get away with: what next step, given those theological starting points, will be plausible as well as novel. Angling for change, the theologian determines which theological materials do the most work in a particular theological configuration and how much interpretive leeway already surrounds them. Thus, if a Constantinian church depends heavily on the idea of Jesus as Lord (in order to suggest that the emperor is a lord to be obeyed like Jesus), perhaps its specialized theological productions (say, the sermons of church officials) already permit the antiimperial interpretation favored by the poor audience for them—the emperor must obey the Lord Jesus who is the loving servant of the people. Permission of that antiimperial interpretation would be a condition for those sermons' popular reception. In such circumstances, it might be relatively easy to construct a theology that demonstrates the reasonableness of such an antiimperial interpretation by showing how it hangs together well with the rest of what Christians properly say and do. In the same way, a baseball pitcher might make the tactical judgment that, while she cannot spit on the ball, she can run her fingers through her hair before throwing. And should it become permissible to run one's fingers through one's hair, she can next try to wipe her sweaty brow. Indeed, in certain circumstances—say, where soaring batting averages threaten to make games less competitive—a pitcher might make the tactical judgment that, despite the reservations of officials, the practice of spitting on the ball will be overlooked and eventually gain official approval. In the same way a clever defense attorney knows that standards of evidence in court cases are liable to go up—and the requirements for reasonable doubt to go down—in circumstances of widespread police corruption. In such circumstances, the clever defense attorney can, indeed, make a good argument that standards of evidence should be so tightened, thereby leading the way to altered judicial practice.

Finally, judgments between competing theological proposals are rarely cinched by outright evidence of fallacious inferences, inconsistency, or unclarity on some party's part. Instead, the issue of whose theological position is most compelling is decided by judgments of an aesthetic sort, ones like those used to determine, say, the best interpretation of a poem.[32] Different readings organize a poem differently so as to highlight different lines that are often understood differently. Proponents of different readings attack one another specifically at those points of different emphasis and interpretation. Such an attack might mean arguing that the interpretation of the lines which one's opponent emphasizes is forced and that the lines so understood make less sense of the rest of the poem than would one's own interpretation. Defense against such attack would require an equally opponent-specific effort to show, say, that the lines in question allow for multiple readings and that the meaning selected illuminates the whole in a way that neither one's opponent's interpretation of the same lines nor his or her competing selection of significant lines can rival. Drawing out the analogy, then, Christianity is one big poem in that the meanings of its elements are subtle and ambiguous, and the connections among them elusive and associative, as matters of practice always are. Moreover, in the Christian case, judgments between competing visions of how to put it all together are even more subtle and complex—and even more unlike, say, demonstrative proof from agreed-upon premises—than is the case with a poem. This is because "the poem" here does not exist as an obvious whole to begin with. It is not clear what lines are to be included in the poem to be made sense of. Some selection among the many potential "lines" has to be made for the poem to be at all manageable as an object of interpretation. In addition, Christian "lines" often square so poorly with one another that one can always argue that some do not belong in the poem at all—they are like corruptions, forgeries, or copying errors. Again, in order to criticize effectively an opponent's decision to exclude certain practices from consideration, one must concentrate on just those points in a way that will address that particular opponent's concerns. One might try, for example, to show how they do indeed cohere with other lines the authenticity of which no one at the time questions, or try to demonstrate that when included they throw a new light on the whole, illuminating other material that one's opponent failed to notice or could make less good sense of.

In sum, when engaging theologies already on the ground—and, as we have suggested, this is almost all the time—theologians use a kind of tact requiring numerous ad hoc and situation-specific adjustments. In contrast to what the values of clarity, consistency, and systematicity might suggest of themselves, even academic theologians do not simply follow logical deductions where they lead or the dictates of abstract principles when arriving at their conclusions. They do not construct their theological positions by applying generalities to particular cases, or emend them by trying to reproduce the same clear meanings in the terms of a new day, so as to convey them across putatively accidental differences in circumstance and vocabulary. Instead, they operate by tying things together—the Latin meaning of *religare*, after all, is to bind. And they do so by way of an innumerable series of discrete disruptions and concrete balancing acts vis-à-vis sets of elements already in play, disruptions and balancing acts that eventually add up to something surprising.

5

Christian Culture and Society

In the last chapter I discussed the nature and operations of theology as part of a Christian cultural context. I availed myself of the modern anthropological idea that culture is the meaning dimension of social action (see chapter 2), while following some of the postmodern modifications of that idea which were discussed in chapter 3. For example, I avoided "high culture" interpretations of the difference between specialized and everyday forms of cultural activity, emphasized cultural process over cultural products, was attentive to contest and struggle within and between such processes, and eschewed quick presumptions of integration and consistency among Christian claims.

The result was a highly constructivist account of the academic theological project. Faced with an incredibly disparate and complex set of materials, the theologian is always ultimately making meaning rather than finding it. No fixed rules or established cultural patterns predetermine proper theological construction or relieve the theologian from responsibility for the decisions he or she reaches. A theologian takes such responsibility by offering situation-specific arguments that he or she knows cannot be immunized against contestation by others; taking responsibility means that a fight by way of good arguments must always be enjoined.

We now need to discuss more thoroughly the nature of the Christian cultural context in which we situated theological operations. In what sense can one talk, as we seemed to in the previous chapter, about Christianity as a particular culture? In what sense is there a specifically Christian way of life?

The question is actually many in one, and raises important issues of Christian identity. First, can one talk about Christian social practices as constituting *a* culture? It seems those practices include both too much and too little to merit such a designation. On the one hand, the incredible expanse of Christian practice across differences of time and place, and the diversity of what Christians say and do even in any one of these times and places, make questionable the status of Christian practices as some sort of whole. Moreover, even if Christian practices do form some whole, it is not at all clear what, if anything, could possibly unify them, make them all of a piece. What keeps the diversity of Christian beliefs and actions from simply fraying off into disconnection, into discrete networks of social practices that have nothing more in common than a name? On the other hand, do Christian social practices include enough to constitute a way of life in the full-bodied, comprehensive sense that the phrase has in anthropological use? The social practices of Aborigines or U.S. residents seem a way of life in that they encompass the full range of human functions—reproductive, economic, political, and so forth—but can Christian social practices plausibly be said to cover anything like the same range?

Second, in what sense is Christianity a *particular* culture, one sort of culture among others? What makes something Christian? On the one hand, this is a boundary issue. How are specifically Christian social practices distinguished from others? What do Christians say and do that others do not? How is Christian identity established with reference to, specifically in contradistinction from, other ways of life? On the other hand, one might try to answer this question about the particularity of Christian culture by describing in positive terms the nature of Christian social practices considered on their own. Can one specify internal connections that bind the elements of Christian practice into some distinctive shape, a characteristic Christian identity? In that case, what do all the elements of Christian practice have to do with one another?

These issues concerning the identity of a Christian way of life, while not always expressed in such overtly anthropological terms, are commonplaces of Christian theology, especially in modern times. They emerge so frequently for several reasons. First, judgments about what is or is not Christian, judgments that often stem from some general sense of what Christianity stands for as a social practice, seem part and parcel of the normative and critical cast of the theological task as we described it in the last chapter. The theologian is fundamentally always asking, "Is this the right thing for Christians to say and do?" Second, questions of Christian identity come up in the face of internal disagreements. Sometimes they are raised in this connection to stay the possibly fissiparous effects of contentiousness. Thus, Paul asks about the character of Christian lives, about the shape that Christian practice takes, in order to prevent the breakup of Christian community along lines that follow differences between Jewish and Gentile practice, between upper- and lower-class lifestyles and privileges, or between those who continue to eat meat offered to idols and those who do not. Thus, the early Christian creeds, while ruling certain practices out of bounds, offered formulas of the faith that helped bridge differences between the opposed theological parties at the time. Sometimes, however, interest in identity issues seems intended to increase the church-dividing potential of theological disagreements by working to characterize the positions of one's opponents as deviations or corruptions of the faith. Thus, identity issues like these—What makes something Christian? How does one distinguish between what is Christian and what is not? What unites Christian practice for all its differences?—came to the fore with the Reformation split between Catholics and Protestants. Third, identity issues arise with the recognition, especially in modern times, of situation-specific differences in Christian social practices that seem to jeopardize claims of Christian unity and wholeness. Thus, questions about the difference between Christian and non-Christian social practices become acute with shifts from minority to majority status, or the reverse. What does it mean to be a Christian if now everyone else is too? How does one's understanding of Christian social practice change if a once-Christian nation is so no longer? In light of such shifts, how can one characterize the relationship between one's Christian commitments and one's allegiances as a member of the wider society? Modernity raises the awareness of situation-specific differences in Christian practice through the development of historical consciousness; the intrinsic character of Christianity seems at risk once one can no longer presume that the Christian practices of the past were the same as those in the present. The intrinsic character of Christianity is also put at risk by the recognition that Christian social practices are pulled in novel directions by their transplantation beyond a Western orbit, and by the modern awareness of affinities between forms of Christian practice and socioeconomic location.

This chapter and the next show how contemporary Christian theology often addresses these issues of Christian identity in ways that reflect a modern understanding of culture. Like a culture according to the usual account of it in modern anthropology, Christian social practices are often taken to be a group-specific, unified whole, sharply bounded to form, at least initially, some sort of self-contained unit. These presumptions are not only contested by postmodern developments in cultural studies; as we will see, they sit uneasily with a number of common claims in Christian theology, and entail, often without adequate theological argument, a judgment in favor of a particular position on substantive theological matters—for example, matters of sin and grace.

In order to explore the way theologians address this many-sided question of Christian identity, we need not try to disentangle its various strands and discuss separately proposals for addressing each one. Typically, Christian theologians offer one sort of answer for them all. To give a simple case, a theologian might say that shared beliefs and values resolve the issue of what holds a Christian way of life together, what makes it a whole. This sort of answer might also do for the question of what distinguishes a Christian way of life from others; Christians maintain just this set of beliefs and values while others do not. The same answer, moreover, could be used to shore up Christian identity in the face of perceived differences in what Christians say and do across time and space: despite those differences, these underlying beliefs and values remain a constant.

The answers that perform these multiple duties tend to be of three sorts.[1] One sort tries to define Christian identity in social terms; a second tries to do so with reference to cultural boundaries; and a third, by looking at intrinsic continuities in Christian belief and action. The first two answers suggest that Christians have a self-sustaining society and culture of their own, which can be marked off rather sharply from others. The present chapter will tackle such ideas. The third sort of answer suggests Christian identity is a matter of cultural commonalities, and will form the subject matter of the next chapter. A variant of this answer, Christian identity in virtue of a distinctive cultural style, is closest to my own proposal. But in the course of criticizing proposals under each rubric, I will gradually construct an alternative theological position, to be summed up at the end of the next chapter.[2]

Christian Identity in Social Terms

This strategy for answering questions concerning Christian identity involves an argument over the sort of social group that Christians form, an argument that goes back to the very beginnings of Christianity. Do Christian social practices form an independent society comparable in its range of functions to the Roman society left behind? Does a Christian way of life mean life in a new and separate community so that Christians constitute a new people comparable to, but different from, Jews, Greeks, or Babylonians? If so, Christian identity would seem to require for its maintenance withdrawal or separation from Roman society, say, in desert communities or in some sort of self-sufficient monastic life. If Christian identity does not require societies like these, need it have a social side at all? Perhaps it just involves ascetic or spiritual practices of individual purification. The Christian could then try to withdraw from social relations altogether in a solitary desert existence or try to remain engaged in social relations while being attentive solely to the state of the interior life. Or, if a Christian way of life does not involve the formation of an alternative society, does it perhaps gain its identity as the religious wing of a Christianized Roman Empire?

The identity of Christianity would then be linked, not to some separate community, but to the Roman society of which it is a part.

These are old questions, involving as they do controversies over Christian identity among Christian sectarians, solitary ascetics, and advocates of a Christian empire. But they are questions that continue into the present in forms that are easily infiltrated by the modern idea of culture. At issue is whether Christianity fits the very old idea that ways of life correspond to distinct peoples or communities. A modern view of culture shares that old idea; it just offers, as we suggested in chapters 1 and 2, a new way of explaining the fact that distinct social groups display different ways of life.

Expressed in a modern anthropological idiom, the question becomes, then, "Do Christians form the sort of social group that can claim to have its own culture?" In other words, do they form their own society set off from others? If so, the difference between what is Christian and what is not, like the difference between distinct cultures, can simply follow a division between social groups; Christian culture breaks off at the same point as Christian society. Christianity maintains its identity, according to this view, by maintaining an alternative social world; it is comparable to any other society in its functions but qualitatively different in its principles. The Christian community is one, say, of peace, joy, and fellowship; all others are ones of power, conflict, and violence. A way of life becomes Christian, rather than something else, then, when it is completely routed by this alternative society, one sort of society being simply substituted for another. A view like this is defended by the contemporary Christian theologian, John Milbank.[3]

Despite the use in Christianity of this sort of language as a rhetorical trope making clear the weighty significance of conversion, the idea that Christian life is led in a new society is difficult to sustain empirically. The majority view in Christianity for most of its history never favored efforts to make Christian social practices into the sort of social group that modern anthropologists would think of as possessing its own way of life. Thus, just as in the modern West, so in the first five centuries of the Common Era Christians continued to participate in many, though certainly not all, of the activities of the wider (in this case Roman) society in which they were placed; they usually withdrew only from those that seemed inextricably linked to pagan religious practices. Christian communities did not try to replace the educational, economic, familial, or political functions served by Roman institutions with their own. Christians may have partaken of meals together, but Christian societies were not literally where they made their bread. Christian communities might have been a family in many ways but nobody was literally born and raised there.

Rather than establishing separate societies in their own right, Christian social practices commonly form something more like an association with initiation rites, a special kind of club unusual in its potential to produce close personal ties—a substitute family in that sense—among people of very different classes and circumstances, and to provide its members with an abiding reference point for the direction of their lives whether in or out of such Christian company. Christians' social relations extend beyond the activities with other Christians that constitute this Christian association or club—the church. And like what happens in an association and not in a separate society, the character of those outside activities also infiltrate it; the social practices that make up this Christian association have to manage the differences in rank and status that its members bring to it in virtue of their other social engagements.

Where efforts are made in Christian history to turn Christian social practices into a full-blown society comparable to that of the Greeks or the Babylonians, the peculiar nature of the effort seems bound to prevent its success. Unlike what is the case with a genuine people, Christian social practices only manage to encompass a fuller range of human functions by incorporating institutional forms from elsewhere. Thus, in the early medieval period, Christian social practices took on the character of a society comparable to the Roman world only by borrowing from it—its laws, its political structures. Unlike the usual case of a social group, when Christian social practices are up and running they do not start with a full complement of institutions they can call their own. In order to become a social alternative to the Roman Empire, Christian social practices must, therefore, borrow from the very society they oppose. There is, one might say, no answer to a question such as, "What is the educational institution of Christian society?" in the same sense as there is an answer to the question "What is the Babylonian one?" Christianity simply does not have a school system of its own in that sense; it takes one over from elsewhere, and shapes it to its own needs, or does without.

Postmodern Critiques

Answering questions of Christian identity by talking about a distinct social group is also contested by postmodern ideas about society and culture. This strategy for addressing the question seems to assume that social groups are objectively demarcated like discrete objects in space lying at some remove from one another. While there may be social groups that lead a completely isolated existence, social groups are generally not demarcated by a natural break in social interactions—that is, in virtue of the fact that these people have only to do with one another.[4] In the main, there are no breaks of that sort; there is just one huge pool of social interaction and divisions among discrete social groups are made on some other basis, as a matter of group identification or allegiance. In other words, members of one group might interact on a daily basis as much or more with members of some other group than with their own; those interactions need not jeopardize group identity because that identity is a matter of allegiance to certain standards or value orientations, a matter of self-definition, and not isolation.[5] Turning one's attention to discrete social groups or communities is not then the way to answer questions about Christian identity; one needs to have answered the question of Christian identity—What makes someone Christian?—in order for Christians and non-Christians to be seen as forming discrete social groups at all.

To put the point another way, this way of answering the question of Christian identity in social terms seems to think of the relations between social groups in terms of relations between physical objects. But while two different objects cannot be made up of the same parts in the same space, two social groups can.[6] People waiting to buy movie tickets make up only one line, but they may constitute, and be actively participating in, any number of different social groups—say, the Jack Benny Society, the 1930s Comedy Society, the Christians-Interested-in-Popular-Culture Society. Christian identity need not exclude, therefore, overlapping activities and memberships. If it does not, its maintenance need not require the sort of alternative society proposed by John Milbank.

Someone like Milbank, who is well versed in postmodern theory, may object that he is well aware of the dangers of localizing social groups in space in this way. Like other "deterritorializing" social movements, the church has no particular place or geographical location—it is a nomad city.[7] But if the Christian community serves all the functions that a so-called secular society does and is organized along entirely different lines, as Milbank affirms, then Christian communities are still being imagined here, like the discrete cultures of modern anthropology, as if they were distributed alongside others in geographical space. They run alongside or occupy the interstices, the spaces left open, by secular society; they can never overlap other social interactions but always have to push them out or replace them.

The strategy of explaining Christian identity in social terms also conflicts with postmodern developments in cultural theory that contest such a simple correspondence between a way of life and a social group.[8] As we saw in chapter 3, no social group has a monopoly on the various elements that make up its way of life; those elements cross social boundaries, being taken up in one way by a particular social group, in another way by some other. One's way of life and one's social location have something to do with one

another but this is not a natural relation. Social location does not find automatic expression in any particular set of beliefs and values, for example; the
relationship between the two has to be established through the active artic-
ulation of one to the other. Thus, nationalism might be characteristic of
certain Christian groups, but this does not mean that nationalism is a simple reflection of their social existence; everything depends on how the resonances and associations of nationalism are developed and made to fit with
Christian preoccupations in a particular context. It is hard to argue, then,
that the character of a Christian way of life is simply determined by the
identity of Christianity as a distinct social organization. Even if that community is clearly demarcated in social terms—say, in virtue of an unusually
diverse membership and organization around rituals like baptism and the
eucharist—how that social identity is fleshed out in a concrete way of life is
not at all obvious on those grounds alone.

Theological objections to the position are also considerable. First, the
claim that Christian identity follows divisions between social groups sits
uneasily with the typical way that Christian accounts of a new identity in
Christ downplay the significance of social distinctions. Christian identity
does not follow divisions between Jew and Greek, or respect the divided
social worlds of men and women, rich and poor, or free and slave, in
Roman society. Why, then, make Christian identity itself dependent on a
new social division? Rather than try to maintain Christian identity by
upholding a sharp difference between Christian social practices and those
of others, Paul, for example, is quite willing to blur the difference between
the two in the interest of Christian fellowship among those whom social
divisions usually keep apart. Thus, simply forbidding Christians to eat meat
dedicated to idols or insisting that Gentile converts be circumcised and follow Jewish laws for daily living would clearly help distinguish Christians
from Romans along social lines: one could claim that their respective social
practices are quite distinct. Paul declines to do so, however: Christian solidarity might be threatened by the usual divisions between social groups
were one to try to establish what it means to be a Christian along that sort
of social line.

Second, for a number of general theological reasons Christian theologians are loathe to make such a sharp distinction between the social practices of Christians and non-Christians. Such a distinction conflicts, for
example, with a belief in the universality of sin and in the capacity of all
persons, however sinful, to be saved by the free grace of Jesus Christ. Unlike
what an account of Christian identity in social terms suggests, Christians
remain threatened by sin despite their acceptance of salvation in Christ;
they have reason to continue to pray for God's forgiveness. They are always

therefore as much outsiders as insiders to a life in Christ, in that they continue to depend, as any sinner would, on God's free grace. Moreover, if anything enables God's grace to find them, it is what they share with those outside the church. God's grace pertains to them in virtue of their status as creatures and as human beings made for an intimate fellowship with God, standings that bridge any division between those inside and outside the church. And God's grace finds them by its own free exercise, in the sense that Christians have not deserved it more than others and in the sense that it may even now find non-Christians through extraordinary means (that is, means that are unknown to Christians).

These ideas about sin and grace blur any difference between Christians and non-Christians drawn on social grounds. According to these ideas, the difference between the two is not a natural or achieved difference—not something that can be lodged or encapsulated, for example, in a particular social organization; it is a difference that always continues to depend on the free offer of grace. When Christian identity is said to depend on the distinctiveness of a social group, those in the church seem, on the contrary, to be different creatures altogether from those outside it: somehow they lead lives, say, of peace and love while the rest of the world wallows in conflict and violence. In dispute here is not the power of the grace of Christ to transform human lives; these ideas of sin and grace and an account of Christian identity in social terms are in agreement on that. At issue, rather, is whether, as the latter seems to imply, that transformative grace is restricted to persons within the church and whether Christians, simply because of their group membership, can congratulate themselves on the possession of some unique perfection.

Christian theologians do commonly talk about conversion as a new birth, as the coming into existence of a new creature. But making sense of that difference in terms of a difference between the way humans live outside and within Christian communities makes the difference so extreme as to jeopardize the oneness of God. The God who brings the church into existence does not seem any longer to be the same God who creates and governs the world that encompasses communities outside it. The world outside is simply left behind rather than redeemed by Christ. Or, one could say God's grace in Christ, along with the church's mission in service and witness to that grace, extends to the whole world only to the extent the world is brought within the church and is therefore no longer the world at all.

Again, Christian theologians do emphasize the difference between a life lived with Christ and life without him, but what makes the difference is a new relationship with what lies beyond the Christian community itself, a new orientation of standards and values around, not the Christian community itself, but that to which the community witnesses—the free grace of God in Christ. In contrast, according to the account of Christian identity at which we have been looking, everything depends on the maintenance of this special society; its superiority and distinctiveness are an overriding theological concern. Such Christian self-concern, alternating as it does between pride and defensiveness, is, if I might hazard a theological judgment, nothing short of idolatrous.

A Social Alternative

If one can muster all these reasons against identifying Christian social practices with the sort of society to which a modern anthropologist would attribute a culture, what is the alternative? If Christian social practices do not constitute their own society, what do they constitute? I have already given a hint by suggesting they form an unusual type of voluntary association. But it is important to see, first, that denying Christianity its own full-fledged society does not force one to define Christian identity simply in terms of a distinctive set of attitudes or motivations.[9] If that kind of definition were the only alternative, Christian practice would not have a social dimension of its own at all; Christian social practices, if they got beyond purely individual pursuits of, say, spiritual self-discipline, would be nothing more than non-Christian social practices accompanied by Christian dispositions, feelings, or motivations. The Christian would do the same old things everyone does but with a different subjective outlook.

Nor, if one denies that Christianity forms its own society and yet wishes to maintain a social dimension for Christian practice, need one make Christian identity hinge on its role in some other, genuinely full-fledged society, say the Roman Empire or the nations of Europe. If Christian identity cannot be determined with reference to a Christian society, one need not look for some other society to fill the same function. In that case, what it means to be a Christian would be bound up inseparably with what it means to be a member of that social group—say, a member of Western society. Ernst Troeltsch seems to have held such a view.[10]

Simply switching in this way the social group at issue from a Christian to a non-Christian one hardly helps. From a theological point of view, this position continues to be oddly preoccupied with the fortunes of a human community—odder still, from a theological perspective, not even with the fortunes of a Christian society but simply a Western one. The threat of idolatry is thereby heightened, since not just Christian social practices but Western societies seem to have reason now for self-congratulatory self-concern. The view that Christianity forms its own society at least had the benefit of permitting criticism of the wider society; here Christian identity is never distinct enough from that of a European identity to get any radical critical purchase on it. Christianity is either the helpmate of Western societies, working to develop the potentials of a distinctively Western way of life, or it must wither altogether as a social force in a Western context.

If these alternatives are inadequate, another remains. As we suggested above, Christian social practices form a voluntary association within a wider society, rather than a separate society in and of themselves. The new point—to add to the other unusual features we mentioned earlier—is that this association shapes its members for altered social relations beyond the interactions constituting the association itself. Because God is the God of the whole world and not just of our religious lives, all social relations outside the interactions that constitute the religious association itself are to be affected by the standards and values to which its members conform. Such an association genuinely shapes, therefore, a whole way of life, without being a separate society. Following the postmodern idea that, as we saw in chapter 3, whole ways of life need not be matched up with separate societies, a whole Christian way of life is brought about by such an action-transforming association, despite the fact that there is no society of its own corresponding to it. Christian social existence is quite literally, then, without a homeland in some territorially localizable society. Christians lead lives as resident aliens in the society of which they are a part, without, however, having migrated from any other society—they have no other homeland—and without setting up an alternative society of their own in a new land.

In contrast, then, to the first alternative I mentioned, this association has a social dimension (and not just a purely personal effect) outside the context of the association itself. And contrary to the second alternative above, these social implications are quite possibly critical of the wider society; the identity of the Christian association is not locked into step with the full-fledged social group with which the members of an association are necessarily also engaged. In short, on this new view, the church would be analogous to a new social movement, an association with a social agenda (but not exclusively so), that takes people in in order to change their ways (say, by consciousness-raising) but that also intends to shake up the social practices of those outside, and not just by bringing them into the fold.

Unlike a new social movement, however, Christian allegiance is not fixed on these new social practices themselves. They therefore are not proposed, as the recommendations of new social movements sometimes are, from a position of indefeasible privilege. In keeping with the theological judgments we made earlier, neither the wider society nor its own practices are to be for this Christian association an idol.

Christian Identity in Virtue of a Cultural Boundary

Rather than look to the character of Christian communities, another way that contemporary theologians account for Christian identity focuses on the idea of a cultural boundary, one that would rather starkly distinguish a Christian way of life, on the one hand, from those of other religions or the wider secular society, on the other. Like cultures according to a modern anthropological understanding of them, Christian and non-Christian forms of life would amount to qualitatively discontinuous wholes, without any obvious common ground between them. Christians have their own language, their own ways of doing, understanding, and feeling; people who are not Christian have some other. On this picture, the cultural forms that constitute Christian identity seem to be, ideally, absent elsewhere. The loci of Christian identity are not, that is, borrowed from elsewhere, but are the spontaneous productions of the people concerned. The New Testament, for example, would be a good case in point. Moreover, such indigenous cultural productions—texts, rituals, peculiar symbolic forms, and patterns of behavior—are said to generate, like all cultures do according to the modern understanding of them, their own world of meaning, a web of significance that is all their own. They can therefore be understood in their own terms without the need for reference to anything outside themselves. Finally, given the purported discontinuity of kind that separates a Christian way of life from others, Christian identity seems properly maintained by avoiding the influences and alterations that might accrue to it by way of intimate involvement with other ways of doing, feeling, and understanding. Christian identity would seem to require, in short, cultural insularity. Like the understanding of cultures in modern anthropology, here a Christian way of life seems a tightly bounded entity, essentially unaffected by relations with others and thereby sustaining its distinctive character.

Such a view of Christian identity, which seems to depend on a Christian way of life's being self-contained and self-originating, is a caricature of the postliberal view offered by its critics.[11] Fueling the caricature are several typical postliberal pronouncements: (1) that the only relevant criteria for determining the meaning and plausibility of Christian practices are ones internal to those practices themselves; (2) that Christian identity is jeopardized when one's primary theological interests are to convey a Christian outlook in terms that non-Christians would find meaningful and plausible; and (3) that becoming a Christian is something akin to primary socialization. This last point means that one does not work from what one already knows in the process of becoming a Christian—say, by translating a new Christian language into the language one already uses. There is no discursive or argumentative transition of that sort. Instead, learning to be a Christian is like learning a second first language. One learns a second native language from the ground up in the same way one learned one's first one—by an intensive immersion in a close-knit group of people who already speak it.[12]

The description offered above of the postliberal account of Christian identity is nonetheless a caricature in that followers of George Lindbeck gladly admit that a Christian way of life is influenced by outside cultures, mixed up with and modified by them. A Christian outlook is a comprehensive one and therefore has its own drive to incorporate or assimilate the cultural practices of others. Other cultures provide the materials to be viewed through a Christian lens or cultural framework. What Christians see through that lens or in terms of that framework is therefore a composite. Even basic Christian doctrines are always reformulated in new terms to reflect the changing cultural scene of the wider society.[13] Moreover, the description of the internal logic of Christian practices, which is one of the theologian's primary tasks, often involves the use of technical conceptualities borrowed from elsewhere.[14]

The caricature remains a good likeness, however, because postliberals interpret the mixed character of Christian discourse and the composite nature of a Christian outlook in ways that again strongly suggest the self-contained and self-originating character of Christian identity. By taking two strategies, postliberals are able to suggest that, while a Christian way may not be self-contained and self-originating, Christian identity still is; though Christian practices are mixed up, for example, with wider cultural spheres, the Christian identity of those practices—what makes them Christian—has nothing to do with such mixing. First, postliberals simply try to exempt from outside influence whatever ensures Christian identity. Thus, the vocabulary or conceptuality of doctrines may be so influenced but not the basic rules by which they abide.[15] The Christian framework is mixed when it extends to outside worldviews, but this Christian lens or framework itself—what ensures the Christian identity of such interpretations of the wider culture—is apparently internally generated and intelligible on its own, independently of them. Scripture, for example, creates its own domain of meaning before it is ever extended to cover the whole of reality as non-Christians understand it.[16] When it comes to the framework or lens itself, therefore, Christian identity once again seems threatened by efforts of translation into non-Christian terms; a distinctively Christian way of life is in danger of being lost thereby. Despite the recognition of outside influences on Christianity, it remains the case that "religions, like languages, can be understood only in their own terms, not by translating them into alien speech."[17]

The second way that postliberals hold onto the idea of a self-contained and self-originating identity for Christianity, despite their admission of a Christian way of life's mixed character, is by appealing to the kind of contextualism typical of a modern understanding of culture.[18] Outside influences may suffuse all aspects of Christianity—even the rules and the framework itself—but reference to what lies outside a Christian context remains irrelevant to Christian identity since any such borrowed material takes on a new sense in a Christian context. Cultural materials from outside mean something else when in Christian use. The only way to unpack that use, and so discover its meaning and assess its credibility, is with reference to the rest of Christian practices. Thus, if one wants to know what Christians mean by "God," looking at the use of the terms outside Christianity is no help; the way the term figures in the stories, beliefs, rituals, and behaviors of Christians is all that matters.[19] There may be, it is true, overlaps in Christian and non-Christian practices. While there is no positive relation in principle between internal and external uses, there is also no need in principle to insist upon a simple opposition between the two.[20] Developing the connections here—whether of resemblance or contrast—is, however, a purely ad hoc, optional matter; developing them is certainly not a condition for understanding Christian uses, nor is it of more than occasional service in highlighting the distinctive features of Christian claims to particular outsiders.[21]

These two moves are not limited to postliberals. The first way postliberals interpret the mixed character of Christianity brings out what they share with correlationist theologians; the second way establishes a kinship with Friedrich Schleiermacher and his liberal Protestant followers. Thus, while correlationist theologians, in contrast to postliberals, think that connections with wider cultural spheres must be developed in order to *assess* the meanings of Christian texts, those connections are not what establishes whether those meanings are Christian. While opposing postliberals by demanding that the meaningfulness and plausibility of Christian claims be proved with reference to general criteria that are not specifically Christian, correlationist theologians share with postliberals the view that Christian texts generate of themselves, and in some at least initially self-sufficient way, a meaning of their own to be so tested. In both cases, Christian texts render or disclose their own world.[22] Their doing so is, indeed, all that prevents loss of Christian identity in the process of correlation. Christianity must already make its own claims to meaning and truth—a seemingly indigenous and self-originating claim in virtue of its classic texts—before being brought before the bar of standards of intelligibilty and plausibility in the wider culture, if its identity is not to be threatened thereby. For a method of correlation to work, it seems it must involve, then, a meeting of independently generated wholes—one constructed by way of a hermeneutical analysis of specifically Christian texts, the other by way of a phenomenological description and transcendental analysis of general human processes. The need for their meeting is disputed by postliberals but the general idea of such independently specifiable wholes is fully compatible with postliberal ideas about Christian identity.

Because of the way aesthetic holism and ideas about individual character inform, as we saw in chapter 1, a German notion of culture, German theology, especially in the Protestant liberal tradition of Schleiermacher, is pushed toward a contextualist rationale, like that used by postliberals, to support a view of Christian identity as self-contained and autonomously generated. German liberal Protestants claim, as postliberals do, that, once outside influences enter a Christian context, they take on an entirely different character from what they had outside; no further reference to what is outside Christianity is therefore necessary to explain what they mean or how they are justified. Thus, according to Schleiermacher, Christian claims have to change with new developments in philosophy and the natural sciences, but borrowed material of this sort never has the same meaning in a Christian context that it had outside it. So much is this the case that Christian theology, despite all its borrowings, is never *essentially* dependent on any outside discipline. All borrowings, once incorporated in a Christian context, take on a Christian character that is utterly individual, a character that therefore can go its own way, developing by an internal impulsion properly immune from outside interference.[23]

Objections

A number of theological and postmodern cultural reasons can be offered for disputing the proposal of a self-contained and self-originating Christian identity in virtue of a cultural boundary. These objections work against the proposal when it is supported by an insistence on the sharpness of the cultural boundary itself that divides Christian from non-Christian, inside from outside (the caricature that effectively captures the dangers of postliberalism when it takes an unnuanced form). They also tell against such a proposal when it takes the more moderate forms typical of the nuanced postliberalism that shares a great deal with its correlationist and liberal opponents. That is, these objections also tell against efforts to exempt those Christian practices that are most responsible for Christian identity from the sort of essential connections with non-Christian cultural spheres that are required in other aspects of the theological project. And these objections effectively challenge the proposal of a self-contained and self-originating Christian identity, too, when it is supported by the claim that what is on the other side of the boundary—whatever its similarities or dissimilarities to Christian practices—is irrelevant for establishing Christian identity. As we will see, Christian identity may have to do with the drawing of a boundary, but that means—contrary to postliberalism, correlationist theology, and the theological heritage of Friedrich Schleiermacher—that Christian identity itself is essentially relational.

Thus, one can argue that, because of several complicating factors, Christian identity simply cannot be secured by a sharp cultural boundary. The first complication hindering such an effort is that it is never clear how to push some practice onto the other side of the boundary, how to exclude it. Say the petitioning of secondary deities found in other religious traditions is to be excluded from Christian practice. Does that mean such practices are to be avoided altogether? That is often the conclusion drawn when Christians identify those deities as demons or devils. Or, does it mean that engagement in such practices is a matter of indifference for Christians since they do not believe those deities exist?[24]

The second complicating factor is that it is rarely clear on what side of the boundary something falls. Say the boundary is supposed to mark a sharp religious difference; Christian practices gain their identity as religious practices that exclude those of any other religion. Still up for grabs is whether any of the practices at issue are religious or not. Are, for example, Greek literature and the educational practices that surround it essentially religious, and therefore to be excluded from Christian practice? Is the caste system merely a social practice or a part of the Hindu religion?[25] Or, looking at matters from the other side, is the way Christian institutions are organized in the West a religious matter or a consequence of following the social imperatives of the wider society? Only in the former case would it make sense to insist that they are required for a Christian identity established by a religious boundary. In short, the drawing of sharp boundaries never seems to settle anything.

The third complication is that where the boundaries are drawn is never fixed; social practices that are excluded at one time and place are included at others. Boundaries therefore seem too fluid to establish the identity of Christian practices. At certain times, in the Western church, for example, Greco-Roman literature was frowned upon, at other times not; and in the West more often than the East. These variations seem to have more to do with situational factors than with any argument about the essential character of Christianity. When and where, for example, there exists a strong pagan aristocracy that treats Greco-Roman literature as an essential feature of its way of life, Christians become more inclined to make the repudiation of that literature a marker of Christian identity.[26]

Moreover, because such decisions are situationally determined, a practice's importance as a boundary marker does not necessarily reflect its importance for a Christian way of life. Depending on the circumstances, almost anything can serve as a boundary marker. For example, if Christians live in a predominantly Hindu society, the fact that they eat beef while their neighbors do not becomes a pertinent boundary marker. That hardly means, however, that beef eating is a matter of any importance within Christian social practices. The practices that mark a boundary need not, then, be good indicators of what is required to maintain Christian identity.

Finally, there is no reason to think that sharp cultural boundaries are necessary to establish the distinctiveness of a way of life. As a postmodern perspective on culture emphasizes, most cultures share a great deal; differences in cultural identity are maintained in more subtle ways.[27] Imported cultural forms, for instance, need not threaten a culture's identity; a difference can be maintained by interpreting those forms differently. Or, both the forms and their basic interpretation in another culture can be taken over by another way of life; their new social and rhetorical contexts will establish a cultural difference. Thus, early Christians incorporated a great deal of the shame/honor code of Greco-Roman morals. Rather than establishing Christian identity by its exclusion, a cultural difference was maintained by changing the goal of such a moral code (the goal is now to do the will of God), by substituting different warrants for the practices (scriptural ones), by making odd content substitutions (humility is now to be honored), and by seeing moral achievement on those terms not as the individual accomplishment of the philosopher but something requiring sustenance from a particular religious community and guaranteed only by God.[28]

Turning to the claim that what is on the other side of the boundary is irrelevant to Christian identity, both theological and postmodern reasons can be supplied to attack directly several additional arguments used by postliberals in support of this claim. Besides appealing to the idea of a contextual determination of meaning and plausibility—an idea I will be qualifying rather indirectly as we proceed—postliberals seem to use the idea of resocialization into a Christian way of life for such support. As mentioned before, if becoming a Christian involves a form of resocialization, what one did before or what one does outside a Christian context is of no direct importance to the process; one's Christian identity can be explained by simple immersion in Christian social practices understood entirely on their own terms. In addition to being empirically improbable—if Christian social practices, as we have said, do not form an independent society, people do not simply discard their other identities when they take on a Christian one—the idea of resocialization is also theologically problematic. It may, for example, capture nicely a Lutheran emphasis on formation by an external word, but it sits uneasily with the idea of justification by faith. Here the Christian seems not the sinner forgiven but a completely new creation. The sins for which one continues to be forgiven as a Christian seem nothing like those for which one would have been justly condemned before, had it not been for God's grace. The failings of Christians seem the far more minor matter of their having to proceed gradually along the often bumpy road of Christian socialization; one needs forgiveness, not because one remains in some quite significant sense the sinner one was before, but simply because one has not fully matured into one's new Christian identity.[29]

Postliberals also try to support the irrelevance to Christian identity of what is on the other side of the boundary by suggesting that the boundary is just an unintended consequence of the tight connection among the elements of a Christian way of life. The boundary does not arise, then, out of any relations with non-Christian practices; it is, instead, just the natural boundary that a Christian way of life forms because it is so highly integrated. Since the elements are all of a piece, relations with what is on the other side of the boundary always threaten to be disruptive, to be an identity-threatening interference, and therefore are best avoided. Postmodern ideas about culture suggest what historical studies of Christianity confirm: that this is a highly unrealistic account of cultural integration.

The postliberal inference of irrelevance is also problematic because, even in the case of the sharpest opposition to other ways of life, opposition is rarely pure. For example, strong opposition to Christian initiation in mystery cults did not mean opposition to water rites in Christian initiation services that were nearly identical in external form to the ones in use there. Christians might make a dualistic distinction between the vices of pagans and the virtues of Christians but the virtues they claimed were often the very same ones that pagans espoused; Christians were simply insisting on the pagan's inability to perform them. Indeed, especially in efforts to turn the tables on an initially more powerful cultural opponent, apparent acculturation is used as a means to effective opposition.[30] Thus, in cargo cults, borrowing of the idea that wealth is to be gained by international trade turns into a millennarian vision for rebellion against the donor-culture. Or in the late fourth century in the West, the Greco-Roman ideal of socialization by way of a literary culture might be incorporated by monasteries in an effort to shape the formation of young men according to the Bible alone.

Christian Identity as Essentially Relational

One might argue, indeed, simply on logical grounds that opposition, no matter how sharp, is essentially relational. One must take into account to what one opposes oneself; what makes an effective opposition depends on what stands out about one's opponent's position.

The nature, then, of any boundary distinguishing Christian from non-Christian ways of life cannot be determined by looking at Christianity alone. As we said before, what functions as a boundary marker at any one time and place may not be apparent simply from the character of Christian practices. Nothing, indeed, about the marked practices themselves makes them suitable for that purpose; almost any aspect of Christian practices can be a likely candidate depending on the circumstances.

Boundaries are determined, in sum, by how a Christian way of life is situated within a whole field of alternatives. The boundaries distinguishing a Christian way of life from others will shift with shifts in the practices of the other ways of life making up the field. For this reason the old boundary markers for Christian identity became problematic with the conversion of large numbers of Greco-Romans; if Greco-Romans are typically Christian, the boundary markers that served when they were not (for instance, the sort of purity of heart displayed in martyrdom or refusals to recant under persecution) will no longer do. It is the same reason for thinking, following Pierre Bourdieu's class analysis of sports, that golf will become problematic as a marker of a middle- or upper-class way of life if large numbers of urban underclass youth, inspired by prominent nonwhite players, take up the game or become enthusiatic spectators of the professional tour.[31]

The contrary postliberal idea that a Christian way of life is self-defining and therefore properly analyzed on its own seems a mistaken inference from the perhaps laudable goal of keeping a Christian way of life from being simply subsumed by some other, as, say, a mere instance of the general run of things elsewhere. As postliberals like to insist, Christian practices—say, the way Christians read Scripture or set standards for intelligibility and truth—are not just instances of a general hermeneutics or of wider cultural norms. The alternative they come up with, however, is often pushed to an unnecessary extreme; especially at its extremes the postliberal position is neither the only alternative nor the most plausible one. In insisting upon a difference postilberals tend to reify it; the plausible idea that Christians have their own way of doing things turns into the problematic claim of an originary autonomy. Postliberals mimic in this way the misguided, but well-intentioned efforts of some scholars in subaltern studies, who suggest that subordinated groups generate their own traditions of discourse and action independently of any one else, in an effort to show that the cultural life of such groups is not dictated to them by more powerful elites.[32] Occluded thereby is the fact of much more complicated relations between them: the ideas and goals of subaltern groups are neither simply given to them by others nor utterly independent of them.

The more complex alternative, generalized by postmodern trends in cultural studies, is that different ways of life take over quite a bit of cultural material from one another; this appropriation, even in the case of groups without much power over their own lives, is not, however, passive. Ways of life show a kind of creativity of consumption.[33] Material borrowed from elsewhere is twisted and turned, used in different ways, when set in a new context.

Differences between ways of life are often therefore established by differences of use and not by the distribution of entirely discrete cultural forms to one side or the other of a cultural boundary.[34] Cultural difference is more a matter of *how* than of *what*; it is not so much what cultural materials you use as what you do with them that establishes identity. Contrary to postliberalism at its extremes, then, differences among ways of life are not attributable to their being formed by cultural materials that have nothing in common. Moreover, contrary to the more nuanced version of postliberalism, identity-establishing differences in the use of the same materials do not simply sit next to one another in supreme indifference, deaf and dumb to one another. Different ways of life establish themselves, instead, in a kind of tussle with one another over what is to be done with the materials shared between them. The distinctiveness of a way of life emerges out of tension-filled relations with what other ways of life do with much the same cultural stuff.

Identity by way of a different use of material shared with others is especially true of Christian social practices, just as it is for the practices of the socially marginalized. Rather than generate cultural artifacts that are all their own, Christian social practices, like those of socially subordinated subcultures, have to make do with materials that they do not themselves produce; they create meaning through a process of consumption.[35] In the case of socially marginalized persons this creative consumption is a function of a lack of power; they are forced to buy the goods, to imbibe the cultural programs, whose manufacture is controlled by those with greater power. But the Christian case holds whatever the power of Christians vis-à-vis their non-Christian neighbors. For the general reasons we discussed earlier, Christian social practices are always forced to incorporate material from other ways of life if they are to constitute a whole way of life themselves. Apart from what they gather from these others, Christian social practices do not amount to a full complement of cultural claims—for instance, on economic, political, or metaphysical matters. They become a comprehensive way of life by working over the practices of others, by transforming what Christians themselves would be otherwise inclined to believe and do if they had only their other sociocultural commitments to go on. Even Christian cultural productions that are specifically religious in a more narrow sense of the term—say, the production of theological statements themselves—depend to much the same extent on other ways of life. Christians do not construct out of whole cloth, or from the bottom up, what they say about God and Jesus or the nature of things in relation to God; instead, they use in odd ways whatever language-games they already happen to speak. *Physis* and *hypostasis*, for example, are common Greek words; it is only their use that is unusual in the early Christian creeds. A Christian way of life is, then, essentially parasitic; it has to establish relations with other ways of life, it has to take from them, in order to be one itself.

Christian language is, then, as Søren Kierkegaard would say, essentially transferred or metaphorical language.[36] And the same holds, as he thought, for all Christian practices. While Christians cannot do everything that non-Christians do—since not all practices can be made Christian (for instance, slavery)—Christian practices are always the practices of others made odd. This is the meaning of Christianity as a second birth; while a second birth means in part the renunciation of prior practices, one's prior life is not simply cast aside but given back to one in a radically different form. It is, indeed, by means of such processes of transference that a world of difference between the two is established. Aside from the practices of others that Christians simply will not perform, the difference between Christian and non-Christian practices is not a matter of direct contrast by way of discrete particulars, say, by way of Christian affirmations or terms that are simply absent from non-Christian outlooks. Christians talk about the Trinity and about salvation in Christ, and non-Christians, let us say for purposes of argument, never even approximate talk like that. Direct contrasts like this would suggest that the difference between Christian and non-Christian is attributable to discrete material added onto all that Christians share with non-Christians. The claim of salvation in Christ would tend to become in that way nothing more than a discrete claim and not what makes all the difference for all that one thinks, does, and says as a Christian.[37]

Besides being impossibly difficult to implement, efforts to repudiate this fact of Christian parasitism are theologically problematic. For theological reasons, one should not try, for example, to purify Christian practices from outside influences out of fear of their possibly corrupting effects. One should not try, say, to keep the worldviews of the wider society at bay when explicating the distinctively Christian import of the biblical story. Such attempts run contrary to the idea that God's grace finds us where we are. As Karl Barth makes the point, if it was not only inevitable but thoroughly in keeping with the idea of God's free grace that the prodigal son arose just as he was, in poverty and rags, to return to his father, then influences from outside Christian social practices are not only unavoidable but theologically legitimate, too.[38]

Moreover, it is theologically problematic to try to evade the idea of an essential dependence on other ways of life by suggesting that such dependence does not go all the way down. Thus, in order to support the idea that Christianity remains in control of the borrowed material it uses, postliberals often seem inclined to give the strong impression that the aspect of Christianity ultimately responsible for keeping this use on a distinctively Christian track—for instance, the biblical story—is simply Christian and not similarly infiltrated by borrowed materials. Otherwise a regress ensues; if borrowed materials are to be made Christian by being subordinated to the Bible and the Bible is also made up of borrowed materials, what keeps it, and the assimilation of all else to the biblical world, on a Christian track? By exempting the Bible from the usual worry about borrowed materials, the postliberal account of the Christian use of borrowed materials suggests that some simply Christian code or story is being brought to bear against what is outside; highlighted thereby is the inadequacy of what is outside for Christian purposes, its need for revision. One could argue, however, that in the process some subset or aspect of Christian social practices is being privileged in a theologically suspect fashion. The only privilege Christian social practices have themselves is the privilege of humility; their own claim to fame is always the ironic one of knowing their own full humanity and therefore their distance from the purity of the Word they witness to. If it is to be in keeping with this sense of humility, the process of transforming borrowed material should be as much about self-criticism as it is about criticism of other ways of life; it should be a self-directed process of transformation in keeping with an awareness of its own need for criticism. That would be the case if, as we have suggested, Christian social practices are never themselves anything other than the transformation of what is outside; if, that is, Christian identity is established from the beginning through the use of borrowed materials.

One can still agree with postliberal theology that the identity of a Christian way of life is formed by a cultural boundary. This is not, however, the sharp boundary of independent cultural contents as postliberalism at its extreme imagines. The boundary is, instead, one of use that allows Christian identity to be essentially impure and mixed, the identity of a hybrid that always shares cultural forms with its wider host culture and other religions (notably Judaism).[39] In contrast, then, to even the more moderate postliberal position, Christianity is a hybrid formation through and through; nothing need be exempted out of fear that the distinctiveness of Christianity must otherwise be lost. Moreover—and most significantly—contrary to moderate postliberalism, the distinctiveness of a Christian way of life is not so much formed *by* the boundary as *at* it; Christian distinctiveness is something that emerges in the very cultural processes occurring at the boundary, processes that construct a distinctive identity for Christian social practices through the distinctive use of cultural materials shared with others.

This last point about the formation of Christian identity at the boundary also cuts against strands of modern theology opposed to postliberalism, for example, those that trace their lineage to Schleiermacher. As the more measured account of postliberalism does, Schleiermacher admits the first point, that the elements constituting a Christian way of life are found elsewhere. Schleiermacher, indeed, can also accept the second point: all the ways of relating to the world that make up a Christian way of living, he says, are to be found in every religion. The distinctiveness of Christian identity is nevertheless explained purely internally, by the centrality in Christianity of one such shared way of relating to the world for the organization of all the others. Without the need for attention to the manner in which those elements function in other religions, elements of Christian practice are shown to be distinctively Christian simply to the extent each of them can be tied up with that central point—as, say, one among many other efforts to express its importance for particular aspects of human life.[40] Despite Schleiermacher's use of a comparative method to pinpoint the place of Christianity within a whole religious field, Christian identity is therefore not actively defined in a back-and-forth of comparison and contrast with anything else; the distinctively Christian use of shared elements does not require direct reference to their different uses in other cultural contexts in order to be intelligible. The boundary between Christianity and other religions or ways of relating to the world is not filled up, so to speak, with active relations among them; it sits empty as they run independently along their nonconflictual parallel tracks. For Schleiermacher, the boundary between them does not emerge out of relations among them, relations in which the use of elements in one cultural field is twisted into some new one; the boundary functions instead to make clear the independent constitution of their respective identities, the autonomous self-determination of those identities, their relations of indifferent exteriority.

The fact that Christian identity is essentially relational means, as well, that both postliberal and correlationist theologians bring relations with the wider culture into the picture too late. Relations with the wider culture are not, as postliberals claim, an at best secondary or at worst purely optional matter of apologetics.[41] Nor are relations with the wider culture merely part of a subsequent task of application, in which one works out the implications

of an already-established Christian perspective by reenvisioning other worldviews in its terms. Unlike postliberals, correlationists make relations with the
wider culture part and parcel of the fundamental theological project; such
relations are necessary to determine the plausibility and intelligibility of the
Christian message. But they, too, fail to make them the crucial determinant
of Christian identity itself. As we mentioned before, for correlationists, relations with the wider culture are primarily necessary simply for the evaluation
of a distinctively Christian way of being in the world. In contrast to both
views, one does not first determine a distinctively Christian message or lens
for viewing the world and then bring it, subsequently, into relation with
other cultural practices for, say, apologetic purposes; those other cultural
practices are there from the beginning as the materials out of which the very
Christian message or lens is constructed. The boundary between Christian
and non-Christian practices is not crossed for the first time with arguments
to show whether, in light of wider cultural norms, what Christians believe
makes sense, seems plausible, or proves illuminating. The boundary has
already been crossed in and through the very processes by which Christians
come to believe anything at all.

A kind of apologetics or polemics with other cultures is internal, then, to
the very construction of Christian sense; this is a new point to add to the
account of basic theological operations offered in chapter 4. Theological
statements themselves amount to a transformative and reevaluative commentary on the wider culture insofar as they are double voiced: theological
statements mouth the claims of other cultures while giving them a new
spin.[42] At one end of the spectrum, the new twist might mean nothing
more than the identification of some aspect of the wider culture with the
truth of Christ; thus, the transcendence of nature which is part of a nineteenth-century ideal of progress might be identified with salvation. At the
other end, the twist might amount to something closer to a reversal; thus,
in the very odd use of an honor code ethics, humility rather than worldly
glory might be said to be cause for honor before God. The presumptions of
the wider culture are visible within or just beneath the surface of the theological statements that trope them, turning them to new uses. Those presumptions are the lure that draws adherents of another culture into the
processes of cultural transformation that produce Christian sense. Because
theological statements are not coming at the claims of that culture from
outside but surreptitiously insinuate themselves within them in this way,
persons inclined to make such claims are likely to follow along undefen-
sively the twists and turns that construct a new culture out of them. To
one's surprise one finds oneself in a new culture without having had any
conscious intention of leaving one's own.

Explicit apologetic or polemical arguments in theology often just take the moves of cultural transformation that are internal to the formation of theological claims and lay them out into discrete argumentative steps: the claims of the wider culture are the premises; the theological claims that embody Christian twists on those premises form the conclusions.[43] Such arguments do not really build on these premises of unbelief, but transform them in the course of the argument. Often, for example, the sense of the terms in the premises will be altered as the argument proceeds. Thus, in Thomas Aquinas's third way for proving the existence of God, a premise about the contingency of particular things in the universe—the optional character of particular beings in view of some worldly context—is used to argue for the contingency of the whole world, a new sense of contingency according to which there might not have been anything at all.[44] Or, sometimes the premises in their ordinary sense are radically revised by being given a surprising significance or a new set of truth conditions. Thus, in Blaise Pascal's *Pensées*, the tendency of humans to become bored and to seek ever-new diversions is given a radically new significance in the course of an argument purporting to show that it is best explained as a sign of the fall.[45] Thus, too, the commonsensical idea that people only receive what they are capable of receiving is radically revised by Barth when he argues that its truth in the case of the reception of grace only holds if God supplies us with new capacities. Because the meaning of premises is often altered in these ways in the course of the argument, theological arguments are often bad arguments if assessed in strictly logico-deductive terms; they do not strictly prove anything, but transpose the ground of argument as they proceed. A bad argument is in this case, however, a good rhetorical strategy. Theological arguments typically start where the audience is and through the manipulations of their use of those starting points, they work to seduce, captivate, or invert the position of the addressee.[46]

Again contrary to both postliberal and correlationist theology, one must say that, because it is always present from the start, Christian engagement with other ways of life rarely involves a face-off between distinct wholes. Christian social practices gradually come to be in such relational processes before there is anything to Christianity to set against some other way of life as a whole. A distinctively Christian way of life was not formed, for example, by any blanket judgment about Roman social practices; it arose in a step-by-step process of engagement with particulars. Transforming the use of shared items from a non-Christian to a Christian one is a piecemeal process, in short; the items of another culture are not taken up all at once but one by one or block by block. Indeed, if they are to be used differently, Christian practices cannot take up the elements of another way of life as

they form a whole; a different use of them requires a form of selective attention by which they are wrested out of their usual contexts in another way of
life. They must be disarticulated, so to speak, taken apart in order to be put
together in a new way, to form a new pool of associations or a new organization of elements with weightings different from what they had elsewhere.
Thus, Christian social practices construct a moral code in which many
pagan virtues are wrested from their usual philosophical context and set in
a religious one, in which they are weaned from their associations with vir-
tuoso achievement and made into an ideal to which all may aspire by God's
grace. Or—to take another example—humility is given a weight that is surprising in a Greco-Roman shame/honor code; and honor is linked, not
with praise by men, but with favor in God's sight.

Because this is a piecemeal rather than a blanket process of transformation, not every item of another culture need be troped in the same way. The
troping process, as we have already suggested, runs the gamut from simple
affirmation (usually on new grounds) to strict opposition (for instance,
"infant sacrifice is contrary to love of God and neighbor"), depending on the
cultural material at issue. Indeed, contrary to modern anthropological procedures, Western Christianity's historical relations with other cultures have
not always involved judgments typifying the practices of those cultures as
wholes; those cultures were not viewed as having a single uniform character
worthy, for example, of either simple condemnation or respect. Although
often all that seemed relevant about another way of life was that it was not
Christian—the basic categories to understand other cultures involved a simple distinction between Christian and heathen—the missionary impulse in
Christianity tended to work against a dichotomous typification, against a
"they are all one way and we are all another" mentality. There had to be
something about the society of others that suggested its openness to grace. It
could not be a single mass of complete depravity absent Christianity. Just as
the Western societies in which Christianity found its initial converts were a
mix of good and bad, so must non-Western ones be. Indeed, to prove the
missionary project to distant lands worthwhile, the character of these other
societies had to be shown to be as open to grace as any Western one. Such a
project required the discrimination of particulars—the search for signs or
movements toward grace, for indications of innocence, despite whatever else
about their way of life made evident their need for improvement by the missionaries' efforts. In this way, the history of Christian relations with other
cultures mirrors for very different—and not altogether laudable—reasons,
postmodern objections to the modern anthropological procedure of com-
paring cultures by summing up their respective characters as wholes, the
practice of viewing them as radically different cultural types.[47]

There are good theological reasons, moreover, for going along with this postmodern idea that cultures are distinguished not by any single sort of relation—say, one of uniform opposition—but by a variety of cross-cutting differences, by a series of different positionalities.[48] Cultures are different in certain respects and not in others. They are different in one way and then in another, depending on the particulars. They are differently situated with respect to one another depending on the aspects chosen for comparison. This suggests, contrary to the influential views of H. Richard Niebuhr, that in the Christian case relations with the wider culture are never simply ones of either accommodation, on the one hand, or opposition and radical critical revision, on the other, but always some mixture.[49] Putting it crudely, the Christian response to a modern Western culture's affirmation of women's rights does not have to be the same as its response to that same culture's practice of sending Jews to concentration camps. Nothing is decided by the simple fact that both practices have figured in the wider culture; everything depends on theological judgments concerning the particulars. Systematic refusals or attacks on other cultures simply as such both underestimate the standing of those cultures and overrate the standing of Christian ones in the light of God's grace. They also err in making God's ultimate victory over sin a matter simply of Christian enforcement. Making adjustment to or symbiosis with other cultures a matter of principle underestimates the depth of the problems to be found in every way of life and overestimates the ease with which they may be remedied by God's grace. The crucifixion suggests, to the contrary, that this is quite a messy, ugly process; it passes through suffering and death. An ad hoc use of various strategies like these, guided by the case-by-case judgment of particulars, makes better sense theologically. It shows a proper willingness to be guided by the Spirit of God, a Spirit that blows freely and not according to prior human presumption, not according to demands for some simple predictable consistency that human beings might take for granted.[50]

6

Commonalities in Christian Practice

Another strategy for accounting for Christian identity takes a more internal tack. There is something about Christian practices themselves, something internal to them, that makes them all of a piece, and therefore identifiably Christian rather than something else. Establishing the identity of Christian social practices means finding what they have in common, what it is about them that makes them all hang together and that brings about their agreement with one another. It involves identifying the coherence or continuity in their character as a way of life that unifies them.

We will criticize three versions of this strategy—the first identifying this agreement or continuity among Christian social practices with a shared understanding of common beliefs and values, the second with tradition, and the third with rules—before turning to what the postmodern modification of the idea of culture might suggest about possible continuity or agreement in style or patterns of use. As usual, throughout the course of the investigation my overall account of Christian identity will be developed gradually.

Before looking at particular versions, however, it is important to see that this strategy in general need not be an exclusive one; it is easily combined with a discussion of Christian identity as a matter of cultural boundaries. In that case, one assumes that what distinguishes Christian from non-Christian is also what makes all the things that Christians do identifiably Christian. The cultural materials that form a boundary with other ways of life are what Christian practices have in common, what makes them Christian rather than something else. Christian practices are unified, for example, by their common reference to cultural claims (say, "Jesus Christ is my Lord and Savior") that non-Christians reject.

I disputed in the last chapter the idea that the way boundaries are drawn always reflects matters of internal importance to Christian practice. Remember the "Christians eat beef" example. But so long as the boundaries have the kind of complex character we discussed, we can admit that this kind of correspondence between external and internal matters of identity frequently occurs. Thus "Jesus is Lord" is a very odd transposition of a claim like "Caesar is Lord" and is not fully intelligible apart from a comparative analysis of the two; in addition to marking a difference with a pagan way of life, it is of central importance to Christian practices themselves. We can even applaud the strategy at hand for avoiding, with this sort of reference to boundaries, the simply self-contained or internal analysis of Christian identity that we criticized in the last chapter.

The problem with this idea of a correspondence between outside and inside is what it often assumes about the unifying character of such claims for Christian practice. Christians may well agree in their use of a claim to symbolize opposition to the wider culture. That does not mean, however, that they agree about it among themselves. Indeed, just to the extent such a claim is a marker of Christian identity vis-à-vis other cultures, the more likely it is to be the focus for disagreement and diversity of opinion within Christian social practices themselves. Because it has this importance, it becomes the stakes in a struggle over competing visions of a Christian way of life.[1]

Such struggles of interpretation need not threaten the stability, the social cohesiveness, of a Christian way of life. Uniformity of belief in general is overrated as a requirement for social stability, according to postmodern understandings of culture.[2] Coordinated social activity need not mean that the parties involved share the same outlook on life; at most, it requires that the parties understand the different points of view from which they operate. Mutual understanding, without substantive agreement, is sufficient to produce a predictable sequence of actions and reactions toward an end that all parties desire though perhaps for quite different reasons. Cooperation may, moreover, hide forms of consent to the espoused values of a social practice that fall far short of enthusiastic commitment; many participants may simply be acquiescing, going along with the practice, because they have no realistic option of doing otherwise or because the costs of a refusal to go along outweigh any possible benefits.[3]

If Christianity is not the involuntary and radically pluralistic way of life just envisioned—contemporary Christians are generally not forced to be so by sanctions and therefore presumably genuinely share (in a sense yet to be specified) the same outlook on life—it is still the case that differences of interpretation need not threaten the stability of a Christian way of life. That is because Christians may yet come together over the form of things if not their substance. They may agree, for example, that Jesus saves or that ritual meals should be eaten in church, even if they do not agree about what those statements or those gestures mean. This is an agreement of a formal sort in that it is primarily agreement on the very statement or basic shape of action itself. They feel solidarity with one another in that each person knows that every other person will gladly affirm, for example, *that* Jesus saves. Such solidarity is achieved despite the fact that no two of them would develop the sense of such a statement in exactly the same way, and despite the fact that they may disagree about what such a statement implies, why they are warranted in making it, and about what it has to do with other aspects of Christian practice. Social solidarity can, moreover, be achieved on this basis without any bother about the extent or depth of such disagreements. The basis for solidarity is, then, a very weak, largely presumed and unexplicated agreement about the meaning of matters of common concern.

One can go further and say, not just that social solidarity could be achieved by Christians in that way, but that it has to be achieved in that way if Christianity is anything like the humanity-comprehensive society it hopes to be. Far from threatening the stability of a Christian way of life, the fact that Christians do not agree in their interpretation of matters of common concern is the very thing that enables social solidarity among them. Solidarity on the grounds of such a formal or weak consensus is a prerequisite for any way of life with the diverse membership of Christianity, a way of life that seeks to include all people everywhere and at all times, whatever their differences of race, sex, national origin, or outlook. Social solidarity in such cases can only be ensured through common concern for very vague, or one might say, very condensed, symbolic forms and acts.[4] Just to the extent they remain ambiguous, amenable to a variety of interpretations, are they able to unify a diverse membership, to coordinate their activities together in the relatively nonconflictual way necessary for a viable way of life. Thus, everyone can participate in an orderly fashion in the baptismal ritual of a church service without bothering about the fact that none of them has quite the same understanding of the whats and whys of the practice.[5]

When this diversity of interpretation comes to the surface—when, that is, the fact of this diversity becomes obvious to the parties concerned—it may, however, prompt potentially divisive conflict. And it does come to the surface quite commonly. Christians must specify what they mean by these forms of statement and behavior whenever critical assessments are made about them (for instance, "Is it really appropriate for Christians to talk about Jesus as their Lord?") or about their further practical implications. Does Christ's lordship, for example, suggest the approbation of human potentates, particularly those who purport to serve God's purposes on earth by, say, routing pagan religious practices? Deciding this question requires the explicit elaboration of the meaning of Christ's lordship and what it has to do with the wielding of this-worldly power or with the success of religious programs. Answering the latter question may mean discussing what Christ's victory over death implies about his own failure to convince others of his mission during his lifetime, and so on.

Differences of interpretation on such matters are worrisome; they have to be taken with utmost seriousness because so much is riding on them. Certainly a great deal is riding on them practically: whether, for example, Christ's lordship brings Christians into association with the powerful or with the powerless makes a potentially huge difference in human terms. But such differences of interpretation are also worrisome and matters for serious concern at an even more basic level in that what is at issue is the very meaning of Christian discipleship.[6] At issue is the very question of what it means to be a Christian: What is one to believe and how is one to live in light of one's Christian commitments? In question is the proper way of being true to God, the proper expression of faithfulness, the meaning of genuine purity of heart. Because so much of both religious and practical importance is riding on the outcomes of interpretation, disagreements tend to become divisive, a threat to the unity or cohesiveness of a Christian way of life.

To put the point even more strongly, as Schleiermacher would, Christianity is polemical within its own borders because Christianity is characterized by an unsatisfied longing to bring the whole of life under a religious viewpoint and to do so ever more completely, ever more purely, at every point. Differences of opinion about how this is to be done are always a source of internal contention or potential strife, even schism, among would-be saints who wish their existence to show forth the fact that they live, move, and have their being in God.[7]

One possible response to such a threat of divisiveness—a very common response in the history of Christianity—is to try to prevent disagreement and enforce a uniformity of conception by setting up a hierarchy of interpretive experts and consolidating their power to transmit a preferred sense. Without going into the complex question of the moral and religious reasons for and against such an attempt, postmodern theories of culture suggest—and history confirms—the futility of the effort. For one, the recipients of the message are never as passive as the project requires if it is to be a success. Another way of avoiding divisiveness—one proposed most commonly in the early church—does not, however, involve such an attempt to discourage diversity of interpretation. Instead, it seeks to avoid divisiveness by encouraging Christian social practices to become *a genuine community of argument*, one marked by mutual hearing and criticism among those who disagree, by a common commitment to mutual correction and uplift, in keeping with the shared hope of good discipleship, proper faithfulness, and purity of witness. This is the sort of unity of mutual admonition and concern that one finds in the letters of Paul.[8] It is something like what Augustine talked about as the new Christian virtue of sociability: a solidarity of love and common hope, which eschews compulsion by allowing all decision to be free, a community ruled by humility and not by way of the advantage of superior power.[9]

Shared Conceptions vs. Shared Concerns

Returning to the question of Christian identity with what we have just said in mind, we can conclude that Christian identity does not mean in any strong sense that all Christians share a common set of beliefs and values. Contrary to the famous opinion of Vincent of Lerins, all Christians have not everywhere and at all times believed the same things. This opinion is certainly empirically untrue if it means that all the claims to which one's Christian allegiances commit one are shared by all other Christians, in all times and places. But it is even untrue for the case of some purported crucial subset—some core deposit or fundamental articles of the faith—if it implies shared conceptions of any depth. Christians can indeed be identified by their tendency to make such affirmations (for instance, God is the maker of heaven and earth), to espouse certain values (for instance, love for God and neighbor), to act along certain ritualized lines in the course of their worship, to feel certain things (for instance, gratitude for God's free grace), but that they all mean the same things by any of it is not the crucial determinant of Christian identity. Again, Christian identity, at this most basic level at least, is more a matter of form than of substance. The understandings of such matters among the variety of Christians past and present may overlap at some very general, vague, and largely unspecified level. Agreement on the central significance of such matters for their lives is in effect what that agreement on meaning amounts to. But because they would not agree on the implications, warrants, or proper elaborations of any of it, one can say Christians are primarily identified by their concern for the bare basic forms of such statements or ritual actions. Christians are identified by the importance they give to distinctive slogans or formulae (like the ones found in liturgical use and often summarized in early doctrinal statements), by the prominence in their way of life of certain patterns of speech or ritualized actions (say, the motif of dying and rising; baptismal and communion rituals), by their penchant for an unusual vocabulary (for instance, Jesus as "the Christ"). They gain their identity in virtue of the way their lives revolve around such things, in virtue of the central significance of these things for determining the course of their lives. Only Christians have this much riding on whether, for example, Jesus is the Son of God, and if he is, on what that might possibly mean.

Because of their importance for Christian life, these materials call each Christian to develop their sense in the effort to determine more specifically the character of Christian identity; particular decisions about what it is that Christians properly do and say are arrived at by way of their elaboration. These are the materials, in other words, with which Christians construct a more nuanced and full sense of what it means to live a Christian life. How these materials are interpreted and organized is crucial to determining what a Christian way of life involves in any more concrete sense.

But it is not the sharing of a particular account of their interpretation or organization that makes one a Christian. After all, Christians, as we have seen, do not commonly agree on that. What makes for Christian identity is the fact that such *investigation* is viewed as crucial, not *agreement* on its outcomes.

Understood as a marker of practices that are social, a marker of a whole way of life with others, this view of Christian identity suggests social practices are identifiably Christian when they form a community among persons who share this same concern. Christian practices are ones in which people participate together in an argument over how to elaborate the claims, feelings, and forms of action around which Christian life revolves.

As we saw in chapter 4, this need not be a highly intellectualist project. It is an argument woven as a matter of course into the simple effort to live one's life in a Christian way; it is an argument that is engaged throughout the whole of Christian social practices, not just in some specialized intellectual sphere. As the argument proceeds, as, that is, varying conclusions are reached and come into conflict, so do the social practices of Christians alter or grow, run together or apart.

In order for such a common project of argument to be viable despite substantive disagreements among its participants, something like the community of solidarity and hope I mentioned before may be required. United in the expectation that a purer witness and discipleship will come of such efforts to work through their disagreements, participants must show a willingness to listen to and be corrected if necessary by all others similarly concerned about the true nature of Christian discipleship. Others are worth listening to—-if not ultimately worth agreeing with—to the extent they have made the effort sincerely; their failings as people cannot preclude the possibility of the success of their efforts by God's grace.[10] Recognizing, however, the disruptive potential of sin and the need therefore to avoid placing judgments so formed in listening to others on the same footing as the Word of God, participants must remain committed to an open debate in which their own judgments are submitted, in turn, to the judgment of others.[11] Sins that would disrupt the community of argument—say, efforts to undermine the full participation of others by imposing one's own views coercively or by using a power advantage to dispel criticism—are countered by a structure of argument in which no one's opinion is exempted from the possibility of salutary admonition and rebuke by one's fellows. Only on conditions like these would there seem to be a point to continued participation in a way of life that amounts to an extended argument with people with whom one does not agree. The Christian identity of social practices may involve additionally, then, a community of argument with a specific shape—one in which participants have the courage of their convictions to dispute the corruptive effects of sin, yet show an openness to being corrected by others in recognition of their own fallibility and possible corruption, brought together in a common project whose realization, they all know, is ever beyond any simple identification with what any of them has achieved.

Besides following postmodern suspicions about shared meanings, this account of Christian identity with reference to matters of form rather than substance can claim good theological grounds. Christian identity in such a case does not revolve around commitment to particular conceptions but suggests allegiance to the object or subject matter of the claims or forms of action at issue. Making those claims or forms of action themselves the center of one's life apart from any particular specification of their meaning can be interpreted theologically as an effort, in short, to make God, rather than some human account of God, the center of one's life. Doing otherwise, making Christian identity a matter of allegiance to certain meanings, threatens to put human ideas about God in the place that only God should fill in Christian life. Most Christian theologians would aver that the two are never conflatable. Replacing the divine with the human or confusing the human with the divine threatens, therefore, to make a Christian way of life an idol. Even in Christ, the human never approximates the divine but remains distinct and unmixed, no third thing approaching the divine by way of the alteration of its own properties. The Word can be identified with a particular human being, Jesus Christ. But his Christian disciples ever follow after him at a distance. And the Incarnate Word is only at best indirectly identifiable with even those human words of the Bible that Christians believe effectively witness to him.

One might suspect, however, that such a threat of idolatry could return with reference to the forms around which Christian life revolves. Are not the forms even without the substance a possible focus for idolatry? Against this objection, one can respond that the argument that revolves around these forms can turn back against them. Getting straight on them is crucial for understanding the meaning of a Christian way of life, but in the process they may be substantially undercut or their form profoundly altered. Christians may be Christians, for example, because so much rides for them on the claim that Jesus is God; that does not mean, however, that some Christians might not decide in the process that the central and overriding significance that Jesus continues to have for human life would be less misleadingly expressed some other way. In short, while they set the terms for argument, the forms themselves are not immune from questioning as the argument proceeds.

Indeed, forms tend to be revised across the board in the course of arguments over what they mean. Thus, the communal meals and baptism rituals around which Christian worship revolves tend to take different forms depending on the interpretations made of them—baptism, for example, sometimes involving children, at other times adults; eucharistic celebrations sometimes stressing the words of institution, at other times not. If Christian identity has to do with a commitment to the importance of certain forms of statement and action, those forms are not necessarily very highly defined; the specific shapes they take vary within certain very general, and often largely inexplicit, parameters.

Nothing much hinges, moreover, on exactly how far the forms at issue extend; nothing much rides on any precise delimitation of the set they comprise. Many of the forms have something to do with Jesus or, if not with Jesus himself, then at least with Jesus' concerns—God's relations with us, the nature of the kingdom—or with the difference Jesus made in human life. That is to be expected given the fact that the distinctiveness of Christian social practices emerged with him and the social practices his actions (and passions) inaugurated. Lots of the forms are codified, too, in written form—in the Bible, in creedal statements, or denominational confessions. These forms—ones that concern Jesus, ones that are codified—need not be exhaustive, however. Almost any element of Christian practice has the capacity to become such a focus of concern; indeed, every part of it has some claim to such a position—as a place, to use specifically theological language, where God's Word or directing Spirit may be heard or felt.

This difference between the object of concern and the Christian conception of it—the fact that on theological grounds they can never be identified—helps to support the point of ongoing argument with those with whom one disagrees. Because one's own point of view is inevitably inadequate, it makes sense to keep in touch with those who have formed other conclusions; one might conceivably be corrected by them. One is concerned, as all other participants in the argument are, primarily with conformity to the object, a concern that outweighs any commitment to the adequacy of the opinions one holds about that object prior to the debate. If those opinions are shown up in the course of argument, so much the better so long as the humbling of one's conception is in the interest of greater purity of witness. The purpose of engaging in argument with others cannot be, then, to bring about conformity with the account of the object one brings to the debate, as if that account were definitive. Consequently, the continued opposition of others to that account is no reason to refuse engagement in the common project.[12]

Tradition

Particularly when it becomes clear that Christians have not always and everywhere believed and valued the same things, theologians often try to talk about Christian identity in terms of tradition. Indeed, for us, too, discussing Christian identity in those terms may be important given what we have just said about the changing shapes of even the forms of statement and action that are the stakes of Christian argument. Talking of tradition enables theologians to show how the many differences in the performance of Christian discipleship can nevertheless be considered one, and to specify the conditions under which some of these differences break that unity. To the extent they are part of the same tradition, Christian social practices remain in agreement despite their diversity. Although not all purportedly Christian social practices do, those that share a tradition may differ among themselves without their Christian identity being jeopardized thereby.

Christianity itself may be called a tradition in the sense that it amounts to a whole ongoing way of life. But in that case, talk of tradition is just a way of formulating the questions about Christian identity we are asking in this chapter and is not a way of answering them. If Christianity is a religious tradition, one is still left with questions about how its identity is established, questions that are often answered, indeed, in terms of the strategies we have already looked at and criticized—strategies that appeal to distinct social groups, impermeable cultural boundaries, or shared beliefs and values as markers of a tradition's identity. The idea of Christianity as a tradition is thoroughly suffused in this way by modern anthropological understandings of culture.

When, however, talk of tradition is an answer to questions of Christian identity—the kind of talk about tradition with which we are concerned here—one is suggesting that Christian identity is sustained across differences of time and place if Christian cultural materials retain their identity when transmitted from one time and place to another and/or if the processes that transmit them do. Tradition refers here both to what is transmitted—the cultural materials—and to the processes by which they are transmitted. One or the other has to remain in some significant sense the same despite all the changes due to lapses of time or transpositions in space, if the social practices that share those materials or that participate in those processes are to retain their identity.[13]

At one end of the spectrum of possible requirements, what is transmitted (tradition in the sense of a store or deposit of treasured materials) has to recur at every time and place. Trading on the idea of the durability of natural objects, tradition amounts to a substance-like stuff that naturally persists across time and displacements of space. While clearly aware of the problems that historical and situational differences throw into the mix, this idea of a self-identical tradition simply collapses into the view that Christians have always and everywhere believed and valued the same things. At most, differences of time and place add situation-specific forms of expression to the recurring substance of such cultural materials. Different words are used to communicate the same ideas to new audiences.[14] Whatever the time or place, the same beliefs and practices therefore form a red thread to be found in all ways of living that are genuinely Christian.[15] Like the view we looked at earlier, this one loses plausibility when historical investigation shows how difficult it is to exempt any Christian belief or practice from substantial change across differences of time and place.

Another way of formulating the requirements of a self-same tradition again looks for identity in what is transmitted but allows for change in it over the course of its transmission. The materials of tradition are ones that can change while remaining the same. Greater attention is given here to the process of transmission, but it is a process in which, it is hoped, an identity of content or substance in what is transmitted is retained. Thus, the process of transmission can be talked about as one of logical explication.[16] The materials of one time and place are different from those at some other time and place but the difference amounts only to making explicit what was implicit before. Or the process of transmission is talked about as an organic one.[17] Later growth is quite different from the original seed or germ, but those later developments are somehow present in a nascent form earlier: they are simply unfolded or unrolled over time with the emergence of supportive environments.

If what comes later is genuinely new, the image here is one of gradual, incremental change. Change is never rapid or extreme in a way that would jeopardize the identity of the material being transmitted. What Christians do, believe, or value at one time and place may be quite different from what they do, believe, or value at some other time and place, but in between there are always the gradual steps of a continuous process of transmission by which the one has turned into the other. Thus, what a body of beliefs implies may not have been, even implicitly, believed prior to its derivation; continuity between the two is nevertheless assured because those implications are drawn out of that body of beliefs in a step-by-step process that builds on itself. Or, the seed may be nothing like the grown plant, but the identity of the two is guaranteed by the gradual process of growth that spans them.

Historical inquiry again enters the picture, however, to disconfirm both the idea that the later is already present in the earlier and the idea that the history of transmission of Christian materials is one of neatly ordered cumulative change by increments. Requirements for the identity of tradition therefore shift away from a concern to show continuity among the diverse outcomes of transmission and look instead to continuity in the process of transmission itself. When Christian materials are transmitted across differences of time and place, the practices that result may have no obvious continuities with one another; there may be no obvious way of arranging them in a neatly ordered incremental sequence according to their contents. Those different results may nevertheless be considered part of the same tradition in that the process of transmission remains in some sense the same.

Thus, one could say that, despite the difference in results, the same cultural materials—the Bible, the Christian idea, the living impression of Jesus—are being applied and appropriated in each case so as to meet the demands of a changing context. Rather than being internal developments of the material being handed down, here diverse results of transmission depend on the changing contexts of the material's appropriation. Diversity of outcomes is the product of outside influences of a cultural or historical sort—though not exclusively so if the process of transmission is to retain its identity across such differences of context. The material transmitted has its own internal richness making it suitable for and applicable to all these varying contexts. The material gives itself to be understood differently in a way that is appropriate for a particular time and place. It need not itself change; it can remain itself while being viewed from multiple perspectives, while addressing new questions or satisfying new needs from its bountiful resources.

This process of transmission, understood as one of situation-appropriate application and interpretation, is the same in that it is ever renewed in the same form. The results may be different but the same Bible, say, is always speaking in the way that is appropriate for a particular time and place. The process of transmission is the same, even if episodic, in virtue of this Christian material's capacity to speak directly to every time and place in a context-sensitive fashion. One can find a view like this in Ernst Troeltsch's work.[18]

Along the same lines, one can claim that different results are part of the same process of transmission because Christian materials are never applied independently of what has been made of them earlier or elsewhere. The process of appropriating Christian materials differently, depending on the context, is continuous in that one is always already influenced by that material's prior effects in history, by the interpretations and appropriations of that material in the circumstances preceding one's own. All the results are therefore incorporated within the same overarching history of the same traditional material's effects. This is the view of tradition that one finds in the work of theologians influenced by the philosopher Hans-Georg Gadamer.[19]

These last two views of the identity of tradition—the episodic and Gadamerian accounts of tradition as transmission—have almost the status of common sense in contemporary theology. Postmodern cultural theory would lodge much the same criticisms against them, however, as it would against the others. It uncovers certain problematic assumptions underlying them all.[20]

First, contrary to the postmodern idea that cultural continuity is always only the temporary outcome of historical struggle (see chapter 3), all these accounts of tradition make continuity in either traditional materials or the process of transmission a presumption by isolating something from the vicissitudes of history to guarantee it. Thus, the continuity of tradition is guaranteed by a timeless deposit or treasury of true propositions, constituting the Christian culture of every age. Or, in a Gadamerian notion of tradition, classic texts or artworks are the paradigm explaining the universal appeal of the traditional materials whose history of effects is overarching and inescapable. The importance of those materials for every time and place need not await the demonstration of history and is not apparently subject to historical disconfirmation. At the root of both understandings of the materials of tradition is the very thing that postmodern theorists of culture try to purge from their own account: a "high culture" view of culture, that is, culture in the form of artifactual productions (ideas, texts, works of art) with a timeless universality.

The notions of tradition we have looked at also take continuity in the process of transmission for granted in an ahistorical fashion. Thus, when organic life is the model for understanding tradition, no amount of diversity in what Christians say and do need dislodge the presumption of their agreement so long as they all seem members of an historically continuous, self-generating sequence of events; historical evidence of conflict and contradiction can always be undercut by the claim of their containment within a higher-order process that remains continuous. Similarly, in Gadamer's case, the fact that one never escapes the influence of the past is used to undermine the seriousness of historical evidence suggesting ruptures and discontinuities in the processes that transmit it; the inevitability of historical influence prevents such evidence from fundamentally disrupting metaphors of continuity in Gadamer's account of interpretive processes over time. Gadamer illicitly slides from the claim that one is never outside tradition, outside the overarching history of traditional materials' effects, to a substantive description of the processes of transmission involved. The former claim—that one is never free from the influence of materials transmitted down or over to one from before and elsewhere—is only plausible when "influence" is understood in the widest and most formal sense, that is, when almost anything counts as "influence," including the fiercest rejection of or indifference to the materials at issue. What that claim must include in order to be plausible Gadamer then tends to exclude from his characterization of the processes of transmission. In a stunningly fallacious inference, Gadamer presumes from the fact that we are never outside tradition that the processes of transmission exclude significant ruptures—say, effective attacks on the universal validity of the materials transmitted—and do not proceed by way of exclusion, domination, and omission.[21]

In short, what a postmodern understanding of culture thinks human beings have to struggle to produce in the messy course of history—cultural continuities—these notions of tradition view as a naturally preexisting reality. According to them, if cultural continuity exists, it exists as an already established fact of the matter in virtue of ahistorical guarantees. Someone who wants to know whether there is any such thing, or what is included in it, has the job of simply uncovering or deciphering such continuity by identifying its signs. If these signs of membership in an identical tradition—signs such as similarity in claims, preservation of shape, or answering the changing needs of the times—are difficult to discern or ambiguous, that need not derail the claim of cultural continuity among the social practices at issue. These signs are only evidence of a reality assured on independent grounds—in virtue of the physical durability of a treasury of traditional materials, the organic life of tradition, its indefatigable spirit or vital force, or the inescapability of its effective history. But from a postmodern point of view, this is all backwards. What these notions of tradition think of as signs manifesting a prior fact of cultural continuity the postmodern interpreter views as contestable proposals for how to arrange the diversity of Christian practices in a continuous fashion. Rather than being indications of a cultural continuity that already exists, they define or construct whatever continuity there is. They are the only things that justify a claim of continuity and therefore difficulties in their verification are always serious challenges that must be met if claims for identity of tradition are to be sustained.

The second problematic assumption underlying all these accounts of tradition is the idea that the various results of transmission maintain their identity by approximating what is transmitted. This presumption is obvious when tradition is understood on the model of a treasury or deposit, on the model of an organism, or a deductive system. What is transmitted can be altered—but not too much all at once if the identity of the tradition is to be safeguarded. What is transmitted may change radically as it is passed down or over to others, but at each step of the process the alteration cannot be much: what comes next must always be quite a bit like its immediate predecessor in the series. The same is true in a more subtle fashion, however, of the Gadamerian and episodic accounts of tradition as a self-identical process. What is transmitted—say, the internally rich depths of a classic text or the Christian idea—already contains the various results of transmission in the sense that those who interpret or apply it anew are merely following this material's own directives or dictates for changing circumstances. What is to come is marked out in advance, everything to come has its place preassigned to it, so to speak, by the already constituted whole of the material to be transmitted. Thus, the Christian idea already incorporates all the sides of itself that will eventually come into view from the new perspectives of different times and places.[22] Or, the rich depths of a classic text's contents are already laid out in a way that enables them to be drawn upon differently as the need arises. When a tradition maintains its identity, the results of transmission line up with or match in these ways the materials transmitted.

The problem with these ideas of identity as approximation is the presumption that the traditional materials approximated are merely found, discovered, or received, and not constructed in a significant sense. Postmodern cultural theory makes the important claim that traditions are invented, meaning by that not merely that traditional materials are often new rather than old and borrowed rather than indigenous, but that they are always products of human decision in a significant sense.[23] The materials that are passed down and over to one time and place from some other time and place are always more numerous than those labeled "tradition." "Tradition" is always a selection from the wide array of materials that could be so designated in virtue of their transmission from before and elsewhere. And even more generally, tradition is always a matter of human attribution; nothing about the materials themselves requires that designation. Even ongoing customary forms of action and belief do not constitute a tradition until they are marked as such and thereby assigned a normative status.

In contrast to this view of traditions as invented, the idea that identity of tradition is sustained by means of approximation trades heavily on a picture of traditional materials as natural objects. Human judgment only seems to enter the picture subsequently, after these traditional materials are already up and running, putting in their own call to human beings to attend to them; human judgment enters late, in the effort to conform to their dictates in changing circumstances. Traditional materials are pictured here as already naturally unified physical wholes, bodies in space. This is obvious when the models for tradition are physical ones—a treasury, an organism. But it is also the case when traditional materials are viewed as ideas or impressions: they are analogous to bodily substances that can be walked around or viewed from different angles. Even in the episodic and Gadamerian accounts of tradition, the materials of tradition seem already laid out in space; they form a depth or expanse of materials to be drawn upon differently. The episodic and Gadamerian accounts of tradition seem to trade, too, on the assumption that what is transmitted has the given unity and wholeness of a natural object. If the material transmitted does not have its own unity, its own arrangements of parts to form a given whole, the identity of tradition is jeopardized. If the unity and wholeness of the original material transmitted are up for grabs themselves in the processes of transmission, one would be hard pressed to say that the markedly different results are really guided to any substantial extent by the same materials.

According to a postmodern account of tradition, to the contrary, there is nothing to approximate before the exercise of human judgment. Which materials are designated "tradition" is a matter for human judgment, a judgment hinging on a contestable claim for their centrality or importance to Christian life. In order to sustain the identity of this tradition across differences of time and place, the interpreter is not called so much to approximate the already given shape of those materials as to organize them in a way that makes clear what else might have a place within them. The materials of tradition have to be first lined up by the interpreter, put in an order, before the appropriate next step can become clear. Thus, whether a contested practice—say, women's ordination—sustains or breaks the identity of the Christian tradition depends on how the materials of tradition are arranged. If, say, the Bible constitutes that material, then everything depends on how, for example, the interpreter connects references to male discipleship in the New Testament with stories about Jesus' violations of social convention.

The third problematic feature that underlies the notions of tradition we have been addressing has to do with the way the results of transmission are taken out of competition with one another by their alignment with different times and places. The different results of transmission are neatly lined up with differences of time and place and are thereby insulated from significant challenge by one another. Because each is characteristic of a different time and place, the rightful inclusion of all these different results in the self-same tradition can be simply assumed: the rightful claim of each one does not need to be proved against the apparent counterclaims of others. Thus, according to an episodic or Gadamerian account of tradition, Jesus may be viewed as a model citizen in one time and place, and a rabble-rouser in some other. So long as one can argue that in both cases the material of tradition has given itself to be interpreted and applied in a way appropriate to the context, the apparent contradiction in results need not be addressed. The history of transmitted material's appearances in this way breaks down into discrete moments to be assessed on their own terms. Requirements for the identity of tradition become purely situation-specific: if justice has somehow been done to both the materials to be passed down and to the circumstances, that is all that matters.

From a postmodern viewpoint, the problem here is the same one afflicting modern anthropological understandings of culture: the idea of a one-to-one correspondence between cultural outlook and circumstance. Like the modern notion of culture, all these accounts of tradition hide the fact of cultural conflict in one and the same historical circumstance. Contrary to what these accounts of tradition assume, when transmitted materials meet a historical context, no one interpretation naturally results from their confluence. Instead, an argument usually breaks out over their interpretation. The historical circumstance itself is not sufficient to establish the propriety of a particular interpretion. Instead, an argument has to be made for one interpretation or application or another—in postmodern jargon, transmitted materials have to be actively articulated to a situation. And as a matter of historical record, there are always various and conflicting arguments, even in a single situation, about how this is to be done. This is so because the history of interpretation, like the history of culture generally, is, as we have said, a history of struggle. Processes of interpretation are always filtered through political conflict in the sense that disagreements over how life is to be lived are being fought there.[24]

There are theological reasons to support all these criticisms of tradition as an answer to questions of Christian identity. First, for theological reasons one should not presume, as most of these views of tradition do, a continuity among the contents of Christian practices over time and space, or, where this sort of continuity seems to be missing, some higher order or deeper level of continuity in the processes of history that span them—as the episodic and Gadamerian understandings of tradition as process of transmission do. What holds all these different practices together as a unity is nothing internal to the practices themselves; the center that holds them all together should remain, as Barth says, empty.[25] What God wants of us is not some part or aspect of Christian social practices themselves; it is not anything that those Christian practices contain or encompass of themselves in a way that might be passed down to others in history. God does not direct the efforts of Christian discipleship in different times and places through some feature of Christian practice that itself controls the movements of Christian history. God's own control of Christian history is not identifiable with some historical aspect of what Christians say and do that is nevertheless exempt from history's vicissitudes. Were any of this to be the case, something about Christian history itself would replace God's own directives to human beings; something human would be illegitimately elevated to the status of God and take God's place as the focus for human obedience. The freedom of God to work in new ways would be thereby inhibited by the illegitimate authority lodged there.

What holds all these different Christian practices together is, instead, their common reference to the God to whom they all hope effectively to witness. They are unified by the effort Christians make to proclaim and be the disciples of God's Word—a unity of task and not necessarily of accomplishment. Although the God Christians hope to obey is one and the same, the results of this common effort are not one in any obvious way, because of the fallibility and sin of these human efforts at discipleship and because of the freedom of God to ask the unexpected of people in new times and places. God is one and God's intentions for us are marked by consistency and faithfulness, but such unity, consistency, and faithfulness are much odder than anything captured by claims for continuity among Christian practices in virtue of shared traditional materials or claims for continuity in the processes that transmit them. Even should the human response to God be properly obedient, this God is one who works by the reversal of human expectations—a God who in Jesus dies rather than triumphs, and then, equally unexpectedly, is risen from the dead—a God who, without being untrue to covenant partnership with Israel, brings Gentiles into the people of God without requiring their observance of Jewish law. There is consistency here—the consistency of a God of free grace—but it is a consistency that, because it could not have been predicted in advance, appears to be such only in retrospect. Ever beyond the control of human expectation, it is a consistency, moreover, that cannot rule out rather outrageous novelty to come, novelty that breaks previous human assumptions about the way it all hangs together. This is not the consistency demonstrated by a continous, unruptured effective history. Nor is it the consistency displayed by a diversity of practices that contain in themselves some vantage point, some specifiable historical principle according to which they can all be surveyed and confidently arrayed in neatly ordered sequences. The latter sort of consistency, in particular, the consistency of a systematically organized whole, hems in God's freedom by restricting the course of what God could conceivably ask of us in future, in some new time and place. One cannot, in that way, master God's free grace by standing outside Christian history and summing it up as some whole; one cannot know in that way in advance what is to come. Instead, one stands at a particular place in the ongoing course of that history and, looking back and across to what others have understood by Christian discipleship, one forms judgments about the consistency of it all so far, to use in assessing the appropriate shape of Christian discipleship now. One knows all the while that these judgments might properly be altered as the history of God's free grace moves through new times and places; one is therefore justified, at most, in believing these judgments are good as they stand for the particular time and place in which they are made.[26]

The theological problems with understanding the identity of tradition as a matter of approximation follow easily from what has just been said. Since God's direction of Christian practices is not a part or aspect of those practices themselves, obeying God is not simply a matter of approximating what Christian have said and done before or elsewhere, a matter of approximating the materials of a Christian tradition, the practices passed over or down from others. That, too, would restrict the free exercise of God's grace; obedience to God would be short-circuited by obedience to something human. Christians must not be bound by what their compatriots have said and done if they are to be free to obey a free God.

This does not mean, however, that one's judgments about appropriate Christian discipleship can be made in isolation from what Christians have done and said before and elsewhere. Here, too, the accounts of tradition we have been looking at are subject to theological critique. If fallibility and sin do not rule out discipleship in one's own case, one cannot presume they rule it out elsewhere. One therefore owes others who have made the attempt of discipleship before and elsewhere a respectful hearing. Although one may ultimately judge that their failures require correction, they have— in virtue of God's free grace, a grace that human sin cannot finally obstruct—a claim to be heard in the course of one's own efforts to establish the meaning of Christian discipleship. One's own judgments then make a similar claim on others; they are submitted, in the same way, for the consideration and judgment of others who are also concerned to establish the meaning of Christian discipleship.

Apparent conflict in the results of these various and ongoing efforts at discipleship is a serious matter that must always be addressed by particular arguments, ones that try actually to show, say, underlying agreement, or nonconflictual complementary of claims in virtue of different circumstances, or some party's error in judgment. Continuity, despite the apparent conflict, cannot be assured in virtue of features that each effort of discipleship may display when considered in isolation from others. Continuity is not assured, for example, by saying that in each case this was, according to their best lights, what the Bible or the living impression of Christ had to say to them in the circumstances in which they heard it. A situation-specific claim like that does not give one sufficient reason to overlook what others have said about Christian discipleship when assessing the propriety of one's own judgment.

One listens to others who have made the effort of Christian discipleship with the expectation, then, that the Word of God is appropriately witnessed to there. One is listening, however, for that to which they witness; one hopes to be obedient to the God one hears there and not so much to the shape their response took. One is obligated to listen to the efforts of others but only insofar as they are witnesses to, simple signs of, what they are not; consequently, the authority of these signs or witnesses does not extend, in any strong sense, to their own substance. One only comes to know the character of one's own discipleship by listening to them, but one is not made thereby their disciple, the disciple of their texts, their words, their deeds. One remains the disciple of God, and not the disciple of God's witnesses. In short, then, no isolation from the judgments of others, but no demand to approximate them either.[27]

Rules

Another way of discussing what unifies diverse Christian practices makes reference to rules; this way of answering questions of Christian identity is the hallmark of contemporary postliberal theology. Christians may say and do different things, but these practices nevertheless agree in that they are all following the same rules for the formation of Christian statements and actions. Christian practices differ because the material governed by these rules varies from situation to situation; the rules, however, remain the same. Thus, one such rule for the formation of discourse might be "whatever is said of the first Person of the Trinity must also be said of the second Person, except that the first is not the second." The results of employing such a rule will obviously differ, perhaps drastically, with the content of "whatever is said." The resulting statements may, indeed, conflict with one another and have no obvious continuities of meaning; their Christian identity is nevertheless assured in virtue of the abiding rules that direct their formation.

From the perspective of both postmodern cultural theory and theology, the problem with this account of Christian identity is much like the last one. Such a strategy for assuring Christian identity is only plausible if the rules can be insulated from the vicissitudes of history. Historical change must be affecting everything but the rules themselves. Such a disjunction between historically changing materials and abiding rules makes little sense if, as postliberals affirm, the rules are the production of historical agents. Rules, according to them, simply follow the historical judgments of Christians in varying times and places about proper Christian practice; they do not have any ahistorical, independent life, but merely encapsulate the principles according to which such judgments are made. The impression of their independence comes from the tendency of postliberals to fetishize them once they have been so established by Christian practice. In the effort to support the claim of a stable Christian identity, postliberals appear to be lifting the rules out of the ongoing historical processes that formed them, as if, once produced, they could not be altered by the same processes in the future.[28]

Other problems are specific to the appeal to rules. A postmodern reading of the favorite philosopher of postliberals, Ludwig Wittgenstein, deflates the postliberal account of Christian identity in terms of rules.[29] On that postmodern reading, Wittgenstein provides no obvious support for the postliberal claim that use of the same rules is the linchpin of Christian identity since one point of Wittgenstein's philosophy was just to problematize what it means to follow a rule. Thus, Wittgenstein maintains there is no way to single out the rule that is being followed by observing purported instances of its application. Even in the apparently least problematic case of rule following—a mathematical one—the numbers in the sequence 2, 4, 6, 8 . . . might be following a variety of different rules—say, add 2 indefinitely, or until you reach 1000 and then add 4, and so on. One cannot conclude, then, that all parties who agree, say, on the propriety of 8 in the sequence are following the same rule. Whether a new number follows the same rule as the preceding ones is, moreover, impossible to determine from the preceding numbers themselves; everything depends on how you frame the rule and the preceding numbers are not sufficient to establish that.

To avoid this problem, one might claim that the rules are formulated in themselves somewhere, that one therefore is not stuck trying to generalize them from their instances of application. Doctrines—say, the early ecumenical creeds—are purportedly formulations of such rules, though in the misleading form of first-order statements. That is, they are like mathematical formulas with the variables (the xs and ys) already filled in; rather than $x + 2 = y$, one finds $2 + 2 = 4$.

One problem with this suggestion is that these doctrines do not seem to function as rules in the way postliberals would like. While the early creeds do seem to rule out effectively the Christian propriety of certain proposals, they do not seem sufficient to establish positively what it is that Christians should say given a particular input and situation. This is very obvious at the time of their formulation; disagreements about the propriety of various Christian statements about Jesus were, arguably, worse after their formulation than before. Rather than having the clear definition of rules, these doctrines attempted to resolve disagreements through the use of rather vague and ambiguous expressions (for instance, *homoousion*) into which a variety of parties could read their own positions. These ambiguities then set the stage for further controversy—say, between Cyrilian and Antiochene factions after the Council of Chalcedon, the very factions united in their acceptance of the Chalcedonian creed to begin with. Rather than supplying rules that specify the shape that Christian affirmation should take in a particular time and place, the creeds conform more to the idea of Christan identity that I have been formulating gradually in this chapter: the creeds, in virtue of their ambiguities, become the focus of an ongoing debate; they are the grounds around which opposed factions unite in argument.

One might argue more generally that the sort of rules postliberals are after are never sufficient to determine the specifics of a practice. The rules that establish the identity of a practice determine what is nonsense or not, but they do not specify positively what it is one should say. Thus, following the rules of English grammar enables one to make a well-formed statement, but it does not direct one to make any particular statement given the input supplied by a particular time and place. Knowing the rules of chess means one knows the moves one can make with the pieces but that is not enough to determine the best move to make at a particular point in the course of a game.

As we suggested in chapter 3 for the directives of culture generally, in between the rule and any specific result is the whole messy process of application by very differently situated people. No formalized or codified set of rules determines of itself the manner of its application. Therefore, no automatic or spontaneous connection exists between a rule and a particular result in any given situation, as the postliberal account of rules seems to imply.

The usual postliberal response to these last two objections is to say that people are trained by others in the game to use the rules in a certain way; and there is much to be said for such a response. Training produces agreement in the application of rules and that agreement in application establishes the propriety of a particular result. Someone skilled in the use of the rules by way of such training, knows not just all the moves that could be made, but what a good move amounts to in a particular situation. Such training also explains why people tend to proceed in the same way on the basis of preceding instances of a purported rule; it explains why they can all be said to be following the same rule in a predictable way. Training by others makes up the short fall: when a player says 12 after 2, 4, 6, 8—and he or she certainly could, since nothing about the preceding numbers rules it out—the others in the game say "No, the right answer is 10," and after a while—by the time one gets to 1000—one is no longer tempted to say 1004.

The postmodern Wittgensteinian would respond in turn, however, that the way postliberals appeal to such communal norms for the use of rules again violates the spirit of Wittgenstein's effort to problematize rule following. While the postliberals are right about what leads to uniformity in the results of rule following, the Wittgensteinian point is that nothing fixes these communal norms in place. They are susceptible to change in the historical course of decisions by the human actors involved. Appeal to communal norms will not guarantee, then, as postliberals want it to, stability underneath the changing forms of history.

Even more to the point in the Christian case, the appeal here to communal norms is only plausible if the problem of diversity in Christian practice is far less serious than it appears to be. Unlike, say, the case of mathematics, this much spontaneous agreement on what are the right Christian moves to make in a particular place and time simply does not seem to exist. Appeal to communal norms for the use of rules helps show the underlying Christian identity of diverse Christian practices when those practices occur in different historical situations—these differences are analogous to the different members of a numerical sequence. But the real problem seems to be that at any point in the sequence, some Christians are saying 8, some 12, and others 102. Instead of a consensus on how to apply the rules in a particular situation, one always seems to find, at least initially, a fight.

There may, indeed, at any one point in time be certain practices that all Christians immediately perceive to be incompatible with their faith (for instance, judgments about slavery are now of that sort). But one certainly cannot assume from that fact that this sort of automatic agreement is the usual state of affairs. One cannot assume from these easy cases that hard ones are rare. Nor can one assume that easy cases now were not hard ones earlier. These easy cases in fact became so by way of earlier disputations among Christians who deliberated differently about what their faith required. Thus, far from being known "intuitively" in any simple sense, the Christian judgment against slavery was preceded by about a hundred years of wrangling—and before that by something more like complacency in judgments about it among even the most "saintly" Christians. From the fact that rules for good judgment are not formulizable—from, that is, the Wittgensteinian point that no explicit rule is sufficient to produce correct judgment apart from training—Lindbeck seems to infer that with training people should always come to the same conclusions without the need for deliberation. In this way Lindbeck replaces the automatic results of a decision procedure—a step-by-step procedure that would guarantee the same results among all who follow it—with the automatic results of training. His appeal to training allows him to keep this sort of claim for automatic agreement in outputs despite the fact that the usual support for it has fallen to Wittgenstein's critique. What Lindbeck fails to see is that Wittgenstein is working thereby to problematize the whole notion of automatism.[30]

Postliberals try to get around the absence of Christian consensus on so many matters at any one time and place by claiming that at least all well-trained Christians will so agree, and that not all, perhaps not even the majority of Christians, are ever well trained.[31] But this is simply question begging. It is a very strange game indeed, if the majority of people playing it never know how.

If postliberals make that claim, then the rules and norms for their application which postliberal theologians formulate do not seem any longer to be capturing the facts of Christian practice; those rules and norms instead amount to a recommendation about how Christians should behave. (The recommendation is, in short, that all Christians should agree with the postliberal judgment about the rules and their proper application in particular times and places.) The postliberal will be saying that not all the players of the Christian game have the same status as data from which to generalize the rules of the game and the norms for their application. There is no point to a general survey of Christian practices when trying to formulate them; the only important data comes from the subset of competent players. The problem with this is that there is no noncircular way of specifying who the competent players are in a situation characterized by this much disagreement. Discrimination between competent and incompetent judgments is usually backed up by referring to a general consensus among players to that effect; but it cannot be supported in this way here. Appeal to competence simply seems therefore to be a rather underhanded way of supporting one faction in an ongoing argument over what Christians should say and do. Rather than allowing a fair fight that might eventually produce agreement in judgments, the very competency of the majority of the players to make such judgments is questioned.[32]

Postliberals might defend the idea that Christianity is a practice that few know how to play by saying that in this unusual practice participants are all like children, always in the process of being formed in a Christian way of life, never fully or truly learning, short of the eschaton, what a Christian way of being involves.[33] The argument between the postliberal and the postmodern Wittgenstein could therefore be formulated in terms of differing recommendations about a return to childhood, differing recommendations about what it means "to become as little children," with all the Christian resonances of that phrase. The postmodern Wittgenstein wants us to return to childhood in the sense that the automatism of training is broken. One realizes that the series of Christian practices could be continued differently by reconceiving the rule they follow. Indeed, one becomes open thereby to the fact that other Christians do continue the series in a way different from one's own training. One becomes open to that fact in the sense that it no longer looks simply like deviance from the unquestioned norm of one's own practice. One becomes wary thereby of simply equating one's own way of being Christian with conformity to the mind of Christ.[34] For the postliberal, return to childhood also means awareness of one's own inadequacy: this is a game for perpetual children, a game that one never fully learns to play. Theologically expressed, the point in both cases is that of justification by faith: even as a Christian, one must be mindful of one's sin and avoid pretensions of perfectionism. In the postliberal case, however, justification by faith loses its usual function as an equalizer. Not everyone is a child; good training requires good teachers who somehow avoid the difficulty—either by natural talent (religious virtuosi) or by dint of constant training (the members of an ecclesiastical hierarchy).[35]

Instead of saying that the majority of Christians have not been adequately trained to play, a more generous reading of the facts of Christian practice—of the fact, in particular, that Christians tend to disagree about what it is proper to do in a particular situation—would be that the rules of the game just do not lead to immediate agreement, not across historical situations or even within any one situation. The rules of the game do not keep Christians who want to bounce the ball out of a game in which others bat it; the identity of the Christian game is not that restrictive.

This inclusiveness does not mean that all the judgments of the participants about what to do in the game are equally proper; it just means that the propriety of their respective judgments will have to be determined in the course of playing the game. If the rules of the game do not lead to immediate agreement, that does not mean then that, when disagreement breaks out, a particular Christian practice does not have the better arguments in its favor. It just means that what identifies all these practices as the same Christian game—the rules that set the game up—is not what determines that any particular practice is the right thing for a Christian to do. Other, more specific arguments in support of particular Christian practices, arguments generated in the course of the game, will have to be offered, in order for that sort of determination to be made.

Style

My own suggestions in the last chapter about the nature of Christian identity might suggest, however, something like Christian identity in virtue of rules. Following the postmodern directives discussed in chapter 3, I argued, when discussing the formation of Christian identity at the boundaries, that what matters is how material borrowed from elsewhere is used. Presumably there might be some distinctively Christian manner of doing so. The materials themselves vary while the way they are used remains much the same.

If rules are too inflexible to capture those similarities of use, perhaps style is a better way to talk about them; indeed style, we remember from chapter 3, is the favored term to discuss cultural identity from a postmodern perspective. Style commonly refers to the specific way a practice is performed when there are other possible options.[36] There are styles in this sense of painting or musical composition. Various artistic practices in the same historical period are often said to share a style; there is, for example, a Greco-Roman style of painting, sculpture and architecture, distinct from that, say, of the Baroque. By extension, one can talk about all the practices of a particular culture—not just its high culture practices—in terms of a shared style. We said in chapter 3 that style, once shorn of its associations with autonomous origination, remains a possible model for cultural distinctiveness. A distinctive way or manner of doing things might, then, unify Christian practices despite their diversity, make them all Christian rather than not.

If what we said earlier about diversity in the Christian use of borrowed matterial is correct, however, one will be able to characterize the style that identifies Christian practices only in the most general terms. We said earlier that Christian practices do not trope all borrowed materials in the same way. Some of these materials seem almost to be left alone, others are directly contradicted, and in the vast gray middle are varying degrees of resistance, contestation, and compromise. At any one time and place there are disagreements about how the same material is to be troped—for instance, one understanding of how to lead a Christian life might allow military action with certain modifications, while the same forms of action are rejected outright by another. Across historical contexts, there is the same sort of diversity about what to do with similar kinds of material—in one context, the economic relations of the society are frowned upon; in another, they seem to be incorporated in Christian practice without a qualm.

Given this degree of diversity, it does not seem advisable to try to characterize the general style of Christian uses of borrowed material by looking for anything that all those uses share, some common denominator that cuts across them all. The different instances of a Christian style just do not seem to be "homologous," that is, to fit together neatly according to a common pattern of transforming the wider culture in the way, say, instances of punk style do. A hole is to a T-shirt, as spitting is to applause, as anarchy is to order. What all these punk alterations of the wider culture share is a refusal to make sense according to the usual demand for order around central values.[37] One could sum up the pattern of the transformations by saying something like: for punk, if the shoe does not fit, wear it.[38] Similar efforts to generalize from Christian cases so as to arrive at their common denominator would produce something very vague indeed—too vague to be of use in distinguishing Christian uses from any other. One might very well be able to say only that, while not troped in the same way, borrowed materials are always troped in some way or other.

Nor does it make sense to try to characterize Christian style as one would a family resemblance, by looking for a set of recurrent features, different subsets of which appear throughout although no one feature does. In this way, the Joneses might be characterized by small noses, buck teeth, black hair, and big eyes, even though no one of those features is common to all of them: Cynthia has buck teeth, black hair, and a small nose; Doug has a small nose and black hair; Ed has buck teeth and small eyes. Specifying the relevant set of features in the Christian case is an impossible task given the incredible number of cases at issue and the fact that the cases to be considered keep multiplying. It is less like specifying what accounts for family resemblances among the Joneses and more like trying to do so for the family of humankind. Moreover, efforts to specify the set of features that account for a family resemblance seem viable only when one is already sure for other reasons who is actually in the family. Thus, only because one knows their parentage ahead of time is it clear that one's account of family resemblances should cover only Cynthia, Doug, and Ed and exclude other people like Missy and Troy. Because who is in or out is the very thing at issue in the Christian case, the situation is more like the extraordinarily difficult one of having first to specify a set of identifying features in order to be able to delimit to begin with the family that is the object of discussion.

One might have more success capturing the nature of Christian style if one stopped looking for similarities across cases and tried instead to form some generalizations about the point of these Christian efforts to trope borrowed material. The point might be the same even if what happens to borrowed material is very different from case to case; indeed, to the extent borrowed materials are themselves diverse, making the same point with them might just require doing different things to them. The very general point of the effort is, one might say, to refer all things to God, and in that way to relativize them.[39] "Relativize" has two senses here: the sense of containing such material within its proper bounds under God, and the sense of setting it in a proper relation to God.[40] In referring all things to God, the resistance of borrowed material to such a reference must be broken, in order for such materials then to be set into the context of the world's relations with God. Thus, for example, when Christians borrow beliefs about the world to be found in secular spheres, it is the Christian understanding of the relationship of things to God that accounts for the difference between a Christian understanding of the world and that of others.[41]

Of course, Christians do not agree on their understanding of God's relationship to the world; they therefore do not have the same understanding of what it means to refer all things to God. For purposes of argument here—just to show how such a reference to God can have rather unpredictable effects on the use of borrowed material—one could summarize in the following way some of the necessarily vague ideas about God's relation to the world that Christians might all share: God's concern for the world is universal in its extent; human beings are made for a special relationship with God as the Word's incarnation in a human being attests; human beings cannot glory in that special standing before God as if it were not the free gift of God. Without worrying about the accuracy of these generalizations and certainly without implying that they are in any way exhaustive, one can see the way ideas like this can have a relativizing function in the senses mentioned. If, for instance, Christians were to borrow the idea common in our culture that human beings are free to determine their own lives as they see fit, such an idea would have to be contained so that it might not imply that humans are free to absent themselves from the arena of divine concern and influence. The idea of human freedom could be set in a positive relation to God by viewing it in terms of the human vocation of fellowship with God and with God's creatures; such fellowship, one could claim, is what freedom is for. Depending on the ideas at issue, similar efforts to relativize them would produce quite different results—alterations, for example, of a much more drastic sort.

Thinking of Christian style in this way, one might be able to formulate some very general resemblances across cases when borrowed materials are of a similar sort. Thus, one might argue that whenever Christians borrow ethical norms from the wider society, they tend to universalize their scope; when Christians find narrowly bounded communities of moral concern, they break those bounds open. (This is the effect of setting such norms in the context of Christian commitment to a God whose own concerns are universal.) Or, whenever Christians take over hierarchical ways of thinking present in the wider culture, they tend to reverse them, thereby raising what was of low regard there and humbling the high. This follows from an understanding of relationship with God in which one glories not in one's privileges but in the God who gives them.[42]

While generalizations like these across cases are all well and good as a help in deciding what one should do and say as a Christian, the reservations we expressed earlier about general efforts to sum up what makes Christian practices all of a piece still hold. One cannot sum up, for more than a particular time and place, the resemblances that tie together the Christian uses of borrowed materials, since the pattern that weaves those practices together may be constantly changing by God's free grace. Moreover—as we implied in the last section about rules—the connections among these various Christian uses of borrowed materials are loose enough, they have enough give or play in them, to make every characterization of them contestable. Of course, that need not stop one from offering the characterization one thinks best, but it is important to see that the better characterization only becomes apparent from how well the variety of Christian practices hang together when viewed in that way rather than some other. It is thus the weave of the practices themselves that does the work when figuring out whether a disputed Christian practice can be included in it. The general characterization itself is not an effective test of Christian identity; everything depends on how things look when one sets that disputed practice next to the rest of what Christians have said and done. The characterization is obviously trying to capture the nature of the pattern, but the pattern itself is elusive enough to make one wary of all such facile substitutes for it. For example, if one includes the ordination of women as part of the mix of Christian practices, what will now stand out about them (perhaps their commitment to social justice?) and how well will the rest of what Christians do and say hang together with that new emphasis? This sort of testing by looking at the weave is clearly more reliable than testing with reference to some general characterization of the identity of Christianity. The only effective support for such a characterization would come from the same sort of evidence.

It probably makes sense, then, to give up any general effort to summarize the resemblances among all the different cases of Christian uses of borrowed materials, a summary that would identify what makes them all Christian. The word *style*, indeed, suggests the very elusiveness of these similarities. One appeals to similarity in style just in case one has difficulty formulating what the similarity is; style is apparent *in* the way things are arranged and cannot be adequately stated in general terms.

Interest might shift, then, to the prerequisites for maintaining a similarity among the Christian uses of borrowed materials—whatever that similarity may be. Thus, one might say, as postliberals do, that the distinctiveness of a Christian use of borrowed materials can be maintained only if Christianity keeps the upper hand over such materials, only if they are thoroughly reworked in Christian terms, assimilated completely to Christian needs, absorbed into a Christian world, rather than the reverse. Here one is not so much specifying what is being done to these materials—for instance, whether they are affirmed or denied or altered in some particular way—as insisting that Christianity is, whatever the case, always directing the show, in complete control of the process. This itself, then, becomes a mark of Christian practice. If borrowed material is not made to submit in this way, there is no chance that a similar use will be made of it. Christian practices would be liable, instead, to be pushed this way and that by the changing materials supplied from the wider society.

There are a number of problems with such a suggestion. First, if our discussion earlier about Christian identity at the boundaries is correct, the Christianity that is supposed to keep the influence of borrowed materials in check is always already infiltrated by borrowed material. Borrowed materials always go to make up Christian words and deeds; no pure Christian something exists, therefore, to direct the process, as seems to be assumed. Second, dominance would appear to be impossible to sustain. Using the materials of others makes that Christian use always susceptible to reversal. The presence of their own materials always gives those others an opening to turn the tables. Thus, pentecostal movements in Western missionizing activity make Christianity attractive to people who already practice forms of spirit divinization, but what is to keep Christian worship from becoming thereby just one more technique in the ad hoc effort to get by in a world of spirits? Because Christian and non-Christian cultural forms are not found side by side but mixed up together when Christianity tropes borrowed material, the logic of the relationship between the two—for instance, which one takes precedence over the other—cannot be laid out explicitly. That relationship is therefore always open to negotiation; it is often not even clear from such double-voiced Christian cultural productions themselves which is the subordinate party.[43] Thus, in the following completely typical cases, how can one tell which party is being absorbed into the world of the other? When the God of Christians is identified with the high God of African religions, is the African high God assimilated to a Christian outlook, or the reverse? If caste rituals are incorporated in Christian worship services in India because issues of social order are viewed as matters of religious indifference, how can one prevent that from signaling simply that Christianity is in service to a particular status-conscious social outlook? When African Christians identify the spirits in control of everyday life with demons and Jesus Christ as the only antidote to their pernicious influence, which is absorbing which—African religious practices or Christian ones? If other African Christians deny the existence of spirits altogether and pray only to God for deliverance from everyday trials, does that mean African practices have been better absorbed into the world of Christian belief than before? What if they now refuse medical treatment, too, as incompatible, like spirit divination, with trust in God? How is the question of who is absorbing whom affected by the fact that it is African religion, and not contemporary Western Christianity, that claims religion infiltrates all aspects of life including the medical?[44]

Given their worries about preoccupations with method in contemporary theology, it is ironic that postliberals often seem engaged in futile efforts to rule out ambiguities and reversals like these through a recourse to method. While they often claim that there is no formulizable rule or method about *how* to subordinate borrowed materials to the needs of Christianity, the subordination itself nevertheless seems an absolute rule.[45] *Theological* method—their own rather than that of their opponents—seems, moreover, to make all the difference if Christianity is to maintain the upper hand. Thus, postliberals commonly say that theologians must not place a priority on translating the Christian message into contemporary terms; they are to avoid defenses of Christianity that make non-Christian standards and norms a benchmark for meaningfulness or plausibility; they must try to keep the assumptions of the outside world from operating as an interpretive framework in their theological work by submerging themselves in the life of Christian communities and the intratextual world of meaning that the Bible supplies. Postliberals also try to guarantee Christianity's dominance in contacts with the wider world and other religions by nullifying theological claims that might put these others on a more equal footing with Christianity. Thus postliberals are no fans of the idea that God's purposes are evident in the world of nature or in the structures of human life generally. Certainly, where knowledge of God is concerned, the particularities of this unsubstitutable person, Jesus, always outweigh discussions of a universal Logos or the possibly far-flung peregrinations of the Holy Spirit; and that preference is backed up by a weighty pessimism about the effects of sin.

Such efforts to ensure the dominance of Christianity in its interactions with other religions and the wider world only make all the clearer, however, more serious problems. In their effort to maintain Christian identity, postliberals are in danger of confusing subordination to the Word with subordination to a human word. Contrary to what postliberals seem to suggest, Christianity does not need to keep the upper hand when using borrowed materials; the Word does.

Christian identity hinges on remaining open to direction from the free grace of God in Christ; that is the organizing principle for its use of borrowed materials and what centers the arrangement of the theological claims that arise in that way. Postliberals, however, are confused about the conditions for this openness. The test for the proper use of borrowed materials is not whether those materials seem to threaten the established character of Christianity. What counts is whether that use distorts that to which Christians are trying to witness, and there is no easy test for that.

For openness to the Word to be possible, it is true, as postliberals remind us, that borrowed materials must lose their fixity; they must be transformable in service to the Word. Keeping borrowed materials open in this way for service to the Word does not, however—as postliberals assume—require the futile effort to keep them from being the interpretive lens or key to the interpretation of Scripture. As Barth affirms, there is always an interpretive lens like that; if one gets rid of one, another simply takes its place. Instead, one must just be willing to alter those presuppositions, to keep them flexible, and admit their provisionality. Some outside interpretive lens or other stays; one's absolute loyalty or unreserved commitment to it is what goes. The lens one employs is never adequate as it stands to the Word to which the Bible witnesses, and even if, after being modified, it is arguably the best lens through which to proclaim that Word at a particular place and time, one must neither foreclose the possibilities for service to the Word that other interpretive frameworks at the time might offer, nor make one's own mandatory for all times and places.[46]

Postliberals also tend to forget that if borrowed materials must lose their fixity, the same must be true for every theological formulation employing those materials. After all, if the concern is to meet conditions for openness to service to the Word, it is not so much the borrowed materials themselves that one is worried about but their use in theology.[47] When theological claims are hardened in a way that obstructs obedience to the Word, they too need to be broken and their provisionality revealed.

Borrowed materials should not, then, always be subordinated to Christian claims; they should be permitted, instead, to shake them up where necessary. If Christianity's having the upper hand over non-Christian materials is made into a rule, this only encourages the Word's enslavement to the human words of Christians.[48]

It is when the Word is given up into the hands of its interpreters that the effort to be true to it becomes the excuse for a power play between competing human words, the rationale for a demand to subordinate one theological position to another. The theologian assumes that obedience to the Word can only be ensured by obedience to a particular theological position. Its superiority has to be secured against the challenges of other competing the-ological claims and those of non-Christian viewpoints. Defense of the Word requires proof—or at least the incontrovertible assertion in the postliberal case—of the superior intrinsic qualities of a particular theologi-cal position and of the Christianity identified with it over other religions and a secular outlook. In a misplaced effort to defend the Word from dis-tortion, the Christian glories no longer simply in the God to whom he or she may, indeed, be effectively witnessing, but, instead, in the importance of the qualities whose possession supposedly enables that witness. Subject to constant external challenge, defense of the Word gradually degenerates into intransigent Christian self-defense.

The same confusion between obedience to the Word and obedience to a human word seems to be behind the fear of a more level playing field between Christianity and the cultural worlds with which it interacts. Unless one is confusing the two, there is no reason to assume when non-Christian influences gain the upper hand on Christianity, that they have thereby wrested control from God's Word. The influences between Christian and non-Christian might very well be reciprocal in many cases if the relation between the Word of God and any human word is never one of equals, if, in short, the Word of God always retains sovereignty over the words in which it is once proclaimed. Even a simple equality between Christian and non-Christian materials need not spell the end of Christian identity, if that identity concerns the effort to be open to God's Word: what is knitting the two together for the Christian might just be confidence in that Word.

Contrary to the good intentions of postliberals, trying to guarantee openness to the Word by human means always ends up making the preten-sions of that method itself an obstacle to openness. The more one tries to prevent obstruction or distortion of the Word through some tactic or tech-nique, the more one turns obedience to God into obedience to a human rule. Ironically, then, doing it right, being genuinely open to the Word, always involves opening oneself to the risk of failure. If the Word of God himself died on a cross, it is foolish to think mere witnesses to that Word can force its triumph in the world by their own exertions. The theologian who wants to remain open to the Word must recognize that there are no human guarantees of faithfulness to it; one cannot ensure such faithfulness by following a rule.

Christian Identity as a Task

We have been rethinking Christian identity in the last two chapters if, as post-modern cultural theory implies, that identity can no longer be determined by group specificity, sharp cultural boundaries, or homogeneity of practices. Christianity becomes a subculture in a world where cultures generally are more like subcultures than the cultures of modern anthropology, in that they are essentially dependent on relations with others. Bringing together postmodern theories of culture with the idea that the grace of Christ is universal in scope and able to find people in any circumstance no matter how apparently hostile or closed to it, I argued first that Christian communities are neither self-contained nor self-sufficient. The character of Christian social relations is sustained, it is true, by some fairly isolated social activities, ones, that is, that involve in the main only Christians—for instance, church services. But Christians always bring with them on such occasions their other social roles and commitments. By infiltrating Christians' activities with other Christians, by being brought inside, those other roles and commitments are reworked in the course of such activities. Christians, moreover, remain in social interactions with non-Christians; they engage with any non-Christian sites of social interaction that might exist. Their Christian commitments remain relevant to these spheres, too, and therefore operate to transform the character of social relations in them. In such fashions, prophetic objections to the wider society are maintained, not by isolation, but by the indefinitely extended effort to alter, where necessary, whatever one comes across through sustained engagement with it, in and out of church.

Second, I argued that, while there are boundaries between Christian and non-Christian ways of life, those boundaries are fluid and permeable. Claims and values that are outside are brought inside (or, much the same thing, what is inside is brought outside) in processes of transformation at the boundary. Christian identity is therefore no longer a matter of unmixed purity, but a hybrid affair established through unusual uses of materials found elsewhere. Nor can Christian identity be understood from isolated attention to Christian practices per se; understanding it now requires the careful situating of Christian practices in the wider field of cultural life on which they are a commentary.

Third, I suggested that what Christians have in common, what unites them, is nothing internal to the practices themselves. What unites them is concern for true discipleship, proper reflection in human words and deeds of an object of worship that always exceeds by its greatness human efforts to do so. What Christians are all trying to be true to is not some element within or character of Christian practices themselves. As a result, Christian identity is not maintained by the anxiously self-concerned effort to protect those elements or that character against corruption; nor does it depend upon the effectiveness of demands for conformity with them.

Christians do believe that Christian beliefs and actions have witnessed to the God whose disciples they also are to be. Exactly which beliefs and actions those are, and, even more so, how they are to be a guide to present discipleship are, however, matters for ongoing assessment and reassessment. What unites Christian practices is not, then, agreement about the beliefs and actions that constitute true discipleship; but a shared sense of the importance of figuring it out.

Scriptures, the creeds, the eucharist, and baptism are places where Christians believe the Word of God is heard, where the Word of God is present. Christian life revolves around matters like these in that Christians always refer back to such matters when moving forward to their own efforts at discipleship. These materials of constant concern are not, however, strictly delimited—for instance, others might be added. The Word's presence or proper reflection in human speech and action cannot be restricted to them; and one's efforts to be a true disciple of the Word heard there do not involve simple repetition. One must do something with them in order to lead one's life in their light. Christians do not agree on how to do that, because the materials that Christians refer back to and forward from are too vague, too many, and too loosely organized of themselves for this ever to be very clear.

In short, then, the diversity of Christian practices are united in a task. Christian practices are engaged in the same task in that, first of all, they tend to revolve around a similar set of claims and ritual actions (for instance, biblical claims, the basic ritual forms to be found in most Christian churches), claims and ritual actions that because of their lack of definition amount in practice to a similar set of questions to be answered in the effort to be true to God. Who and what Jesus was, the difference he made in human life, the practices and beliefs that came into the world with him, are understood to be of crucial significance for how one is to live. There are affirmations here, which give these questions sense: for example, a strong enough belief in the significance of Jesus and of initiation into the community of his followers to put one's life in motion around the question of what exactly this person and that initiation means for it. But the affirmations are so vague that they amount, in practice, to a project requiring a solution. The immediate problem is to specify a meaning for them that is sufficiently definite to direct a whole way of life. The very lack of definition that enables the claims and ritual practices at issue to be of concern to large numbers of very differently situated people prompts an extended argument about how to interpret them in the course of a life led in their light.

Great diversity and conflict of particular interpretations are more often than not the result. There are no rules here to bring about proper interpretation; there is no agreement about methods of investigation that will produce agreement in results. When agreement about the nature of true discipleship is reached—when, say, agreement is reached about the impropriety of slave-holding—that is not so much because a majority of the Christians of the time were finally socialized well into abiding norms for the interpretation and use of Christian claims. Instead of following rules for the settlement of disputes about the meaning of Christianity, a majority of Christians finally were in a position to make the more ad hoc judgment that such a practice fit uneasily with the rest of Christian beliefs and practices; the rest of what Christians had come to believe and to think proper as forms of action was finally such as to make slavery seem anomolous.

When some agreement is reached about the meaning of the initially vague fundamental claims and ritual actions of Christian commitment, that agreement again tends to be based on a vagueness of formulation that allows for a diversity of interpretation. Certain practices are ruled out—say, by a creed or a rule of faith that garners widespread affirmation—without specifying positively the positions compatible with it. Arguments break out over whether a position is sufficiently like the agreed-upon one to be ruled legitimate; arguments break out, too, over whether particular positions are sufficiently like those the agreed-upon one clearly rules out, to be ruled out themselves.

Despite continuing diversity and conflict, community of argument about the meaning of true discipleship is nevertheless assured to the extent competing judgments about it claim to be based on plausible interpretations of materials in which all parties put some stock. What all parties are fighting over form normative reference points for the argument, even if their interpretation is part of what is subject to debate. There are some common standards for the assessment of judgments about true discipleship that come simply from the willingness of all parties to enter into debate about certain matters as if their lives depended on it; those matters amount to standards of argument, even if those standards are vague and subject to review as the argument continues. To the extent a plausible interpretation is offered of them, one is obligated to take seriously the arguments based on them.

Community of argument is sustained, too, to the extent all parties offer their interpretations for the consideration and judgment of the other participants. Despite their disagreements, Christians are united in argument in that they believe that the project of interpretation, which leading a Christian way of life requires, is properly pursued by way of an extended argument with everyone else engaged in the same project. If sin does not rule out one's own contributions to the enterprise, it can never entirely rule out anyone else's either. The most warped Christian practice is at least a beneficial reminder of errors one should avoid. The seriousness, moreover, of sin on all sides makes the prospect of mutual correction a salutary one; one's own contribution is never likely to stand just as it is. Even without agreement in results, unity among Christian practices is therefore sustained by a continuity of fellowship, by a willingness, displayed across differences of time and space, to admonish, learn from, and be corrected by all persons similarly concerned about the true meaning of Christian discipleship. All Christians are in this project together. Such a relationship of mutual accounting and responding is therefore to be kept up in a continuous fashion, so as to include all Christians in every historical and geographical location. Ideally, there are no breaks here, whereby some parties to the argument fall irretrievably out of the arena of further Christian consideration. Coming to terms with the viewpoints of other Christians past and present and offering up one's own judgments for the consideration of others who live beside one or who will come after, each Christian who struggles with what it means to be a Christian takes up his or her place within the historical body of Christians similarly concerned.

In the end, then, how the identity of Christianity should be summed up is an unanswerable question in that Christianity has its identity as a task; it has its identity in the form of a task of looking for one. The theologian must not be timid in his or her judgment about what the Word of God requires at a particular place and time. But one function of theology—particularly of theology as a specialized practice of intellectual production with some autonomy from the immediate demands of everyday practice—is to remind people making such judgments about the need for openness to a free Word. Theology in this capacity is the reminder that, no matter how true and right those judgments are, one must not lose contact with their object in a kind of self-satisfied slumber but remain open for new movements of faithfulness to a free Word. One may sum up what Christianity stands for in the process of judging what one must do here and now. But, since the Word of God is a free Word, the meaning of discipleship—what it really means to be a Christian—cannot be summed up in any neat formula that would allow one to know already what Christian discipleship will prove to include or exclude over the course of time.

7

Diversity and Creativity in Theological Judgment

Def.
$\quad$ y conclusions in the last chapter about Christian identity—that it is
$\quad$ constituted most fundamentally by a community of argument concerning the meaning of true discipleship—suggested that Christian identity need not be jeopardized by ongoing disagreement about what Christians
should say, feel, and do. We have yet to ask, however, whether there is any
positive significance to such ongoing disagreement. The whole point of the
argument over what constitutes Christian identity seemed, as I described it,
to hinge on some discomfort with diversity in theological judgments: the
fact of it cannot be accepted with complete equanimity; the point of the
argument is to do something about it. Diversity in theological judgments is
worrisome because Christians believe that it is possible to go seriously
wrong in one's understanding of Christian discipleship and that the stakes
of such error are high—one's standing before God and the existence of
effective witness to God's rule on this earth are, for example, at issue. Diversity of judgment is also always at least dangerous in that it could give rise to
a divisive sectarianism sufficient indeed to break the Christian fellowship
on which Christian identity depends. Do these worries mean that consensus is the goal of the argument? Does "doing something about it" entail,
that is, an effort, over the course of such argument, to achieve uniformity of
belief and evaluation and thereby eradicate diversity from Christian judgments about proper Christian practice? Or might there be something of
value in the failure to reach agreement? If there is, can one specify the
extent to which or the mode in which agreement remains a desideratum?

$\quad$ Closely bound up with the question of the positive significance of a failure to agree on the meaning of Christian discipleship is the question of the
value of theological creativity. Creativity in theological judgment leads to
novelty and change; especially if given free rein, it is one likely source of disagreement in theological judgments about what it means to lead a Christian life. To what extent do worries about those disagreements properly

translate into worries about creativity and therefore prompt efforts to restrain its exercise?

Responses to both questions have been an undercurrent in the last two chapters, but they need now to be offered explicitly and developed. As we will see, postmodern trends in cultural theory seriously modify the usual way these questions are answered by theologians who understand theological activity in specifically Christian cultural terms. When one understands theology as a part of Christian cultural contexts, the answers one gives to these questions vary according to whether a modern or postmodern view of culture informs them.

The Interpretation of Diversity

How one accounts for diversity in theological judgments obviously affects one's ability to view diversity—and by extension, theological creativity—in positive terms. Because it thinks that cultures require consensus, a modern understanding of culture makes diversity in theological judgment a function of either improper socialization or a difference in cultural contexts. Thus, according to the first sort of explanation, Christians draw different conclusions about what it means to lead a Christian life because at least some of them lack the social training to enable them to do so appropriately. The second sort of explanation has less uniformly negative consequences for how diversity is understood. Diversity is the product of the effort to be a Christian in different cultural contexts. What it means to be a Christian should not look the same from one cultural context to another—say, from pagan ancient Rome to contemporary Catholic Spain. One lives a Christian life differently depending on the cultural materials with which one has to work and the challenges to the Christian faith specific to that context. Sometimes, however, in the effort to be a Christian in a new situation, the cultural context that directs theological judgment shifts illicitly from a Christian to a non-Christian one. One is then no longer viewing the new situation from out of a Christian cultural context but the reverse; one is fitting a question that comes up in the course of the effort to lead a Christian life into, say, a secular cultural framework operating according to different socially enforced norms and standards. One finds explanations like these for theological diversity in George Lindbeck's *The Nature of Doctrine*.[1]

A postmodern understanding of culture would of course dispute the sharp boundary between Christian and non-Christian cultures that is presupposed in the last point. Employing norms of the wider culture need not mark a shift in cultural contexts, if Christianity does not form a way of life apart from the wider society and establishes its own identity through the use of non-Christian cultural materials. Such a criticism only, however, makes the worry about shifts from Christian to non-Christian cultural contexts more acute; it would be far harder to tell when they occur.

A more serious problem is that this position refuses to see the extent to which diversity of theological judgment is propelled by Christian practice itself. Contrary to this position, diversity results not so much from a failure to internalize Christian culture as from proper socialization into the kind of practice Christianity is. The position does see that the universalizing tendencies of a Christian life—propensities, that is, to make a Christian way of life cover everything—prompt diversity. The effort to be Christian in changing cultural contexts prompts diversity in theological judgments, as would, it might be added, the Christian penchant to live in a Christian way throughout the whole of one's life—all its dimensions—at any one time and place. But for Lindbeck the diversity of theological judgment seems to have its roots solely in external influences; without them, properly socialized Christians would, it seems, form the same judgments. The position does not see that features of Christian practice itself make agreement in theological judgment enormously difficult. Because their function as a unifying focus for diversely situated persons requires them to be, the cultural materials of Christianity are too vague to steer theological judgment apart from the exercise of theological judgment. Moreover, because those materials are constructed piecemeal in the messy course of social relations, they do not emerge with sufficient consistency among themselves to prompt uniformity in the judgments that appeal to them. Some selection from them has to be made if there is to be a consistent basis for judgment; and the rest remain as a resource for different principles of selection. Finally, because of the complexity of the situations in which they must be employed, rules for the use of Christian materials—say, rules for the use of biblical precedents—can amount to no more than opportunities for improvisation. In order to deal with contingencies as they arise, with unanticipated occurrences whose nature is not fully understood at once, rules have to leave room for maneuver, for ad hoc adjustments and for elaboration of their import to suit particular occasions and the various needs and concerns of the actors involved. The rules cannot be either fully spelled out or rigidly prescriptive.[2] They must have, in short, the sort of flexibility that makes uniformity in their application even at a single place and time unlikely.

If the very nature of Christianity seems to encourage them, it would seem, on the one hand, that different understandings of how to lead a Christian life—even when they occur at the same time and place—are not necessarily a bad thing. They may be just the product of sincere, equally uncorrupted, and fully capable Christian efforts to lead a Christian life.

Persons equally skilled and faithful to Christian culture no longer seem required by that culture to come up with the same conclusions about Christian discipleship in any given circumstance. The same facts of human existence might prompt, it seems, a valid diversity of opinion about how to make Christian sense of them. Christian culture would just not be the sort of culture that demands uniformity of practice.

On the other hand, if Christian culture has its own internal prompters of diversity, one cannot render diversity harmless, as Lindbeck does, by parceling it out to different times and places. His position would have us believe that legitimate diversity in theological judgment can never be worrisome. Differences that are legitimate, in that they do not result from improper socialization or corrupting outside influences, can never for him produce genuine disagreement, because they are just what the same Christian cultural directives require in different settings. Different judgments are kept from coming into conflict with one another by claiming their suitability for different cultural materials in different times and places. If Christianity itself prompts diversity in judgment, however, it is as likely to erupt in the same time and place as across different ones; indeed, it is likely to erupt over the very same matters. And when it does, it becomes implausible to attribute the fact solely to some parties' improper socialization or seduction by outside cultural forces. Differences in theological judgment can suggest therefore the possibility of genuinely conflicting understandings of discipleship among equally "good" Christians. If the requirements of Christian culture are loose enough not to enforce uniformity, they may also be loose enough to give rise to a genuine fight about what they imply. One cannot rule out the possibility, then, that Christian discipleship is an essentially contested notion.[3] The position we have been looking at tries to do so by pushing sources of conflict out of Christianity proper. Conflict among Christians is always attributed either to corrupting outside influences or to all parties' not really being full participants in Christian culture to begin with. According to our more postmodern account of Christian culture, to the contrary, conflict may arise through the simple effort of all parties to follow the directives of Christian culture; the possibility of conflict is, in short, inherent in the kind of culture Christianity is. Diversity again then becomes more problematic on a postmodern reading of culture than before, in the sense that the possibility of genuine conflict among Christians cannot be hidden.

Implications for Theological Creativity

Postmodern criticisms of the account of diversity we have been investigating also suggest that the areas where theological creativity has to be

exercised are far more numerous than it admits. The position we are looking at restricts the exercise of creativity to the assimilation of, or application and adjustment to, changing non-Christian cultural circumstances.
The theologian has to be creative when redescribing in Christian terms
the shifting worlds of different times and places, when giving a Christian
meaning to new domains of human existence, when figuring out how to
reinterpret a Christian outlook in contemporary terms or how to reconstitute it in ways that meet current challenges. Considered apart from
such efforts of application and reconstruction, at any one place and time
Christian cultural materials are definite and internally consistent, there
are clear rules for the use of those materials, and those rules, when properly followed in a particular situation, produce uniformity of results. The
position also assumes that all of this—a well-defined and organized
Christian outlook on life and rules for its uniform use—has been passively internalized by well-socialized Christians.

Postmodern cultural theory disputes this whole set of assumptions. Theological judgment has to be exercised in order to give meaning and structure to the cultural materials that figure in Christian social practice; those
materials are vague and circulate in many different versions, with many different potential or actualized associations with other cultural materials and
with particular patterns of social action. Though there may be rules establishing certain negative boundaries of acceptable practice (at any one time
and place certain beliefs and actions will prompt widespread opprobrium),
there are no rules establishing positively what Christians should say and do.
The situations to be addressed are too complex for the simplicity of a general rule—say, a rule requiring that beliefs about Jesus be used to oppose the
taken-for-granted certainties of the day, or an equally simple rule requiring
accommodation to them. Or, if there are general rules—say, a rule requiring one to keep the subject matter of Christian proclamation from being
made captive to a particular human outlook—it is never beyond dispute
when a rule like that is actually being followed.

For all these reasons, Christian culture does not have the clear definition
and consistency of shape sufficient for socialization into it to be entirely passive. Being a Christian at all, in even the simplest of circumstances, requires
theological judgment; one must either take responsibility for that judgment
oneself or decide to acquiesce in someone else's judgment. When particular
parties lend Christianity a clearly defined and consistent shape, the effort to
get others to go along with it is not, moreover, properly characterized as
socialization. One is not talking about socialization into Christianity, since
Christianity is far more amorphous than that, but the effort to bring about
conformity with a selected range of meanings, values, and practices favored

by a particular segment of participants in a Christian way of life. Far from being simply transmitted, that selection will, therefore, always face potential resistance from those favoring other meanings, values, and practices to be found in Christian life. To be accepted by others, a particular Christian viewpoint will have to work actively to overcome or control such resistance. That work does not, moreover, simply emerge after the fact—once, that is, a particular account of Christian beliefs and values, and of their implications for the organization of Christian life, is already on the ground. Instead, the fact of counter-interpretations usually has to be taken into account in the very process of constructing a viable version of Christianity for general dissemination. Even when backed up by institutions controlling the production and distribution of "the" Christian message and by a "police arm" of Christian practice with the power to exclude resisters from Christian fellowship, a particular account of Christianity generally does not precede resistance in a way that would make such resistance merely reactive. Instead, such an account itself emerges through the effort to incorporate potentially resistant beliefs and values in a way that will both ensure its attractiveness to the people who hold them while effectively neutralizing their capacity for trouble. That might be done, say, by establishing symbolic connections between these beliefs and values and its own while breaking their associations with other ideas and forces of potential opposition. Thus, one might construct a telling of the Christian story in which the Virgin Mary is associated with submission to the will of superiors, and the glorious reversal of high and low which she proclaims in her Magnificat is lost from view. In short, here we have something closer to the mutuality of a contest than to unilateral imposition on a blank slate, something more like a power-riven negotiation than the training of people into a way of life of which they are otherwise bereft.[4]

Postmodern culture theory does not just widen in this way the arenas in which creative theological judgments figure, extending the questions to be addressed creatively from what to do with one's Christianity given the wider world and historical changes, to the even more fundamental ones of what to make of Christianity to begin with and of the competing accounts of it given by those around one. Postmodern cultural theory also gives theological judgment greater interpretive leeway in all these areas by making its exercise seem genuinely creative.

Thus, Christian directives for how to address the contemporary situation become looser because the situation itself fails to dictate any particular Christian response. The theologian has the responsibility for interpreting the cultural materials of Christian life in a way that either meshes into or fits uneasily with the practices of a particular time and place. Those judgments are, moreover, always potentially contestable according to a different selection, explication, and organization of Christian cultural materials.

Furthermore, as I suggested in the last chapter when looking at tradition, no deep underlying or hidden depth to Christian texts or practices guides the course of Christian life over time and space. Theological judgment is not guided by God in that fashion, but by the shifting ways the material surfaces of Christian practices may be linked together to form intelligible chains. The Holy Spirit moves over the surface of the waters and not in their depths. This is the way, for example, it makes sense on some Christian readings of its Scriptures for God's steadfast faithfulness to Israel to be supplemented by God's grace to Gentiles in Christ. What Christianity takes over from Judaism and what Christians affirm alone— God's free grace in Christ to Gentiles—are linked, on this reading, as if they were faces brought near enough together to see their resemblances, linked by way of the sort of surface connections that make a pun or a homonym, and not through the discovery of a meaning running underneath them, a meaning they all instantiate.[5] One could say that the notion of free grace bridges what God does for the Jews and what God does for Gentiles now that Christ has come, but what that means is only apparent in retrospect, from the swerves in the chain of events that Christians have dared to put together.

Since what matters is how the materials of Christian practice are put together, one should not talk about already existing Christian practice as a constraint on theological creativity, or about the demand for approximating it (changing it but not too much) as a limit on theological creativity. It is not clear what "continuity with what went before" amounts to before theological judgment establishes how the different things Christians say and do relate to one another to begin with. Whether a new proposal seems continuous with what went before depends on how that earlier material is put together. The theologian has to give shape to the cultural materials of Christianity before they can work as a constraint on novelty. Thus, contemporary white feminist and womanist theologians often question the propriety of saying that Jesus' death was saving in itself; saying so might appear to validate the suffering of the innocent as a remedy for the faults of their oppressors. Nothing is served by arguments over how far such a suggestion strays from past Christian practice of talking about the atonement; everything depends on the relative plausibility of their respective construals of how past and present Christian materials hang together. If atonement theories do threaten to justify suffering in contemporary times, would that be harder to integrate with the way these Christian practices hang together than if one were to drop such theories instead?

In a similar fashion, our discussion of tradition suggested the impropriety of using appeals to tradition to foreclose innovation by serving as conversation-stoppers. Nothing is settled by a simple appeal to tradition; one cannot simply say "that is the Christian tradition," and leave it at that. Materials designated "traditional" are, we said, always a selection from those that could be so designated. The ones selected are those that figure centrally in the organization of Christian materials favored by the party that puts them forward; therefore, what is labeled "tradition" always has links to a preferred course of Christian behaviors now. Defending that designation means, then, not an argument over which materials are truly traditional— there are too many appropriate candidates for that. Most of the Christian cultural materials that circulate in the present also circulated in the past. Instead, one has to defend directly the organization of Christian materials that the claims to tradition serve. How well does that organization make sense of the different things that Christians have been prone to say and do? Does it make sense of the things that Christians tend to value most? What is lost when materials are organized in that way? What is gained, in apparent truth, beauty, intelligibility, or the advancement of the good?

To generalize, our discussion of tradition in the preceding chapter suggests the impropriety of limiting the exercise of theological creativity by demanding conformity with any human authority deemed a pure and inviolate stand-in for God's Word itself. The identity of Christian culture may be defined by its revolving around a body of human words and practices— for instance, the Bible, certain forms of ritual activity and pronouncement—where it expects the Word of God to be heard. But, as we said in chapter 6, this does not mean that God's Word directs the course of Christian practices by being a part of them, by setting up some aspect or element of Christian practice as a sacrosanct center according to which Christian practice might be judged. The freedom of Christian discipleship to follow God's Word where it leads is blocked by any human claim that refuses to allow itself to be criticized or altered in the course of the ongoing argument about true discipleship that Christianity is. Binding the freedom of theological interpretation to a human authority in that way actually threatens to interrupt the obedience of Christians to the Word.

Finally, interpretations and organizations of Christian materials that have come to be established in the course of the argument over discipleship—interpretations and organizations that are established in the sense of garnering widespread approbation from participants—do not set any firm limits on future theological creativity. The cultural processes, from out of which agreement arose, continue apace; any agreement remains vulnerable, then, to the same processes that produced it. Modifications to what

Christians have agreed upon until now cannot be ruled out by considering that agreement as if it were some sort of fixed fact. While consensus reached after long, inclusive argument among opposing Christian factions is a good indication of the propriety of a judgment about the character of true discipleship—some process of mutual correction would presumably have occurred—even Christian consensus of that sort is never equivalent to the Word to which Christians are trying to be true. It is always possible that a minority opinion might properly enter the scene to disrupt achieved consensus. One certainly need not, moreover, wait for consensus before forming a judgment of one's own. A minority view thereby has room to rebuke a majority opinion. Especially where one can argue that beliefs and values central to Christian practices are at stake, a minority stance might properly hold out against a common or increasingly common Christian viewpoint.

Postmodern cultural theory makes one wary, moreover, of facile judgments that agreements are really as widespread as advertised. The claim of consensus may, for example, simply be a power play. Any interpretation and organization of Christian materials is bound to be selective and therefore to be opposed or simply inattentive to other aspects of Christian practice. One cannot prejudge that such opposition or inattention will always turn out to be warranted. That is, one cannot assume, in the first place, that opposed cultural materials have not been simply kept out of the argument over Christian discipleship through force and disdain; in that case the purported consensus is not a genuine one. Nor can one assume, in the second place, that, if a present consensus is genuine, the future will not see serious modifications to it through the incorporation of materials that are not taken seriously at present (say, those, like the communism of the early church, that are merely a distant memory of past Christian practice) or ones that are just beginning to emerge as the cultural dimension of new Christian practices (say, the ritual practices of women's worship services).

The very nature of cultural processes, on a postmodern understanding of them, means, moreover, that it will be very difficult in any case for established interpretations and organizations of Christian materials to set firm limits on future theological creativity. For the following reasons, established productions are always prone to dissolution, to be taken apart, reorganized, and their elements reinterpreted in the process.

First, established productions have internal fissures or fault lines that make them vulnerable to revision. Because they emerge in the messy, conflictual course of history, the materials included in such productions are bound to be inconsistent and in tension with one another, and capable of being held together, therefore, only through the exertion of pressure. One cannot simply get rid of such tensions and inconsistencies by making of these materials anything one likes. Instead, one must always struggle with the meanings and associations that history has already secured for them to some extent. Thus, since moral and spiritual discipline is historically associated in a Hellenistic milieu with social elites or individual philosophical virtuosity, Christian practices that combine advocacy of such discipline with more egalitarian hopes are always faced with a struggle against those associations. Those associations remain in tension with a more egalitarian practice, encouraging an ongoing fight between Christians who favor the institution of different spiritual classes of Christians and those who do not. As we suggested in chapter 5, internal to any Christian interpretation and organization of materials is a contest with different uses of many of the same materials in non-Christian social practices. Moreover, as we suggested in chapter 4, internal to any account of how Christian beliefs, values, and actions hang together is the active effort to wrest such materials from their contrary interpretation and organization at the hands of other Christians. The resulting internal strains may be held in check in any particular case through powerful material and ideological pressures—for instance, by efforts to monopolize institutions of Christian education or specialized practices of theological production. But the existence of internal strains always holds the potential for change; it establishes a hook on which to anchor efforts to break up the elements under strain and reconstitute them in some other form.[6]

The second reason that established interpretations and organizations of Christian materials can never set a firm limit to theological creativity is that, no matter how successful they may be in the struggle against them, rival interpretations and organizations are rarely entirely routed; they at least remain historically recoverable pieces of the past. In short, established positions cannot set a firm limit to future theological creativity because they never exhaust the theological field. The struggle with alternatives is always either actively enjoined or threatening to erupt.

Third, established interpretations and organizations of Christian materials never have those materials fully under their control. As postmodern cultural theory puts it, signifiers tend to "float." Without active efforts to keep them fixed—efforts whose successes are always only temporary—the meanings and associations of terms tend to drift with the changing circumstances of their use and the differently situated persons employing them. Although such contexts of use may help delimit the meaning of cultural materials, no particular context has an absolute hold on them; like all meaningful materials, it is part of their very nature to be able to be abstracted from one context and inserted into another.[7]

In short, established cultural productions cannot control what others will make of them. They cannot, for example, prevent a selective attention that would dislodge the elements from their present organization and divert them to a new use, perhaps one in which cultural materials ignored by them are given a prominent place. Thus, nothing can prevent healing stories that have an insignificant place in an established interpretation and organization of Christian materials from being seized upon and closely associated with those techniques in popular practice for solving everyday problems upon which this interpretation and organization of Christian materials frowns. One can *try* to prevent this sort of diversionary attention to an established way of understanding Christian materials, but such efforts are always testimony to the fact that such processes are a constant, ineradicable threat.

What has just been said against putative constraints on theological creativity suggests something about the nature of theological creativity. It does not seem to amount to any "pure," freewheeling expression of creative drives. It seems, instead, to be the creativity of a postmodern "bricoleur"—the creativity, that is, of someone who works with an always potentially disordered heap of already existing materials, pulling them apart and putting them back together again, tinkering with their shapes, twisting them this way and that. It is a creativity expressed through the modification and extension of materials already on the ground.[8]

This sort of creativity does not necessarily bring with it, however, a plodding reformism. The effects of such tinkering can be genuinely revolutionary. Small changes, first of all, can have a major effect. What matters is how the material that is changed figures in the prior organization of Christian materials. Materials subject to cultural contest are usually those that carry a great deal of weight in the overall organization of Christian materials. Tinkering with them will tend therefore to make the whole construction wobble and threaten it with collapse. For example, in present-day arguments against women's ordination, the significance of Jesus' being a man tends to carry weight. Feminist theologians who tinker with that significance—saying, for example, that God was incarnate in a man to show how social privilege must be relinquished out of solidarity with the oppressed—aim to overthrow two thousand years of Roman Catholic practice.

Second, tinkering with what already exists can be revolutionary when it draws upon materials of the cultural field overlooked or suppressed by established interpretations and organizations of Christian materials. Tinkering in that case might mean pushing forward cultural materials from the Christian practices of minority populations—say, the complex and nuanced ideas about God's justice and grace to be found in African American spirituals. It might mean, too, helping to bring to explicit expression the cultural dimensions of such Christian practices when they have hitherto remained at their most implicit—lived but not expressed in ways that might rival established accounts. One could elicit, for example, understandings of God from the stories that Hispanic women tell about their lives. Finally, tinkering can be revolutionary when it helps to develop the cultural dimension of Christian social practices that are just beginning to emerge—again, the innovative prayers, rituals, and storytelling of women's worship services come to mind. Emerging practices might produce in this way cultural materials with the capacity to shake up established forms in surprising ways, since these established forms have not yet had the chance to incorporate and neutralize their oppositional potential.[9]

Is the Idea of Cultural Conditioning Necessarily Conservative?

If theological creativity is always shaped by culture, that fact all by itself might be viewed as an objectionable infringement on its freedom. The individual Christian's ability to follow his or her theological imagination where it leads might seem to be hemmed in by the dead weight of oppressive cultural restraints. Rather than starting and ending where it wills, one's theological creativity always seems to have to make do, initially at least, with materials supplied by the history of the cultural processes in which one participates, and the innovations it can achieve seem limited to those that will make sense given one's formation in a particular culture.

This impression of cultural restraint operates, however, with traces of the complex history of the notion of culture that, as we saw in chapter 1, run contrary to its anthropological use. Informing this objection to cultural conditioning in the name of creative freedom is an Enlightenment opposition to the rigidities and thoughtless habits of custom. Tired routines of social intercourse are to be escaped through the free flight of either reason, as Enlightenment paeans to civilization would have it, or the imagination which their Romantic heirs affirm. Forgotten, thereby, is the cultural conditioning of the reason or imagination that makes the escape.

Or, one might say that informing the objection is an understanding of culture that fuses a high culture and anthropological idea of it in much the way we saw Matthew Arnold did. What Arnold applauded, this objection fears. Underlying the objection is something like an Arnoldian view of culture as a social overlay, disciplining already formed persons. Like high culture, culture according to the Arnoldian understanding is a self-conscious effort to refine or develop the capacities and tendencies that persons already display; in common with an anthropological appreciation for social conditioning, the purpose of such a pursuit is to discipline the unruly and anarchic inclinations of a whole populace, and its achievement requires social means, a truly social discipline of institutional scope.

In contrast to this Arnoldian view, culture, according to the anthropological idea of it detailed in chapter 2, constitutes the very humanity of persons. Some culture or other therefore shapes all the desires or tendencies one has; culture does not enter the picture after the fact of them as some sort of restraining or redirecting force. Although there certainly are biologically based needs, they do not take a human shape apart from cultural conditioning. There are, then, no humanly intelligible desires or tendencies to be constrained by the fact of cultural conditioning; one's imaginative impulses, for example, are always already culturally conditioned. It is true, of course, that a particular culture might be restrictive of those impulses in the sense that it enforces uniformity of practice and expels innovators; but it makes no sense, on an anthropological understanding of culture, to be worried about the simple fact of cultural conditioning as a repressive, freedom-deadening force. One has to start somewhere and where one starts influences where one can go. As culturally conditioned beings, there is no help for that, because there is no human alternative.

Opposition to the idea of cultural conditioning in the name of individual freedom is not simply, however, an intellectual error brought on by ignorance of the complex history of the anthropological notion of culture. It is an understandable reaction to the primary mistakes made by proponents of a culturally conditioned theological imagination. Many of those proponents certainly give the strong impression that theological creativity is reined in by Christian culture; one might argue that their intent in talking about theological activity in a cultural context is just to obstruct innovation.

The idea of cultural conditioning can be pushed in this conservative direction by making a number of different moves. First, one can ignore cultural process and all but identify culture with finished fixed products—ideas on the ground, texts already written, stories already told, agreed-upon rules for conduct. Fixed forms (and even a mere selection of those in cultural circulation at that) then monopolize the domain of the social. Free-moving, inchoate, or active processes—or just-established cultural forms that are not included in the selection made—are pushed outside of culture and deemed mere personal, idiosyncratic, or private matters. This move simply encourages those who advocate innovation to assume that the processes necessary to produce it are not culturally conditioned, that they do not amount to social practices of cultural production in their own right. But they do.[10]

Abstracting cultural products from cultural process also allows one to hide the fact those products can be altered as cultural processes continue. By deflecting attention from the cultural process of which they are a part, one gives the impression that the hardening or immobility of cultural productions is just a natural fact over which human beings have no control. Nothing, however, keeps such cultural productions in place, with the shape they have, except the continuing commitment to them of the participants in the culture. As we suggested in the last chapter, once set, the rules governing a cultural practice do not become independent of the future decisions and behaviors of the players; decisions can be made in the course of the practice that change the rules. The rules themselves do not establish in advance what players can do; they merely sum up how the practice has been performed so far.

Moreover, the ossification of cultural products, which results from abstracting them from cultural process, runs directly counter to the moral tenor of an anthropological idea of culture, discussed in chapters 2 and 3. The point of that idea is to get us to see that our lives are our own construction, and that we must therefore take responsibility for the shape they take. The way we live could be different. If it is not, that is because it is held in place by the decisions made everyday about how to live it. Established meanings and rules have no power of themselves to resist alteration; the human beings committed to them are responsible for that. They are held in place through the exercise of human power—by the will of the participants, by human institutions of social control, by the sanctions of human authorities, and by penalties against deviance.

The other major move made by conservative advocates of cultural conditioning is to pass off a particular kind of cultural practice as the condition for having any viable culture at all. Cultural practices are of all different sorts; not all of them insist on uniformity of practice or resist change to the same degree. At one end of the spectrum are, say, the cultural practices of mathematics where every effort is made to spell out fully the rules of its operations and uniformity in their applications is insisted upon. Most practices, however, lack the sort of abstract simplicity of subject matter that is a prerequisite for such efforts. At the other end of the spectrum are cultural practices in which a variety of responses is the very thing called for—say, cultural practices of having fun or airing family disputes on talk shows. Insisting on agreement among the participants or rigid rules of cultural production here would mean one simply did not know what one was doing. Conservative advocates of cultural conditioning, nevertheless, try to suggest a culture is not viable at all unless it imitates practices at the mathematical end of the spectrum. The choice is either that sort of discipline or anarchy.[11]

But this is surely incorrect: the simple idea of cultural formation does not establish the shape any particular cultural practice should take—

whether it should be a static or dynamic one, whether it should allow diversity of response among its participants or try to exclude it.[12] Forcing a choice between chaos or a monotonous, severe discipline just enables those who favor conservatism in Christian practice to hide their responsibility for trying to make it a conservative practice. They can claim that the very conditions for a viable culture require a Christianity of static rules and rather rigid uniformity, when in fact practices with those features are the product of contingent choice. When something new emerges that is hard to reconcile with previous ideas about the rules for Christian practice, there is always the option of either excluding its propriety or rethinking the rules so as to include the new item more easily. The question here is not one of law and order—Will anarchy reign or not? The question instead is a political one, in the broad sense—How will Christian life be organized from now on and who decides?

In defense of the conservative position, one might admit the logical sleight of hand just mentioned but still insist that Christianity is the sort of practice in which uniformity of practice and stasis are proper goals. The rules already established should not be changed in the course of the practice, and they should be such that all parties following them in a particular situation will arrive at the same results. The viability of any cultural practice does not require those things, but the viability of the specific practice that Christianity is does.

A major problem with this suggestion is that it seems to involve a historical fabrication. Christianity simply does not seem to be a practice like that. While it is not like the practice of having fun—Christians do not simply revel in their diverse practices but tend to worry about them—Christian cultural materials and rules for their use never seem definite or internally consistent enough to make clear when diversity of response is a matter of some parties having broken the rules or contravened the meanings of those materials. General agreement on particular practices that constitute error is, moreover, far harder to come by than the account of Christian culture given by advocates of Christian conservatism would lead one to expect.

Advocates of Christian conservatism cannot, then, simply be suggesting that one renounce restless desires for innovation and sink back into established practice, satisfied with the state of Christianity as it is: the status quo is too messy and confused for that. Instead, they must themselves be recommending a change in Christian practice, a change that moves it closer to the mathematics end of the spectrum of cultural practices and farther away from the fun end.

Moving it closer to that end would mean, however, altering the conditions that promote diversity in Christian practice. For example, getting rid of the indefinite and inconsistent character of the materials around which Christian practice revolves would help. Those messy biblical books are a problem—so many versions concerning even the most crucial details of Jesus' life and death! Some consistent telling of the story would have to replace the established biblical canon if greater theological uniformity were to be achieved. Given, however, the status of these biblical books in Christian practice, one could hardly expect to garner general Christian agreement for a proposal like that. Reducing the complexity of the cultural materials to which Christians appeal would, moreover, severely inhibit the reach of a Christian way of life; Christian cultural materials would lose the sort of flexibility that enables them to address new and changing circumstances.[13]

Furthermore, the very fact of diversity in Christian judgments about proper behavior is the major culprit interfering with the proposal of a more orderly Christian practice. Given the enormous range of existing positions, it is hard to see how remaking Christian practice along more uniform lines could avoid coercion and repression. Something would have to be done to corral the dangers posed to a more conservative Christian practice by Christian practices that abide by looser norms and by the common occurrence of particular practices that this more rigid understanding of Christianity suggests are improper. Such practices might, for example, be physically repressed, demeaned, or simply ignored. At the very least, if the facts are to support a conservative Christian practice, apparent dissensus would have to be turned into the required consensus by excluding large numbers of Christians from the count. The temptation would always be to break the bonds of Christian fellowship by designating some segments of the population unruly upstarts—those segments that favor a more flexible practice or that hold particular judgments about Christian discipleship incompatible with a now-tightened account of Christian cultural materials and the rules for their use.

The Proper Mean

The questions we have just been addressing lead us back to the questions with which we started this chapter: What kind of practices are Christian ones? To what degree do they seek consensus or view diversity as a good?

Being of one mind about the nature of true discipleship might be a laudable ideal—something to expect in heaven perhaps, something that should be welcomed here and now where it can be found, even something that it makes sense to strive for when the conditions are right. One can make a strong case, however, that insistent and persistent pursuit of consensus under present conditions brings with it unacceptably high costs.

Worries like those just expressed about proposals of a conservative Christian practice return here.

Thus, in situations where there is so much disagreement to start with, it seems likely that any simple effort to enforce uniformity of belief and action will only magnify the very dangers of factionalism and division that make Christian diversity worrisome. The insistence that there is only one right way of being a Christian is even more likely to rupture Christian fellowship, to make a mockery of the unity of love and peace of Christ, than the existing diversity of practice for which it is the supposed remedy. Moreover, since there is no single universal culture, such an effort can only mean imposing a particular cultural practice on everyone.[14] Doing that hampers the catholicity of Christian practice; a Christian way of life cannot speak easily to persons of every time and place if it is simply identified with the view from one time and place. It also threatens to absolutize a particular cultural formation in preference to the God to whom it hopes to witness; it threatens to make an inviolable idol out of a fallible human practice.

Of course the search for agreement need not be an all or nothing affair—just as the acceptance of diversity need not be total. The problem is to find the proper mean, in both the manner and goal of the pursuit. Thus, while Christians have the obligation to put forward their own views about Christian discipleship for the general edification of their fellows, the awareness of their own fallibility, if nothing else, should make them wary of simply bringing others around to their own point of view. Moreover, rather than being of such urgency that it needs to be imposed, agreement should be looked for with the utmost patience; the beliefs and actions that are to make Christian practice uniform must be ones that all parties, and not just some, come to agree upon. Wary of the dangers of assuming consensus where it does not really exist and knowing that the future can always test its adequacy, one must simply wait, without drawing precipitous conclusions, for consensus among Christians to arise in the course of the argument that Christianity is.

The extent of the agreement one expects might be tempered, moreover, by a limited respect for the value—or, if not value, at least inevitability—of disagreement. Given the existence of cultural diversity, it makes no sense to expect people the world over to live out their Christian commitments in the same way. Differences of situation will always warrant some diversity in Christian practice. Although we have said it is very difficult to tell when it is the case, those differences may be just that—differences, without amounting to any fundamental disagreement in what Christianity stands for. One should not seek, then, a uniformity of Christian action and affirmation across the board. Perhaps mutual recognition is the more reasonable expectation where simple agreement in affirmation and action cannot be had. Continuing to say and do the different things that are made appropriate by differences in their situations, the various parties might nevertheless come to see in one another a concern for the same beliefs and values. In the same way, people who come to know each others' languages without being able to speak them might recognize that they are in agreement in the course of a conversation in which they never speak anything but their own.[15] If what we have said in previous chapters is on the mark, however, this is still too sanguine an expectation where differences among Christian practices remain. Christians may all be revolving around much the same materials— say, a simple rule of faith to be found in the Apostle's Creed. But if they always affirm it only under very different, often opposed, formulations (since no one holds the worldview or precise theology of bygone times that inform that creed), one would be hard pressed to say they are of a common mind about it. The common affirmation of a verbally identical formula provides no evidence in that case of common understanding.[16]

Common formulations of the proper way to fill out the meaning of such cultural materials are unlikely to ensue, since such formulations would require the same conceptual framework and philosophical and theological worldviews among all parties.[17] Future agreements are more likely, then, to go backward than forward—that is, they are likely to concern, not refinements, but the even more basic (and vaguer) claims that such cultural materials presumed without bothering to state—for instance, there is a God (of some sort or other), Jesus is of crucial significance (in some unspecified sense) for knowledge of God and for the proper orientation of human life in light of God's existence.[18] Moreover, we have said that if further agreement on the interpretation and application of Christian materials is reached in the course of argument, that agreement will itself continue to allow for a range of conflicting interpretations and applications: the shared understanding will rule some things out without specifying a particular shape to Christian beliefs and actions that conform to it. Rather than aiming to establish positively what all Christians should say and do by restricting such room for maneuver, Christians should be content in their search for consensus with the most that progress in Christian argument would seem to accomplish on that front: negatively, the ruling out of bounds of certain judgments about the meaning of Christian discipleship whose erroneous character has becomes a matter of uncontroversial recognition, while, positively, simply setting the direction for further controversy to move in.

In a similar effort to find a mean, disagreements might be permitted but kept within bounds so that the result is neither chaos nor sectarian conflict. There cannot, of course, be disagreement about everything. In order to be viable, every practice must restrict the reign of diversity, for example, by ruling some things out of bounds; otherwise it would not be a practice at all, but a completely amorphous mush. Agreed-upon boundaries of Christian practice can and do, however (as I argued in chapter 5), shift to meet situational needs. While at any particular point there must be some agreement about them, that agreement should not, then, keep argument over where they should be drawn from arising. This is what I have been arguing all Christian agreements are like: they are agreements about how to have an argument, an argument that can, at any particular point, turn back against what was initially agreed upon, in an effort to rework it.

Efforts to contain disagreement by deeming some things out of bounds should, moreover, be made very cautiously, especially where proposals about Christian discipleship just coming onto the scene are at issue. Unless the proposal is very much like one whose exclusion has passed the test of time without great controversy (and therefore is really not very new), the judgment of a new practice's impropriety should be less like an anathema that pushes the perpetrator out of the community of Christian argument and more like a strong warning to reconsider one's judgments in light of the objections of one's fellow Christians.[19] Good judgment concerning a new practice's propriety always requires, moreover, a nuanced appreciation for the sort of alterations it makes to the cultural materials it borrows in a particular time and place, and an equally nuanced appreciation for how that practice looks next to the Christian practices that have preceded it or ones that compete with it in similar circumstances. To some extent, then, Christians in the particular situation out of which it arises are the best judges of it—not their fellow Christians at a distance.

Conflict is best contained not by trying to ignore it or smooth things over. Instead, its existence must be honestly recognized if its possibly harmful effects on Christian fellowship are to be averted. Sectarian divisions (for example) are prevented not by pretending that conflicts among Christians do not exist or by ruling them out of bounds by sheer fiat—by saying, for instance, that genuine conflict among Christians is only ever due to poor socialization or corrupting outside influences. Sectarian division is prevented by the way conflict is handled, by a fellowship that can be sustained despite controversy—a fellowship of mutual concern and admonition, based on the recognition that Christianity is just the sort of thing that prompts a controversy with no clear pointers on how to settle it.

One should not try to contain diversity by getting rid of it because diversity involves certain positive goods. Human judgment is fallible and therefore the chance for correction by others who disagree with one is a valuable thing. True discipleship is more likely to come out of a wrangling with others about its nature than it is to spring simply from one's own head and heart fully realized. Diversity is a salutary reminder, moreover, that Christians cannot control the movements of the God they hope to serve.[20] It helps them remain open to the Word by keeping them from taking their own view of things for granted. Just as a postmodern understanding of culture makes internal divisions in a culture as much a spur to self-criticism as the knowledge of different cultures, so here the recognition that Christian discipleship is an essentially contested matter leads Christians away from complacency in their respective judgments. The recognition of God's free and uncontrollable Word, which respect for Christian diversity spreads, desocializes Christians, so to speak; it breaks the habit of the normal, and thereby frees them for renewed attention to the Word.

If the point of Christian argument about the nature of true discipleship is not agreement or uniformity, what is it then? Are there other goods, besides consensus, that might be sought?[21] Among such goods might be included the mutual understanding that remains even when uniformity of affirmation and action cannot be achieved. In the course of argument, one simply begins to understand better the nature of one's disagreements. Continuing the argument is all by itself, moreover, a way of reaffirming a shared commitment to the importance of the materials over which one is arguing; commitment to them is deepened as the argument continues even if there is never any final agreement about their import. Finally, a reachable goal of great value is simply the strengthening of the bonds of Christian fellowship. Through the ongoing practice of choosing dialogue over monologue, there emerges a strengthening of the commitment to search for the meaning of Christian discipleship together, with both seriousness about the stakes and an eagerness to make something good come of conflict.

Notes

Preface

1. Alfred A. Kroeber and Klyde Kluckhohn, *Culture: A Critical Review of Concepts and Definitions* (Cambridge, Mass.: Papers of the Peabody Museum of American Archaeology and Ethnology, Harvard University, 1952), 3.

2. See, for example, Robert Darnton, *The Great Cat Massacre* (New York: Basic Books, 1984); and Natalie Z. Davis, *Society and Culture in Early Modern France* (Stanford: Stanford University Press, 1975).

3. See Robert Berkhofer, "Clio and the Culture Concept: Some Impressions of a Changing Relationship in American Historiography," in *The Idea of Culture in the Social Sciences*, ed. Louis Schneider and Charles Bonjean (Cambridge: Cambridge University Press, 1973), 8.

4. Stephen Greenblatt, *Renaissance Self-Fashioning: From More to Shakespeare* (Chicago: University of Chicago Press, 1980), 4, 5.

5. See Charles Sabel, *Work and Politics* (New York: Cambridge University Press, 1982); and Michael Taussig, *The Devil and Commodity Fetishism in South America* (Chapel Hill: University of North Carolina Press, 1980).

6. See, for example, Daniel Bell, *The Cultural Contradictions of Capitalism* (New York: Basic Books, 1976); Christopher Lasch, *The Culture of Narcissism* (New York: W.W. Norton, 1979); and for the Frankfurt School, Max Horkheimer and Theodor Adorno, *Dialectic of Enlightenment* (New York: Herder and Herder, 1972).

7. See, for example, Stuart Hall, "Cultural Studies: Two Paradigms," *Media, Culture, and Society* 2 (1980): 57–82; and John Thompson, *Ideology and Modern Culture* (Stanford: Stanford University Press, 1990).

8. Margaret Mead, *Patterns of Culture* (New York: Houghton Mifflin, 1934), xi.

1. The History of "Culture"

1. Raymond Williams, *Keywords* (Oxford: Oxford University Press, 1976), 76.

2. Zygmunt Bauman, *Legislators and Interpreters* (Oxford: Polity Press, 1987), 81–83.

3. Cicero, *Tusculan Disputations*, Book 2, 5 (13), cited by W. H. Bruford, *Culture and Society in Classical Weimar 1775–1806* (Cambridge: Cambridge University Press, 1962), 432.

4. See, for example, M. H. Abrams, *Natural Supernaturalism: Tradition and Revolution in Romantic Literature* (New York: W.W. Norton, 1971).

5. C. M. Wieland, "Koxkox und Kikequetzel" (1770), cited by Bruford, *Culture and Society*, 38.

6. See Robert Muchembled, *Popular Culture and Elite Culture in France 1400–1750* (Baton Rouge: Louisiana State University Press, 1985); Bauman, *Legislators*, chaps. 4–5; and Jacques Revel, "Forms of Expertise: Intellectuals and 'Popular' Culture in France (1650–1800)," in *Understanding Popular Culture*, ed. Stephen Kaplan (Berlin, New York, and Amsterdam: Mouton Publishers, 1984), 255–73.

7. See Raymond Williams, *Marxism and Literature* (Oxford: Oxford University Press, 1977), 11–14.

8. This phrase is used to describe the quasi-ethnology of English missionaries in George Stocking, *Victorian Anthropology* (New York: Free Press, 1987), 104–5.

9. See Revel, "Forms of Expertise," 265–70.

10. Stocking, *Victorian Anthropology*, 19.

11. Bruford, *Culture and Society*, 4; Alfred A. Kroeber and Klyde Kluckhohn, *Culture: A Critical Review of Concepts and Definitions* (Cambridge, Mass.: Papers of the Peabody Museum of American Archaeology and Ethnology, Harvard University, 1952), 13.

12. See Norbert Elias, *The Civilizing Process*, vol. 1: *The History of Manners*, trans. Edmund Jephcott (Oxford: Basil Blackwell, 1978), Part One.

13. Ibid., 5–6.

14. See Herder, *Reflections on the Philosophy of the History of Mankind*, abridged with introduction by Frank E. Manuel (Chicago: University of Chicago Press, 1968).

15. Ibid., 98, 78, 7. The last quotation from *Reflections*, Book 9 (in *Werke*, ed. Suphan, vol. 13) is cited by Bruford, *Culture and Society*, 207 (italics mine).

16. *Reflections*, 59; and *Reflections*, Book 9 (*Werke*, vol. 13) cited by Bruford, *Culture and Society*, 205.

17. *Reflections*, 44, 116, 97.

18. See Raymond Williams, *Culture and Society 1780–1950* (New York: Columbia University Press, 1958).

19. Matthew Arnold, *Culture and Anarchy*, ed. with introduction by J. Dover Wilson (Cambridge: Cambridge University Press, 1932), 70, 48, 48–49.

20. Ibid., 163.

21. See Fritz Ringer, *Decline of the German Mandarins* (Cambridge, Mass.: Harvard University Press, 1969), esp., 123–27.

22. Arnold, *Culture and Anarchy*, 204 (italics mine).

23. First quotation: Robert Owen, *Observations on the Effect of the Manufacturing System* (London, 1815), 5, cited by Williams, *Culture and Society, 1780–1950*, 27. Second quotation: Robert Owen, *The Life of Robert Owen by Himself* (repr. London, 1920), 122–23, cited by Williams, *Culture and Society, 1780–1950*, 28.

24. See John Stuart Mill on Coleridge in *Mill on Bentham and Coleridge*, introduction by F. R. Leavis (Cambridge: Cambridge University Press, 1980), 132.

25. Arnold, *Culture and Anarchy*, 52.

26. See Christopher Herbert, *Culture and Anomie* (Chicago: University of Chicago Press, 1991), 35–36.

27. George Stocking, *Race, Culture and Evolution* (Chicago: University of Chicago Press, 1987), 87.

28. Tyler, cited without reference in ibid., 81.

29. Stocking, *Victorian Anthropology*, 192–93.

30. Ibid., 174.

31. Stocking, *Race, Culture and Evolution*, 205, 210–11.

32. Ibid., 210; see also J. G. Merquior, *The Veil and the Mask: Essays on Culture and Ideology* (London: Routledge and Kegan Paul, 1979), 40–45.

33. Stocking, *Race, Culture and Evolution*, 210, citing Boas, "Limitations of the Comparative Method of Anthropology," *Science* 4 (1896): 905–8 (no exact page reference given).

34. Stocking, *Race, Culture and Evolution*, 203.

35. Ibid., 229.

2. The Modern Meaning of Culture

1. For overviews of the major schools, see George Stocking, "Ideas and Institutions in American Anthropology: Toward a History of the Interwar Years," in *Selected Papers from the "American Anthropologist" 1921–45*, ed. George Stocking (Washington, D.C.: American Anthropological Association, 1976), 1–53; and Sherry Ortner, "Theory in Anthropology since the Sixties," *Comparative Studies in Society and History* 26 (1984): 127–32 (on symbolic anthropology), and 135–38 (on structuralism). For classics of the various schools, see Ruth Benedict (a leading student of Boas), *Patterns of Culture* (New York: Houghton Mifflin, 1934); Bronislav Malinowski, *Myth, Science and Religion, and Other Essays* (New York: Doubleday Anchor, 1954) (functionalism); Claude Lévi-Strauss, *Structural Anthropology* , trans. Claire Jacobson and Brooke Grundfest Schoepf (New York: Basic Books, 1963) (structuralism); Clifford Geertz, *The Interpretation of Cultures* (New York: Basic Books, 1973), and Victor Turner, *The Forest of Symbols* (Ithaca, N.Y.: Cornell University Press, 1967) (symbolic or interpretive anthropology).

2. See George Stocking, *Victorian Anthropology* (New York: Free Press, 1987), 289; and Peter Burke, *History and Social Theory* (Ithaca, N.Y.: Cornell University Press, 1992), 119.

3. Geertz, *Interpretation of Cultures*, 45–46.

4. John Bennett and Melvin Tumin, *Social Life* (New York: Alfred A. Knopf, 1948), 209, cited in Alfred L. Kroeber and Klyde Kluckhohn, *Culture: A Critical Review of Concepts and Definitions* (Cambridge, Mass.: Papers of the Peabody Museum of American Archaeology and Ethnology, Harvard University, 1952), 51.

5. Ibid.

6. Melvin Herskovitz, *Man and His Works* (New York: Alfred A. Knopf, 1948), 625, cited by Kroeber and Kluckhohn, *Culture*, 44.

7. Robert Redfield, *The Folk Culture of the Yucatan* (Chicago: University of Chicago Press, 1941), 133, cited in Kroeber and Kluckhohn, *Culture*, 61 n.16.

8. Edward Reuter, *Race and Culture*, ed. R. E. Park (New York: McGraw-Hill, 1939), 191, cited in Kroeber and Kluckhohn, *Culture*, 64.

9. L. J. Carr, "Situational Psychology," *American Journal of Sociology* 51 (1945): 137, cited in Kroeber and Kluckhohn, *Culture*, 65.

10. Margaret Mead, *Cooperation and Competition among Primitive Peoples* (New York: McGraw-Hill, 1937), 17, cited in Kroeber and Kluckhohn, *Culture*, 47.

11. John Dollard and Allison Davis, *Children of Bondage* (Washington, D.C.: American Council on Education, 1940), 4, cited by Kroeber and Kluckhohn, *Culture*, 47. The phrase "passive porters" is from John Dollard, "Culture, Society, Impulse, and Socialization," *American Journal of Sociology* 45 (1939): 50–63, cited, without specific page reference, by Kroeber and Kluckhohn, *Culture*, 49.

12. Benedict, *Patterns of Culture*, 46–47.

13. Ibid., 52.

14. Franz Boas, "The Aims of Anthropological Research," in *Race, Language and Culture* (Chicago: University of Chicago Press, 1982), 255.

15. See Kroeber and Kluckhohn, *Culture*, 152; and J. G. Melquior, *The Veil and the Mask: Essays on Culture and Ideology* (London: Routledge and Kegan Paul, 1979), 48–49.

16. See Kroeber and Kluckhohn, *Culture*, 31–38.

17. See Geertz, *Interpretation of Cultures*, 14, 44.

18. Benedict, *Patterns of Culture*, 16.

19. Edward Evans-Pritchard, *Social Anthropology and Other Essays* (New York: Free Press, 1962), 19.

20. Ibid., 99.

21. Geertz, *Interpretation of Cultures*, 130.

22. See Benedict, *Patterns of Culture*, 46.

23. See Claude Lévi-Strauss, "The Structural Study of Myth," in *Structural Anthropology*, 206–31.

24. See Malinowski, *Myth, Science and Religion*, 47–53.

25. Evans-Pritchard, *Social Anthropology*, 98, 99.

26. Geertz, *Interpretation of Cultures*, 152, 153.

27. See Kroeber and Kluckhohn, *Culture*, 160–61; this whole paragraph is a paraphrase.

28. See Geertz, *Interpretation of Cultures*, 142–69.

29. Benedict, *Patterns of Culture*, 10.

3. Criticism and Reconstruction

1. See Emiko Ohnuki, "Introduction: The Historicization of Anthropology," in *Culture through Time*, ed. Emiko Ohnuki (Stanford: Stanford University Press, 1990), 1–20.

2. See George Marcus and Michael Fischer, *Anthropology as Cultural Critique* (Chicago: University of Chicago Press, 1986), chap. 4.

3. Ibid., 98.

4. See James Clifford, *The Predicament of Culture* (Cambridge, Mass.: Harvard University Press, 1988), 201–2; Bernard McGrane, *Beyond Anthropology: Society and the Other* (New York: Columbia University Press, 1989), 94, 111; and also Johannes Fabian, *Time and the Other* (New York: Columbia University Press, 1983).

5. See Margaret Hogden, *Early Anthropology in the Sixteenth and Seventeenth Centuries* (Philadelphia: University of Pennsylvania Press, 1964), 332.

6. See Roy Wagner, *The Invention of Culture* (Chicago: University of Chicago Press, 1981), 22–23; and Clifford, *Predicament of Culture*, 217.

7. For this sort of criticism of Geertz, see Clifford, *Predicament of Culture*, 39; and John Thompson, *Ideology and Modern Culture* (Stanford: Stanford University Press, 1990), 134–35.

8. See Pierre Bourdieu, *Outline of a Theory of Practice* (Cambridge: Cambridge University Press, 1977), 37–38, 105–10.

9. See Edward Evans-Pritchard, *Oracles and Magic among the Azande*, abridged with introduction by Eva Gillies (Oxford: Clarendon Press, 1976), 221.

10. Christopher Herbert, *Culture and Anomie* (Chicago: University of Chicago Press, 1991), 5–6.

11. Ruth Benedict, *Patterns of Culture* (New York: Houghton Mifflin, 1934), 47.

12. See, for this whole paragraph, Nicholas Thomas, *Colonialism's Culture: Anthropology, Travel and Government* (Princeton: Princeton University Press, 1994), 79–98.

13. Clifford Geertz, *The Interpretation of Cultures* (New York: Basic Books, 1973), 408.

14. See Dan Sperber, *On Anthropological Knowledge: Three Essays* (Cambridge: Cambridge University Press, 1985), 48.

15. Bourdieu, *Outline of a Theory of Practice*, 18–21.

16. See Anthony Easthope, *Literary into Cultural Studies* (London and New York: Routledge, 1991), 22.

17. Ibid., 22–23, 34–35.

18. Ibid., 141.

19. See Edmund Leach, *Social Anthropology* (Oxford: Oxford University Press, 1982), 142.

20. Clifford, *Predicament of Culture*, 39–40.

21. Bourdieu, *Outline of a Theory of Practice*, 37.

22. See Clifford, *Predicament of Culture*, 46; and idem, "Introduction: Partial Truths," in *Writing Culture*, ed. James Clifford and George Marcus (Berkeley: University of California Press, 1986), 15, showing the influence of Mikhail Bakhtin.

23. See A. P. Cohen, *The Symbolic Construction of Community* (London and New York: Tavistock Publications, 1985), 14–21.

24. See Chris Weedon, *Feminist Practice and Poststructuralist Theory* (Oxford: Basil Blackwell, 1987), chap. 2.

25. See Sperber, *On Anthropological Knowledge*, 47–60, for the range of possibilities.

26. See Daniel Cottom, *Text and Culture* (Minneapolis: University of Minnesota Press, 1989), 78 *et passim*.

27. Roger Keesing, "Anthropology as Interpretive Quest," *Current Anthropology* 28, no. 2 (1987): 165.

28. Jonathan Friedman, "Retorts and Invective," *Antropologiska Studier* 35–36 (1984), cited without page reference in ibid., 169.

29. Renato Rosaldo, *Culture and Truth* (Boston: Beacon, 1989), 94–95.

30. Bourdieu, *Outline of a Theory of Practice*, 96.

31. See, for example, Ernesto Laclau and Chantal Mouffe, *Hegemony and Socialist Strategy* (London: Verso, 1985).

32. Cottom, *Text and Culture*, 36.

33. Bourdieu, *Outline of a Theory of Practice*, 29; J. G. Melquior, *The Veil and the Mask: Essays on Culture and Ideology* (London: Routledge and Kegan Paul, 1979), 64.

34. Bourdieu, *Outline of a Theory of Practice*, 17, following Max Weber.

35. Merquior, *Veil and the Mask*, 64.

36. Thompson, *Ideology and Modern Culture*, 8.

37. Ibid., 91–92.

38. See Alain Touraine, *Return of the Actor*, trans. Myrna Godzich (Minneapolis: University of Minnesota Press, 1988), 41 *et passim*.

39. See Raymond Williams, *Marxism and Literature* (Oxford: Oxford University Press, 1977), 37, 39, 75–82, 99, 112–14; and Merquior, *Veil and the Mask*, 70–73.

40. Williams, *Marxism and Literature*, 33–40.

41. Ibid., 14–15.

42. See Margaret Archer, *Culture and Agency* (Cambridge: Cambridge University Press, 1988), 186, 135 *et passim*.

43. Michel De Certeau, *The Practice of Everyday Life* (Berkeley: University of California Press, 1984), 166.

44. See Archer, *Culture and Agency*, 82, 87, 89. I am modifying Archer's account to avoid her "Three Worlds" analysis of cultural systems; she fails, in my judgment, to see the degree to which meaning is dependent on social use.

45. Bourdieu, *Outline of a Theory of Practice*, 8.

46. Rosaldo, *Culture and Truth*, 125.

47. See Sabina Lovibond, *Reason and Imagination in Ethics* (Minneapolis: University of Minnesota Press, 1983), 66, 179, 195.

48. Cottom, *Text and Culture*, 18–19, 59, 83.

49. See Eric Wolf, *Europe and the People without History* (Berkeley: University of California Press, 1982), 387; Ernest Gellner, *Nations and Nationalism* (Ithaca, N.Y.: Cornell University Press, 1983); Benedict Anderson, *Imagined Communities* (London and New York: Verso, 1983); and E. J. Hobsbawm, *Nations and Nationalism since 1780* (Cambridge: Cambridge University Press, 1990).

50. Gellner, *Nations and Nationalism*, chap. 2.

51. Clifford Geertz, "The Uses of Diversity," *Michigan Quarterly Review* 25, no. 1(Winter 1986): 115.

52. See Stuart Hall, "Some Paradigms in Cultural Studies," *Estratto da Anali-Anglistica* 3 (1978): 30, citing, without page reference, Nicos Poulantzas, *Classes in Contemporary Capitalism* (London: NLB, 1975).

53. See Laclau and Mouffe, *Hegemony and Social Strategy*.

54. See Roger Chartier, "Texts, Printing, Reading," in *The New Cultural History*, ed. Lynn Hunt (Berkeley: University of California Press, 1989), 171.

55. See Wolf, *Europe and the People without History*, Introduction and Conclusion.

56. See Cottom, *Text and Culture*, 60; and Tzvetan Todorov, *On Human Diversity* (Cambridge, Mass.: Harvard University Press, 1993), 331.

57. See Herbert, *Culture and Anomie*, 21, quoting Robert Lowrie.

58. See Adam Kuper, *Anthropologists and Anthropology: The British School 1922–1972* (London: Allan Lane, 1973), 146–47.

59. Wolf, *Europe and the People without History*, 3, 4, 7.

60. McGrane, *Beyond Anthropology*, 120–29.

61. Geertz, "The Uses of Diversity," 108–14, attacking Richard Rorty.

62. Cottom, *Text and Culture*, 67–69.

63. McGrane, *Beyond Anthropology*, 119–22.

64. Todorov, *On Human Diversity*, 340–41; Marcus and Fischer, *Anthropology as Cultural Critique*, 157–60.

65. Clifford, *Predicament of Culture*, 192 n.3.

66. See Cottom, *Text and Culture*, 37–38.

67. See Clifford, *Predicament of Culture*, 258, on the application to anthropology of Edward Said's account of Orientalism.

68. See Stuart Hall, "Toad in the Garden: Thatcherism among the Theorists," in *Marxism and the Interpretation of Culture*, ed. Cary Nelson and Lawrence Grossberg (Urbana and Chicago: University of Illinois Press, 1988), 52–53; and Laclau and Mouffe, *Hegemony and Social Strategy*, 112. They (and I) are describing what Antonio Gramsci means by hegemony.

69. See Hall, "Toad in the Garden," 52–53; Williams, *Marxism and Literature*, 112–14.

70. See Hall, "Toad in the Garden," 52–53; idem, "Some Paradigms," 38–39, 46–47; and idem, "Notes on Deconstructing the 'Popular,'" in *People's History and Socialist Theory*, ed. Raphael Samuel (London: Routledge and Kegan Paul, 1981), 232–33.

71. See Catherine Bell, *Ritual Theory, Ritual Practice* (Oxford and New York: Oxford University Press, 1992), 193, 200–1, discussing Michel Foucault.

72. Ibid., 191.

73. For this idea of common stakes, see Touraine, *Return of the Actor*, 27, 54–55.

74. Cohen, *Symbolic Construction of Community*, 15–21.

75. See Dick Hebdige, *Subculture: The Meaning of Style* (London and New York: Routledge, 1979); and Chartier, "Texts, Printing, Reading."

76. See Clifford, *Predicament of Culture*, 10–11, 14–15, 58–59, 178–80, 274–75, 302–6, 342–44; see also Edward Said, *Culture and Imperialism* (New York: Alfred A. Knopf, 1993).

77. See Hebdige, *Subculture*; and De Certeau, *Practice of Everyday Life*, 100–1 *et passim*.

78. See Said, *Culture and Imperialism*, 239–61, on the "voyage in"; and Clifford, *Predicament of Culture*, 175–81, on Aimé Césaire.

79. See Marcus and Fischer, *Anthropology as Cultural Critique*, 132–40, 157–60; and Cottom, *Text and Culture*, 89, 100–1.

4. The Nature and Tasks of Theology

1. H. Richard Niebuhr, *Christ and Culture* (New York: Harper Colophon, 1951).

2. See, for example, Ernst Troeltsch, "The Place of Christianity among the World Religions," in *Attitudes toward Other Religions*, ed. Owen Thomas (New York: Harper & Row, 1969), 73–91.

3. See Friedrich Schleiermacher, *On Religion*, trans. John Oman (New York: Harper & Row, 1958), speech five; H. Richard Niebuhr, *The Meaning of Revelation* (New York: Macmillan, 1941), 5–16; Karl Rahner, "Reflections on Methodology in Theology," in *Theological Investigations*, vol. 11, trans. David Bourke (New York: Seabury, 1974), 77–84; and George Lindbeck, *The Nature of Doctrine* (Philadephia: Westminster Press, 1984). Schleiermacher, of course, antedates modern anthropology but works with the direct German precursors of the idea in aesthetic and organic holism; see above, chap. 1.

4. Neo-orthodox theologians are followers of Karl Barth; Protestant liberals are often followers of Friedrich Schleiermacher. See Gordon Kaufman, *In Face of Mystery* (Cambridge, Mass.: Harvard University Press, 1993).

5. See David Tracy, *Blessed Rage for Order* (New York: Seabury, 1978).

6. See Gustavo Gutiérrez, *A Theology of Liberation* (Maryknoll, N.Y.: Orbis, 1973).

7. The idea of Christian theology as a culture-specific activity is a view closely associated on the contemporary theological scene with the postliberal followers of George Lindbeck and Hans Frei; it is a defining moment of the postliberal stance. As my discussion in this chapter of theology as a feature of Christian communal practices suggests, I do not, however, think such a view is limited to them. Schleiermacher, the father of liberal Protestant opponents of postliberals, can, for instance, be read in the same terms (as Frei himself argued, perhaps too timidly, in his *Types of Christian Theology* [New Haven: Yale University Press, 1992], 34–38). The postliberal version of the position will, moreover, come in for concerted criticisms in this chapter and the next.

8. See Gordon Kaufman, *In Face of Mystery* , esp. chaps. 1–5.

9. See, for the first, Paul Tillich, *Systematic Theology*, vol. 1 (Chicago: University of Chicago Press, 1951); for the second, Karl Rahner, *Foundations of the Christian Faith* (New York: Seabury Press, 1978); and for the third, David Tracy, *Blessed Rage for Order*.

10. See Kaufman, *In Face of Mystery*, 19–31, for this suggestion about "confessional" or "tradition-focused" ways of doing theology.

11. Ibid., 26.

12. Ibid., 40.

13. See Rahner, *Foundations*, 10–11. For more on an interpretation of Rahner like this, see Nicholas Healy, "Indirect Methods in Theology: Rahner as an Ad-hoc Apologist," *The Thomist* 56, no. 4 (October 1992): 613–33. Saying that theology generates a philosophy does not mean that Christians are the only ones able to propose such a philosophy or to find it plausible.

14. In this way my recommendations are similar to those made by liberation and feminist theologies. See, for example, Gustavo Gutiérrez, *A Theology of Liberation*; and Ada María Isasi-Díaz, *En la Lucha* (Minneapolis: Fortress Press, 1993).

15. See Friedrich Schleiermacher, *The Christian Faith*, ed. and trans. H. R. MacIntosh and J. S. Stewart (Philadelphia: Fortress Press, 1976), 81–85.

16. Ibid., 77–78, 81–93.

17. Karl Barth, *Church Dogmatics*, I/1, trans. G. T. Thomson (Edinburgh: T&T Clark, 1936), 1.

18. See, for example, Gutiérrez, *A Theology of Liberation*.

19. See, for example, Isasi-Díaz, *En la Lucha*.

20. See, for example, Ronald Thiemann, *Revelation and Theology* (Notre Dame: University of Notre Dame Press, 1985), 72–73.

21. See Hans Frei, *Types of Christian Theology*, 88.

22. See, for example, ibid., 2, 20–21, 124; the ideas in this book of his represent in many ways the founding ideas of postliberalism.

23. Ibid.

24. Compare Schleiermacher, *Christian Faith*, 120–21.

25. See Henry Staten, *Wittgenstein and Derrida* (Lincoln and London: University of Nebraska Press, 1984), 101–2.

26. Here I am diverging from some feminist theologians, such as Isasi-Díaz in *En la Lucha*.

27. See Pierre Bourdieu, *In Other Words: Essays towards a Reflexive Sociology* (Stanford: Stanford University Press, 1990), 100.

28. Ibid., 48, 87–88, 110–11.

29. For more on the ideas to follow, see Kathryn Tanner, "Theology and Popular Culture," in *Changing Conversations*, ed. Sheila Davaney and Dwight Hopkins (London and New York: Routledge, 1997), 101–20.

30. The same sort of blurring between everyday and theoretical practice occurs in postmodern anthropology: the operations of everyday practice become the model for, and not just the object of, theoretical inquiry; the latter becomes a kind of continuation of the former, despite the differences between the two. Recommendations for changes in the style of anthropological reportage follow. See Renato Rosaldo, *Culture and Truth* (Boston: Beacon Press, 1989), part two; Pierre Bourdieu, *Outline of a Theory of Practice* (Cambridge: Cambridge University Press, 1977); and Michel De Certeau, *The Practice of Everyday Life* (Berkeley: University of California Press, 1984), 77–78, 80–81.

31. *Institutes of the Christian Religion*, trans. Ford Lewis Battles, ed. John T. McNeil (Philadelphia: Westminster Press, 1960), 2 vols.

32. See Basil Mitchell, *The Justification of Religious Belief* (New York: Seabury, 1973), 45–51. The processes I describe are also typical of legal and historical reasoning when they are themselves understood to involve something more like aesthetic judgment than demonstrative proof. See ibid., 51–57.

5. Christian Culture and Society

1. The reader should be aware that the typology of positions I offer is, like all typologies, a simplification for practical purposes. It does not necessarily capture the complexities of individual theologians' work nor provide a general overview of the present theological scene.

2. My own position has therefore a very complex relation to the other proposals. It is not simply the construct of postmodern cultural trends, but develops out of the proposals criticized.

3. John Milbank, *Theology and Social Theory* (Oxford: Basil Blackwell, 1990).

4. For postmodern criticisms of "society," see Michael Mann, *The Sources of Social Power*, vol. 1 (Cambridge: Cambridge University Press, 1986), 1–14; and Ulf Hannerz, *Cultural Complexity* (New York: Columbia University Press, 1992), 39, 51, 71–74.

5. See Frederick Barth's Introduction in *Ethnic Groups and Boundaries*, ed. Frederick Barth (Boston: Little, Brown, 1969), 9–38.

6. See David-Hillel Ruben, "Social Wholes and Parts," *Mind* 92 (1983): 219–38.

7. See Milbank, *Theology and Social Theory*, 208, 392, 416; and idem, "The End of Dialogue," in *Christian Uniqueness Reconsidered*, ed. Gavin D'Costa (Maryknoll, N.Y.: Orbis, 1990): 179–80.

8. See, for example, Stuart Hall, "Gramsci's Relevance for the Study of Race and Ethnicity," *Journal of Communication Inquiry* 10, no. 2 (Winter 1985): 5–27.

9. Milbank strongly suggests that denying Christianity its own society necessarily means "spiritualizing" it: "Members of the Church . . . on the whole remained in their existing political communities and must therefore have regarded the Church as simply a spiritual association of souls" (*Theology and Social Theory*, 399); see also his treatment of Clodovis Boff in the same book, 245–52.

10. See his "The Place of Christianity Among the World Religions," in *Attitudes toward Other Religions*, ed. Owen Thomas (New York: Harper & Row, 1969), 79–91.

11. The *locus classicus* for the caricature that postliberalism recommends a kind of Christian cultural insularity is James Gustafson, "The Sectarian Temptation: Reflections on Theology, the Church, and the University," *Catholic Theological Society Proceedings* 40 (1985): 83–94. See also David Tracy, "Lindbeck's New Program for Theology: A Reflection," *The Thomist* 49 (July 1985): 65; and Gordon E. Michalson, "The Response to Lindbeck," *Modern Theology* 4, no. 2 (January 1988): 113–14, 116.

12. The phrase "a second first language" is from Alasdair McIntyre. See *Whose Justice? Which Rationality?* (Notre Dame: University of Notre Dame Press, 1988), 370–88. Cited approvingly by George Lindbeck in "The Gospel's Uniqueness: Election and Untranslatability," *Modern Theology* (forthcoming): 8 (of typescript).

13. See Hans Frei, *Types of Christian Theology* (New Haven: Yale University Press, 1992), 4: "it is important to . . . constantly restate doctrinal statements in light of cultural and conceptual change."

14. Ibid., 81.

15. George Lindbeck, *The Nature of Doctrine* (Philadelphia: Westminster Press, 1984), 82–83.

16. Ibid., 117.

17. Ibid., 129.

18. For a good expression of this contextualist interpretation of outside influences, see Ronald Thiemann, *Revelation and Theology* (Notre Dame: University of Notre Dame Press, 1985), 74–75.

19. Lindbeck, *Nature of Doctrine*, 42, 114.

20. Frei, *Types of Christian Theology*, 45–46.

21. Ibid., 161.

22. See Lindbeck, *Nature of Doctrine*, 116, for a postliberal discussion of classics. The distinction between "render" and "disclose," which is important for other issues of biblical interpretation, makes no difference to the point I am making here.

23. For Schleiermacher's contextualism and its implications, see his *The Christian Faith*, Fortress Texts in Modern Theology, ed. and trans. H. R. MacIntosh and J. S. Stewart (Philadelphia: Fortress Press, 1976), 81–85, 119–21.

24. See J. D. Y. Peel, "Syncretism and Religious Change," *Comparative Studies in Society and History* 10, no. 2 (January 1968): 121–41; and Birgit Meyer, "Beyond Syncretism: Translation and Diabolization in the Appropriation of Protestantism in Africa," in *Syncretism/Anti-Syncretism*, ed. Charles Stewart and Rosalind Shaw (London and New York: Routledge, 1994), 45–68.

25. See David Mosse, "The Politics of Religious Syncretism: Roman Catholicism and Hindu Village Society in Tamil Nadu, India," in *Syncretism/Anti-Syncretism*, 85–107.

26. See R. A. Markus, "Paganism, Christianity, and the Latin Classics in the Fourth Century," in *Latin Literature of the Fourth Century*, ed. J. W. Binns (London and Boston: Routledge and Kegan Paul, 1974), 1–21.

27. See A. P. Cohen, *The Symbolic Construction of Community* (London and New York: Tavistock Publications, 1985).

28. See Wayne Meeks, *The Origin of Christian Morality* (New Haven: Yale University Press, 1993); idem, *The Moral World of the First Urban Christians* (Philadelphia: Westminster Press, 1986); and idem, *The First Urban Christians* (New Haven: Yale University Press, 1983).

29. See, Lindbeck, *Nature of Doctrine*, 60–62.

30. See George Devereux and Edwin Loeb, "Antagonistic Acculturation," *American Sociological Review* 8, no. 2 (April 1943): 133–47.

31. See Pierre Bourdieu, "Programme for a Sociology of Sport," *In Other Words: Essays towards a Reflexive Sociology* (Stanford: Stanford University Pres, 1990), 156–69.

32. See Rosalind O'Hanlon, "Recovering the Subject: Subaltern Studies and Histories of Resistance in Colonial South Asia," *Modern Asian Studies* 22, no. 1 (1988): 189–224.

33. See Michel De Certeau, *The Practice of Everyday Life* (Berkeley: University of California Press, 1984), xi–xvii, 21, 43.

34. See Roger Chartier, "Texts, Printing, Reading," in *The New Cultural History*, ed. Lynn Hunt (Berkeley: University of California Press, 1989), 154–75.

35. See De Certeau, *Practice of Everyday Life*, 34–35.

36. Søren Kierkegaard, *Works of Love* (New York: Harper Torchbooks, 1962), 199–200. In contrast to the position I spell out in the next few sentences, Kierkegaard seems to think almost any practice is suitable for a transferred Christian use.

37. This point is made by Schleiermacher in *The Christian Faith*, 45–47.

38. Karl Barth, *Church Dogmatics*, I/2, ed. G. W. Bromiley and T. F. Torrance (Edinburgh: T&T Clark, 1956), 729.

39. For the notion of hybridity, see James Clifford, *The Predicament of Culture* (Cambridge, Mass.: Harvard University Press, 1988); and Edward Said, *Culture and Imperialism* (New York: Alfred A. Knopf, 1993).

40. For this account of individuality in terms of the same elements differently organized insofar as one of them becomes the distinctive angle or fundamental viewpoint on the whole, see Schleiermacher, *On Religion*, trans. John Oman (New York: Harper & Row, 1958), speech five.

41. See William Placher, *Unapologetic Theology* (Louisville: Westminster/John Knox, 1989), 167, for differences among postliberals on this score. Even, however, for postliberals who make it a required component of theology (for instance, Placher himself, *Unapologetic Theology*, chap. 7; and William Werpehowski, "Ad Hoc Apologetics," *The Journal of Religion* 66, no. 3 [July 1986]: 282–301), apologetics is still a secondary theological task, one subordinate to the primary task of explicating the logic of Christian belief itself.

42. For the concept of "double-voiced" language, see Mikhail Bakhtin, *Problems of Dostoevsky's Poetics*, ed. and trans. Caryl Emerson (Minneapolis: University of Minnesota Press, 1984).

43. More on this account of theological arguments can be found in my unpublished manuscript, "Two Types of Apologetics."

44. For this interpretation of Thomistic proofs, see Victor Preller, *The Divine Science and the Science of God* (Princeton: Princeton University Press, 1967), 126–31; and John E. Smith, *The Experience of God* (New Haven: Yale University Press, 1968), chap. 5.

45. Blaise Pascal, *Pensées*, trans. with introduction by A. J. Krailsheimer (London: Penguin Books, 1966).

46. De Certeau, *Practice of Everyday Life*, 39.

47. See Nicholas Thomas, *Colonialism's Culture: Anthropology, Travel and Government* (Princeton: Princeton University Press, 1994), 72–77, 128–29.

48. See Stuart Hall, "What Is This 'Black' in Black Popular Culture?" in *Black Popular Culture*, ed. Gina Dent (Seattle: Bay Press, 1992), 21–33, discussing processes of identification around race, gender, sexuality, and class differences: "We are always in negotiation, not with a single set of oppositions that place us always in the same relation to others, but with a series of different positionalities" (31).

49. See Jan Pranger, *Tradition and Enculturation* (Ph.D. diss., University of Groningen, 1997); and James Cone, *The God of the Oppressed* (New York: Seabury Press, 1975), 91, 96.

50. See Karl Barth, *The Christian Life: Church Dogmatics* IV/4, Lecture Fragments, trans. Geoffrey W. Bromiley (Grand Rapids, Mich.: Wm. B. Eerdmans, 1981), 197–202; and C. S. Song, *Jesus in the Power of the Spirit* (Minneapolis: Fortress Press, 1994).

6. Commonalities in Christian Practice

1. See Pierre Bourdieu, *In Other Words: Essays towards a Reflexive Sociology* (Stanford: Stanford University Press), 87–88, 110–11; and Lamont Lindstrom, "Left-amap Kastom: The Political History of Tradition on Tanna, Vanuatu," *Mankind* 13,

no. 4 (August 1982): 318, discussing struggles over the definition of custom that ensue once custom becomes a marker of national identity.

2. See Nicholas Abercrombie, Stephen Hill, and Bryan S. Turner, *The Dominant Ideology Thesis* (London: Allen and Unwin, 1980).

3. See Nicholas Rescher, *Pluralism: Against the Demand for Consensus* (Oxford: Clarendon Press, 1993), 137–55.

4. This is a major thesis of A. P. Cohen, *The Symbolic Construction of Community* (London and New York: Tavistock Publications, 1985).

5. See James Fernandez, "Symbolic Consensus in a Fang Reformative Cult," *American Anthropologist* 67, no. 4 (1965): 902–29.

6. See Stephen Sykes, *The Identity of Christianity* (Philadelphia: Fortress Press, 1984), 23–26.

7. Friedrich Schleiermacher, *On Religion*, trans. John Oman (New York: Harper & Row, 1958), 242–45.

8. See Wayne A. Meeks, *The First Urban Christians* (New Haven: Yale University Press, 1983), 113, 123, 191.

9. See R. A. Markus, *The End of Ancient Christianity* (Cambridge: Cambridge University Press, 1990), 78–82. An ideal that Augustine fell short of himself—for example, in the Donatist controversy.

10. See Karl Barth, *Church Dogmatics*, I/2, ed. G. W. Bromiley and T. F. Torrance (Edinburgh: T&T Clark, 1956), 593.

11. Ibid., 588–91.

12. See Rescher, *Pluralism*, 138–47.

13. See J. G. A. Pocock, *Politics, Language, and Time* (Chicago: University of Chicago Press, 1960), 220–71, for a helpful typology of the complex historical intersections between these two understandings of tradition.

14. For this view of tradition, see the discussion of J. B. Bossuet in Owen Chadwick, *From Bossuet to Newman: The Idea of Doctrinal Development* (Cambridge: Cambridge University Press, 1957), 19–20.

15. Adolf von Harnack used the term "red thread" to discuss that part of Christian belief and practice that remained the same whatever else Christianity included in different times and places. See Sykes, *Identity of Christianity*, 133–35, for references and discussion.

16. See the discussion of the seventeenth-century Spanish Jesuits L. Molina, F. Suarez, Gabriel Vasquez, and John de Lugo, in Chadwick, *From Bossuet to Newman*, chap. 2.

17. See, for example, Alfred Loisy, *The Gospel and the Church*, trans. Christopher Home (Philadelphia: Fortress Press, 1976).

18. See Troeltsch's "*Logos* and *Mythos* in Theology and the Philosophy of Religion," and "The Dogmatics of the History-of-Religions School," in *Religion in History*, Fortress Texts in Modern Theology, trans. James Luther Adams and Walter F. Bense (Minneapolis: Fortress Press, 1991), 46–72, 87–108; and idem, "What Does 'Essence of Christianity' Mean?" in *Ernst Troeltsch: Writings on Theology and Religion*, trans. and ed. Michael Pye (Louisville: Westminster/John Knox, 1990), 124–81.

19. See Hans-Georg Gadamer, *Truth and Method*, 2d rev. ed., trans. Joel Weinsheimer and Donald G. Marshall (New York: Crossroad, 1989).

20. For postmodern criticisms of Gadamer in particular, see John D. Caputo, *Radical Hermeneutics* (Bloomington and Indianapolis: Indiana University Press, 1987), 111–15, 148–50; idem, "Gadamer's Closet Essentialism," in *Dialogue and Deconstruction*, ed. Diane Michelfelder and Richard Palmer (Albany: SUNY Press, 1989), 258–64; Mary McClintock Fulkerson, *Changing the Subject* (Minneapolis: Fortress Press, 1994), 137–42; and Sheila Briggs, "The Politics of Identity and the Politics of Interpretation," *Union Seminary Quarterly Review* 43, no. 1–4 (1989): 163–80.

21. For this argument, see John Brenkman, *Culture and Domination* (Ithaca and London: Cornell University Press, 1987), 30–56.

22. See John Henry Newman, *An Essay on the Development of Christian Doctrine* (Baltimore: Penguin, 1974), 95: "Ideas are . . . like bodily substances, which . . . can be walked around and surveyed on opposite sides and in different perspectives. . . ."

23. See Eric Hobsbawm and Terence Ranger, eds., *The Invention of Tradition* (Cambridge: Cambridge University Press, 1983); Richard Handler and Jocelyn Linnekin, "Tradition, Genuine and Spurious," *Journal of American Folklore* 97, no. 385 (1984): 273–90; and Jocelyn Linnekin, "Defining Tradition: Variations on the Hawaiian Identity," *American Ethnologist* 10, no. 2 (May 1983): 241–52.

24. For an attack on the one-to-one correspondence view of culture and circumstance, see, again, Hall, "Gramsci's Relevance for the Study of Race and Ethnicity," *Journal of Communication Inquiry* 10, no. 2 (Winter 1985): 5–27.

25. Barth, *Church Dogmatics*, I/2, 864–71.

26. See ibid., 594–96, 632, 862. Here I am closer to Barth and the later Troeltsch (see the 1913 essays mentioned in n.18) than I am to Schleiermacher and Sykes on the question of the need for and status of judgments about the essence of Christianity. Compare Sykes, *Identity of Christianity*, 174–208.

27. Barth, *Church Dogmatics*, I/2, 828.

28. This is a common criticism of postliberalism. See David Bryant, "Christian Identity and Historical Change: Postliberals and Historicity," *The Journal of Religion* 73, no. 1 (January 1993): 31–41; and Fulkerson, *Changing the Subject*, 158–64. For a more moderate statement of the criticism by a postliberal sympathizer, see James Buckley, "Doctrine in the Diaspora," *The Thomist* 49 (July 1985): 443-59.

29. Henry Staten, *Wittgenstein and Derrida* (Lincoln and London: University of Nebraska Press, 1984).

30. For the idea of automatic agreement with training, see Lindbeck, *The Nature of Doctrine* (Philadelphia: Westminister Press, 1984), 36, 79, 82–83, 100, 130, esp. the discussion in this connection of an analogy with computer codes, 83. Compare the account of Wittgenstein in John McDowell, "Virtue and Reason," *The Monist* 62, no. 3 (July 1979): 331–50.

31. See Lindbeck, *Nature of Doctrine*, 100.

32. See similar criticisms of the appeal to communicative competence by reader-response literary theorists in Mary Louis Pratt, "Interpretive Strategies/Strategic Interpretation: On Anglo-American Reader-Response Criticism," in *Postmodernism and Politics*, ed. Jonathan Arac (Minneapolis: University of Minnesota Press, 1986), 26–54.

33. See Lindbeck, *Nature of Doctrine*, 60–61.

34. 1 Cor. 2:16; compare Lindbeck, *Nature of Doctrine*, 36.

35. See ibid., 100–1, for a discussion like this of who is competent.

36. See Alfred L. Kroeber, *Style and Civilizations* (Berkeley: University of California Press, 1963).

37. See Dick Hebdige, *Subculture: The Meaning of Style* (London and New York: Routledge, 1988), 120.

38. Ibid., 107.

39. This is basically the Thomistic idea of defining theology by its formal object. See Clodovis Boff, *Theology and Praxis* (Maryknoll, N.Y.: Orbis, 1987), 67, 75, 88–89. I am mixing that account of theology's formal object here with Karl Barth's general understanding of what happens to borrowed claims in Christian use, see Barth, *Church Dogmatics* IV/3, 1, trans. G. W. Bromiley, ed. G. W. Bromiley and T. F. Torrance (Edinburgh: T&T Clark, 1961).

40. Barth, *Church Dogmatics*, IV/3, 1, 163–65.

41. For more on this, see Kathryn Tanner, "The Difference Theological Anthropology Makes," *Theology Today* 50, no. 4 (January 1994): 567–79.

42. For an extended argument like this, see ibid.

43. See John Fiske, "Television: Polysemy and Popularity," *Critical Studies in Mass Communication* 3, no. 4 (December 1986): 391–408.

44. For African and Indian forms of Christianity, see again the references in nn. 24 and 25 of chap. 5.

45. See Frei, *Types of Christian Theology* (New Haven: Yale University Press, 1992), 40–41, 80–86, 153–56.

46. Barth, *Church Dogmatics*, I/2, 728–30.

47. Ibid., 734.

48. Ibid., 734–36.

7. Diversity and Creativity in Theological Judgment

1. George Lindbeck, *The Nature of Doctrine* (Philadelphia: Westminster Press, 1984).

2. See Thomas McCarthy, *Ideals and Illusions: On Reconstruction and Deconstruction in Contemporary Critical Theory* (Cambridge, Mass.: MIT Press, 1991), 30, 58, 158; and Pierre Bourdieu, *Outline of a Theory of Practice* (Cambridge: Cambridge University Press, 1977).

3. See Stephen Sykes, *The Identity of Christianity* (Philadelphia: Fortress Press, 1984), 250–61.

4. For criticisms of the idea of socialization like those found in this paragraph, see Alvin Gouldner, *The Coming Crisis of Western Sociology* (New York: Basic Books, 1970), 421; and Nicholas Abercrombie, Stephen Hill, and Bryan S. Turner, *The Dominant Ideology Thesis* (London: Allen and Unwin, 1980), 50–55. For the idea that dominant discourses are constructed with popular ones in mind, see Stuart Hall, "Notes on Deconstructing the 'Popular,'" in *People's History and Socialist Theory*, ed. Raphael Samuel (London: Routledge and Kegan Paul, 1981), 227–40.

5. See David Dawson, "The Grammar of the Spirit: Christian Reading of Scripture in Auerbach, Boyarin, and Frei," *Modern Theology* (forthcoming).

6. For the idea of internal strain, see R. G. Collingwood, *An Essay on Metaphysics* (Oxford: Clarendon Press, 1940), 74–77.

7. See Ernesto Laclau and Chantal Mouffe, *Hegemony and Socialist Strategy* (London: Verso, 1985).

8. For more on bricolage, see Michel De Certeau, *The Practice of Everyday Life* (Berkeley: University of California Press, 1984); Dick Hebdige, *Subculture: The Meaning of Style* (London and New York: Routledge, 1988); and Jeffrey Stout, *Ethics after Babel: The Languages of Morals and Their Discontents* (Boston: Beacon, 1988).

9. See Raymond Williams, *Marxism and Literature* (Oxford: Oxford University Press, 1977), 125, 129–34, for his account of structures of feeling.

10. See ibid., 128–29, 133, 187.

11. This is a major argument of Sabina Lovibond, *Reason and Imagination in Ethics* (Minneapolis: University of Minnesota Press, 1983).

12. Ibid.; again, one of the major arguments of the book.

13. See Delwin Brown, *Boundaries of Our Habitations: Tradition and Theological Construction* (Albany: SUNY Press, 1994), 135–37.

14. See Nicholas Lash, "Theologies at the Service of a Common Tradition," in his *Theology on the Way to Emmaus* (London: SCM, 1986), 25.

15. Ibid., 29–30.

16. Karl Rahner, "On the Theology of the Ecumenical Discussion," in his *Theological Investigations*, vol. 11, trans. David Bourke (New York: Seabury Press, 1974), 36–37.

17. Karl Rahner, "Pluralism in Theology and the Unity of the Creed in the Church," in ibid., 19–20.

18. See Rahner, "On the Theology of the Ecumenical Discussion," 52–53; "Foundation of Belief Today," in *Theological Investigations*, vol. 16, trans. David Morland (New York: Seabury Press, 1979), 8, 10; and "Reflections on Dialogue within a Pluralistic Society," in *Theological Investigations*, vol. 6, trans. Karl-H. and Boniface Kruper (London: Darton, Longman and Todd, 1969), 35–36.

19. See Rahner, "Pluralism in Theology," 3–23; and idem, "On the Theology of the Ecumenical Discussion," 43.

20. See Stephen Sykes, "Barth on the Centre of Theology," in *Karl Barth: Studies of his Theological Method*, ed. Stephen Sykes (Oxford: Clarendon Press, 1979), 53: "a plurality of theological positions are not merely . . . inevitable, but desirable. For in their very plurality is guaranteed the fact that theologians will not be thought to control their object, rather than in any personal disclaimers they may make."

21. See Michael Perry, *Love and Power: The Role of Religion and Morality in American Politics* (Oxford: Oxford University Press, 1991), 125.

Recommended Reading

1. The History of "Culture"

Bauman, Zygmunt. *Legislators and Interpreters*. Oxford: Polity Press, 1987.

Elias, Norbert. *The Civilizing Process*. Vol. One: *The History of Manners*. Trans. Edmund Jephcott. Oxford: Basil Blackwell, 1978.

Herbert, Christopher. *Culture and Anomie*. Chicago: University of Chicago Press, 1991.

Stocking, George. *Race, Culture and Evolution*. Chicago: University of Chicago Press, 1982.

————. *Victorian Anthropology*. New York: Free Press, 1987.

2. The Modern Meaning of Culture

Benedict, Ruth. *Patterns of Culture*. New York: Houghton Mifflin, 1934.

Geertz, Clifford. *The Interpretation of Cultures*. New York: Basic Books, 1973.

Kroeber, A. L., and Klyde Kluckhohn. *Culture: A Critical Review of Concepts and Definitions*. Cambridge, Mass: Papers of the Peabody Museum of American Archaeology and Ethnology, Harvard University, 1952.

3. Criticism and Reconstruction

Bourdieu, Pierre. *Outline of a Theory of Practice*. Cambridge: Cambridge University Press, 1977.

Clifford, James. *The Predicament of Culture*. Cambridge, Mass.: Harvard University Press, 1988.

Keesing, Roger. "Anthropology as Interpretive Quest." *Current Anthropology* 28, no. 2 (1987): 161–76.

Marcus, George, and Michael Fischer. *Anthropology as Cultural Critique*. Chicago: University of Chicago Press, 1986.

Williams, Raymond. *Marxism and Literature*. Oxford: Oxford University Press, 1977.

4. The Nature and Tasks of Theology

Bourdieu, Pierre. *In Other Words*. Stanford: Stanford University Press, 1990.

Kaufman, Gordon. *In Face of Mystery*. Cambridge, Mass.: Harvard University Press, 1993.

Thiemann, Ronald. *Revelation and Theology*. Notre Dame: University of Notre Dame Press, 1985.

Tracy, David. *Blessed Rage for Order*. New York: Seabury Press, 1975.

Williams, Raymond. *Marxism and Literature*. Oxford: Oxford University Press, 1977.

5. Christian Culture and Society

Clifford, James. *The Predicament of Culture*. Cambridge, Mass. Harvard University Press, 1988.

De Certeau, Michel. *The Practice of Everyday Life*. Berkeley: University of California Press, 1984.

Hannerz, Ulf. *Cultural Complexity*. New York: Columbia University Press, 1992.

Lindbeck, George. *The Nature of Doctrine*. Philadelphia: Westminster Press, 1984.

Milbank, John. *Theology and Social Theory*. Oxford: Basil Blackwell, 1990.

Niebuhr, H. Richard. *Christ and Culture*. New York: Harper & Row, 1951.

6. Commonalities in Christian Practice

Barth, Karl. *Church Dogmatics*. I/2. Ed. G. W. Bromiley and T. F. Bromiley. Edinburgh: T&T Clark, 1956.

Cohen, A. P.. *The Symbolic Construction of Community*. London and New York: Tavistock Publications, 1985.

Hebdige, Dick. *Subculture: The Meaning of Style*. London and New York: Routledge, 1988.

Hobsbawm, Eric, and Terence Ranger, eds. *The Invention of Tradition*. Cambridge: Cambridge University Press, 1983.

Sykes, Stephen. *The Identity of Christianity*. Philadelphia: Fortress Press, 1984.

7. Diversity and Creativity in Theological Judgment

Lovibond, Sabina. *Reason and Imagination in Ethics*. Minneapolis: University of Minnesota Press, 1983.

Rahner, Karl. *Theological Investigations*. Vol. 11, chaps. 1–3, 9. New York: Seabury Press, 1974.

Index

Anthropology, types of, 25, 178 n.1; cognitive, 31; cultural, 25–37 *passim*; functionalist, 25, 34, 178 n.1; social, 26; structuralist, 25, 33–4, 178 n.1; symbolic (interpretive), 25, 31, 39, 47, 178 n.1; *see also* Culture (in anthropological sense)

Apologetics, 115–17, 187 n.41

Argument (concerning Christianity), 125, 135; community of, 123–24, 125–26, 127–28, 136–38, 153–55, 172–75
    agreement in results of, 154, 156, 159, 164, 171–72, 175; conflict within, 137, 156, 159, 173–74, 175; inclusiveness of, 155, 164, 171, 172
    inconclusiveness of, 143, 153, 155, 170, 173, 174; *see also* Consensus, cultural: in Christianity; Discipleship (Christian); Judgment, theological

Arnold, M., 4, 12–15, 16, 17, 19, 20, 48, 167–68

Augustine, Saint, 124, 188 n.9

Bacon, F., 4

Barth, K., 72, 113, 117, 135, 150, 189 n.26, 190 n.39

Bell, D., ix

Benedict, R., x, 25, 29, 42

Bible, 72, 87, 88, 104, 105, 106, 109, 110, 113–14, 126–27, 130, 134, 138, 149–50, 153, 158, 162, 163, 171; interpretation of, 111, 113, 150, 186 n.22; in relation to Word of God, 126, 153

Bildung, 4–5, 9

Biology, 23, 26, 28, 30, 34, 36, 43, 51, 52–53, 70, 168; discipline of, ix

Boas, F., 19–21, 23, 25

Boundaries, cultural, of Christianity, 104–19, 152, 157–58 (*see also* Identity [of Christianity]: as a distinct culture); modern anthropological understanding of, 32, 36
    criticized, 53, 99, 108–10; established by internal organization, 32, 110; socially or geographically defined, 21, 32, 34–35, 99
    postmodern account of, 53–54, 57–58, 109, 111–12, 114–15, 144; *see also* Culture (in anthropological sense): differentiating function of; Hybridity

Bourdieu, P., 111

Bricolage, 166, 191 n.8

Burke, P., ix

Calvin, J., 83, 88

Church. *See* Identity (of Christianity): as a society

Cicero, 4

Class, social, 4–6, 7, 8, 13, 27, 38, 48, 51, 111, 165; in Christianity, 94, 98, 100, 165, 187 n.48

Clifford, J., 25, 39

Colonialism, 9, 21–22, 38, 39, 42–43, 47, 54, 56, 58

Communities, Christian. *See* Identity (of Christianity): as a society

Community of argument. *See* Argument (concerning Christianity): community of

Competence, 79, 142, 189 n.32

Consensus, cultural, 27, 32, 40, 56–57, 78, 157; in Christianity, 124–28, 129, 159, 169; of form, not substance, 46, 57, 121–22, 124, 126–27, 153; idea of, criticized, 45–47, 48, 121; *see also* Culture (in anthropological sense): polysemy in

Conservativism, 168–71

Contextualism (in modern anthropological sense), 19, 21, 22–23, 34–35, 37; in Christian theology, 77, 106–7; reconceived as unanchored, 77–79; reconceived in wider field, 39, 54, 111–12, 115, 121, 152

Conversion, 101, 109–10, 113, 118

Correlationist theology. *See* Theology, types of: correlationist

Creeds, 75, 76, 83, 88, 94–95, 113, 124, 127, 139–40, 151, 154, 173

Cultural studies, ix

Culture (in anthropological sense); change in, 35–36, 51–52, 129; and civilization, 4, 6–11, 13, 16, 17, 30, 41 (*see also* Enlightenment); and comparison, 11, 20, 22, 30, 35, 36, 54; contingency of, 28, 37; conventional character of, 28, 37, 40; correlation with social groups, 6, 9–10, 21, 26–27, 97; criticized, 53, 98–100, 103, 185 n.4; defined, 25–42; differentiating function of, 5, 9, 16, 26, 53–53, 57–58, 67, 112, 119 (*see also* Boundaries, cultural); Hybridity; and discipline, 4–5, 7, 8, 13–14, 27–28, 167–68; and high culture, 4–6, 7, 10, 11, 12, 13–14, 16, 19, 30–31, 37, 39, 41–42, 44–45, 48, 50, 70, 93, 131, 144, 167; as human universal, 25, 36–37, 64–66; integration of, 32–34, 44, 56, 74; likened to a game, 47, 52; likened to an individual person, 8, 10, 29, 33, 54, 107; likened to a language, 33, 34, 50; likened to a machine, 34, 44; likened to an organism, 12, 34, 36, 38, 43; likened to a text, 33, 34, 37, 38, 42, 44–45, 47; likened to a work of art, 29, 33, 37, 38, 42, 45; and political struggle, 40, 50, 56, 57, 74–75, 121,